Tim Burton

ALSO EDITED BY JOHNSON CHEU

Diversity in Disney Films: Critical Essays on Race, Ethnicity, Gender, Sexuality and Disability (McFarland, 2013)

Tim Burton

Essays on the Films

Edited by JOHNSON CHEU

McFarland & Company, Inc., Publishers
Jefferson, North Carolina

LIBRARY OF CONGRESS CATALOGUING-IN-PUBLICATION DATA (new form)
Names: Cheu, Johnson, 1969– editor.
Title: Tim Burton : essays on the films / edited by Johnson Cheu.
Description: Jefferson, North Carolina : McFarland & Company, Inc., Publishers, 2016. | Includes bibliographical references and index.
Identifiers: LCCN 2015045635 | ISBN 9780786498000 (softcover : alk. paper)
Subjects: LCSH: Burton, Tim, 1958– —Criticism and interpretation.
Classification: LCC PN1998.3.B875 T68 2016 | DDC 791.4302/33092—dc23
LC record available at http://lccn.loc.gov/2015045635

BRITISH LIBRARY CATALOGUING DATA ARE AVAILABLE

ISBN (print) 978-0-7864-9800-0
ISBN (ebook) 978-1-4766-2391-7

© 2016 Johnson Cheu. All rights reserved

No part of this book may be reproduced or transmitted in any form or by any means, electronic or mechanical, including photocopying or recording, or by any information storage and retrieval system, without permission in writing from the publisher.

Front cover: Tim Burton and Mia Wasikowska on the set of the 2010 film *Alice in Wonderland* (Walt Disney Pictures/Photofest)

Printed in the United States of America

McFarland & Company, Inc., Publishers
Box 611, Jefferson, North Carolina 28640
www.mcfarlandpub.com

*To the memory of
Diana, Chris, and Rob—
colleagues and dreamers
gone too soon*

Acknowledgments

Thanks to all my contributors for their steadfastness and wanting to get it right. My students, too. There are too many to name, but trust me when I say that all the talking, writing, and good thinking that happens with all of you is reflected in these pages.

My respect and gratitude to my colleagues at Michigan State, particularly Sarah Gibbons, for working through all the mythology stuff with me. Roger Bresnahan, Deborah Carmichael, Cheryl Ceaser, Jeff Charnley, Mary Cook, Kate Fedewa, Richard Manderfield, David Medei, and Elizabeth Spence for the willingness to stop and listen whenever I needed it. Jeffrey Grabil (fearless leader) for enduring support with this project and in all things. Douglas Noverr and Gary Hoppenstand who support me down this road and who always make time. Marsha Edington, Diana Shank, Melissa Arthurton, and Karly Mitchell who make sure everything's always running. John Dowell, who, once again, came through with both friendship and his technical expertise. The library staff at MSU is beyond reproach. At Ohio State, I am grateful for the continued conversations with Linda Mizjewski and Debra Moddelmog who, likewise, always make the time.

Matt Wanat and John McCombe, who answer every email. Edna Poore who makes sure I'm up on all the movies and that I'm well fed. Brian and Ed for coffee and talk. Robert, Pat, and Carolyn, who always talk things through. And, of course, my family for all manner of love and support in all things.

Table of Contents

Acknowledgments   vii

Introduction: Movies and the Art of Humanity
    JOHNSON CHEU   1

Section One: Outsider Characters and Other Oddities

"Why Spend Your Life Making Someone Else's Dreams?": *Ed Wood* Comes Out and Makes His Own Dreams in a Fluffy Pink Angora Sweater
    GAEL SWEENEY   8

An Odd Quest Continued: The Heroes of Tim Burton
    RACHEL S. MCCOPPIN   21

Mixed Assortment: The Typical and Atypical Body in *Charlie and the Chocolate Factory*
    ELIZABETH LEIGH SCHERMAN   36

Corporeal Mediation and Visibility in *Sleepy Hollow*
    LORI PARKS   54

Capitalism and Its Discontents: Gender, Property and Nature in *Batman Returns*, *Sleepy Hollow* and *Corpse Bride*
    SUSAN M. BERNARDO   70

Section Two: The Nature of Adaptations

Becoming the Stories: Indefinite Play in *Big Fish*
    LISA K. PERDIGAO   86

Mixing Man and Monkey in *Planet of the Apes*
    KIMIKO AKITA *and* RICK KENNEY   102

"A Stranger in a Sea of Familiar Faces": Self-Referentiality, Bodily Hauntings and Materializing Identity in *Dark Shadows*
    LANCE NORMAN   117

"Attend the Tale": Burton's Transformation of *Sweeney Todd*
from Stage Epic to Screen Intimacy
 BRIAN D. HOLCOMB   134

Navigating the Risks of Re-Adaptation: Burton's *Charlie and
the Chocolate Factory* After Dahl and Stuart
 PAMELA KRAYENBUHL   150

The Kids Aren't All Right: Childhood Liminality and the
Monstrous-Cute in Burton's Roald Dahl Adaptations
 SARAH DOWNES   165

Section Three: Technology, Artistry and Stardom

Converging Worlds: Neo-Victorianism in the Stop-Motion
Films
 KARA M. MANNING   184

The Use of German Expressionism and American
Exceptionalism
 PETER C. KUNZE   198

"I'm Not Finished": Gender Transgression and Star Persona
in *Edward Scissorhands*
 DEBORAH MELLAMPHY   212

Films Referenced   229
About the Contributors   233
Index   237

Introduction: Movies and the Art of Humanity

Johnson Cheu

In the weeks following the racially motivated massacre in Charleston, South Carolina, on June 17, 2015, I find myself shaken and, like many others, I suspect, caught up in the motions of work, trying to get back into the grind of things. For me, that means writing this introduction to an essay collection on the work of Tim Burton (I'll get to him, I promise). It's not what I can write now, though Burton's films with their misfit characters now seem particularly poignant. Being a person of color, these killings weigh heavily because they're a reminder that we are vulnerable to other people's predilections and beliefs, that our safety and worth are fragile commodities indeed. More than that, though, this massacre shakes my core because I'm a teacher and a humanist, a professor of humanities. My adult life has been spent working with the young and examining questions that form the foundation of the humanities: "Who are we?" "What does it mean to be human?" "Why do human beings treat other human beings the way that they do?"

Discussing these questions through works of art, literature, film and other media, and through classroom essays would not have prevented the tragedy in Charleston. But for me, a humanities curriculum is where we explore the nature of who we are—our motivations, our dreams, our fears, our beliefs. And yes, as a young man in my twenties, I was drawn to the humanities—African American literature in particular, because it spoke to the disenfranchisement I felt then. I was looking for a way to stop people from slurring me (both in terms of disability and in terms of race). The humanities was where people were writing about those issues, and largely still are.

I can't say for certain that the students I teach today feel the way I once did—looking for someone, something to validate them, to say that who they are is important as they are finding their way, coming into their own. I can say that over the last twenty-odd years of teaching, I've noticed a few things.

Particularly over the last few years, students who have come of age in the middle of the self-esteem, no-bullying movement seem simultaneously more assured of themselves, and less assured, unsure of what to say or feel. Social media helps and hurts, too. Students express themselves more, but actually interact less with each other face-to-face. Colleagues comment on how, when walking into a classroom now, the lights are off and no one's conversing. Everyone is just staring at their phone.

And we educators are as beholden to technology as anyone, using it to supplement or enhance our teaching. There isn't a way to detach ourselves from technology, it seems, and maybe that isn't the point. This concern about isolation through connectivity in our dizzying-paced society isn't a new worry; it's been examined in works like Susan Maushart's *The Winter of Our Disconnect* and Joshua Mohr's new novel, *All This Life*. Students live with this connective disjuncture of being plugged in, yet somehow cut off. As some students say, "Yeah, Dr. Cheu, sometimes I've got to remind myself that, 'Hey, I've binged-watched *Scandal* for six hours, maybe I ought to go outside.'" And they worry, regardless of whether they express themselves more through social media or in person. They worry about the economy, about finding jobs, about dating, about who they are, who they are becoming, and the world in which they live.

A humanities class won't solve all of that, surely, but neither will talking about those human issues *less*. It's no secret that the United States has underfunded education across the board. It's no secret that the states have slowly divested more and more money away from state colleges, particularly as we look for other sources of corporate or private funding. It's no secret that the American public has decried the high cost of college, while the numbers of lower-paid "contingent" faculty rise. Through it all, the liberal arts get the short end of the stick, in relation to the STEM disciplines (science, technology, engineering, and math). And indeed, the advent of social media and online courses may make it seem like not much is lost in terms of the humanities, since movies and media are critiqued on blogs and people tweet and post their opinions. Communication is happening, but on a screen where the writer is, or can be, invisible. We seem to be talking *at* people, but maybe we're saying *less*. We are seeing other people less, as we constantly look down at our phones or have earbuds in our ears. As a humanities scholar, this is scary, for how can we understand each other better if we can't even bother to look up or outside or to unplug ourselves?

The truth is there's always been consternation about the humanities and what it is we do. (If I only had a nickel for every time someone said, "You get paid to study Disney?" Never mind that Disney has affected the thoughts and beliefs of generations.) It may seem frivolous to some, but art and artists have always endeavored to say something about the human condition, about what we feel and why we act the way that we do. Grappling with these questions in sustained and substantial ways seems particularly paramount after, sadly, events like Charleston. Lately, the millennial generation that I work with, for all the whiz bang of technology and social media, has been feeling unsure, some even despondent, like Outsiders in a precarious post–9/11 world.

Tim Burton has always worked with the theme of Outsiders (as well as other themes too, of course). From Pee-wee Herman to an angst-ridden Batman and Joker, to the oddity of his Willy Wonka, his Alice, his Sweeney Todd, and of course to Edward Scissorhands. His latest, *Big Eyes* (2014), deals with the Keanes—Walter, a larger-than-life presence riddled with insecurity, and Margaret, a true talent unable to claim her own art, her own life. Outsiders both. Burton is, too, as highlighted by this bit from an interview in *The Guardian*:

> Burton's accounts of his own growing up have generally been fairly circumspect, though he has never left much doubt that his career has been in part an imaginative retort to the emotional privations of those years. (The detail that tends to surface is the strange fairy-tale fact that his parents bricked up the windows of his bedroom, leaving only a small chink of light for him to see out of, and leading him to identify with those Edgar Allan Poe heroes who were buried alive).[1]

Filmgoers may look at his artistic output and exclaim, "He's just so weird!" when they watch a film like *Corpse Bride* or *Frankenweenie*. Weird his films may be, even ghoulish at times. But they are never without heart, without humanity. They never stop arguing for the misfit, the outsider, to find a way and a place for him or her to be.

There have been few scholarly collections devoted to the work of Tim Burton, though he has been a fixture of popular culture for the better part of thirty years. In editing this collection, I've tried to choose not only essays which explore recurring themes in Burton's work, but also those which speak to his other fascinations—his collaborations and relationship with Johnny Depp, his work with musicals and Roald Dahl, and, of course, his love for ghoulish stories. Though by no means exhaustive, I hope these essays will provide new insights into his art and artistry.

Section One, "Outsider Characters and Other Oddities" opens with Gael Sweeney's essay, "'Why Spend Your Life Making Someone Else's Dreams?' *Ed Wood* Comes Out and Makes His Own Dreams in a Fluffy Pink Angora Sweater," in which she looks at both the film and the life of Ed Wood as a (sort of) coming out narrative. Rachel S. McCoppin's essay, "An Odd Quest Continued: The Heroes of Tim Burton," uses Joseph Campbell's work to look at the nature of the hero in Burton and the idea of inclusivity. "Mixed Assortment: The Typical and Atypical Body in *Charlie and the Chocolate Factory*" by Elizabeth Leigh Scherman examines disability and its constructions through various bodies in the text. Lori Parks' essay, "Corporeal Mediation and Visibility in *Sleepy Hollow*," looks at bodies and medicine in the time of *Sleepy Hollow*. Susan M. Bernardo's essay, "Capitalism and Its Discontents: Gender, Property and Nature in *Batman Returns*, *Sleepy Hollow* and *Corpse Bride*," closes out the section, focusing mostly on gender and its relationship to economics as a Burton theme.

Section Two, "The Nature of Adaptations," wrestles with the themes and issues of some of Tim Burton's cinematic adaptions of other works. Lisa K. Perdigao's essay, "Becoming the Stories: Indefinite Play in *Big Fish*," looks at dreams, truth, reality, relationships and the nature of story in *Big Fish*. "Mixing Man and Monkey in *Planet of the Apes*" by Kimiko Akita and Rick Kenney invests us in questions of identity in relation to dominance, nature, and time. Lance Norman's "'A Stranger in a Sea of Familiar Faces': Self-Referentiality, Bodily Hauntings and Materializing Identity in *Dark Shadows*" deals with haunting identity and voice in one of Burton's newer films, *Dark Shadows*. Brian D. Holcomb's "'Attend the Tale': Burton's Transformation of *Sweeney Todd* from Stage Epic to Screen Intimacy" compares and contrasts changes in the stage and film versions of *Sweeney Todd*, positing a more individualized Todd in Burton, much like present-day notions of the lone gunman. Pamela Krayenbuhl's "Navigating the Risks of Re-Adaptation: Burton's *Charlie and the Chocolate Factory* After Dahl and Stuart" considers the general nature of adaptations and places Burton's *Charlie* squarely in the realm of current cultural and social concerns. "The Kids Aren't All Right: Childhood Liminality and the Monstrous-Cute in Burton's Roald Dahl Adaptations" by Sarah Downes uses the idea of "monstrous-cute" (think Disney's *Hunchback* or Pixar's *Monsters* series) to explore childhood, what's scary and what isn't.

Section Three, "Technology, Artistry and Stardom," considers specific technology Burton employs, his use of German Expressionism, and his working relationship with actor Johnny Depp. "Converging Worlds: Neo-Victorianism in the Stop-Motion Films" by Kara M. Manning examines Burton's use of stop-motion technology in his films and how that impacts context and meaning. "The Use of German Expressionism and American Exceptionalism" by Peter C. Kunze takes a look at Burton's nod to German Expressionism and how that movement influences the visual nature of his work and contributes to a heightened sense of American Exceptionism. "'I'm Not Finished': Gender Transgression and Star Persona in *Edward Scissorhands*" by Deborah Mellamphy closes out the collection with an exploration of Depp's star persona, particularly as it has been shaped by Burton, largely though the film *Edward Scissorhands*.

* * *

I'm not naïve enough to believe that the study of film or literature or rhetoric will solve the issues of despondent teens, worried twenty-somethings, or any of us with our own issues and foibles. But the young man I once was found solace and a community in books, art, music, and films where there existed people who seemed to feel just a little bit like me. *Edward Scissorhands* was a favorite of my college years, as I was grappling with understanding bodily difference and social acceptance in both a scholarly and real-world way. This I also know: that I have a life filled with books and music and movies and art and students because American society's beliefs changed, or perhaps, more pointedly, were legally forced to change. The move to desegregate the educational system, as well as the move to mainstream the disabled in the educational system, have had direct impact on my life. It likely saved me, and countless others, from an institutional or house-bound life. Those moves, like all social, cultural or political changes, were shaped by many forces, among them the humanities, where we examine the value and worth of one another and our ways of life.

In the end, we may never fully know the mind of Dylann Roof and what caused him to commit those heinous acts. We may never understand how he could so devalue human lives or what it means to be human. This tragedy, like others, will recede in our collective memory. We'll purge the symbols of hate, perform the rituals of mourning, bury the dead, satisfied (or not) with the lessons we've gathered. Such is the nature of humans, stuck in a perpetual drive forward. Long after we've moved on to yet another tragedy, the discipline of the humanities and the movies will still be here to teach us something about who we are, about how we treat others, and about the nature of the world we inhabit. We'll be watching, but will we look beyond entertainment to embrace the lessons they hold for us?

Note

1. Tom Adams, "Tim Burton: the Love, and Life and Death Stuff was Stewing from the Start," *The Guardian*, Oct. 6, 2012. http://www.theguardian.com/film/2012/oct/07/tim-burton-frankenweenie-interview.

Bibliography

Adams, Tom. "Tim Burton: The Love, and Life and Death Stuff Was Stewing from the Start." *The Guardian*. Oct. 6, 2012. http://www.theguardian.com/film/2012/oct/07/tim-burton-frankenweenie-interview.

Maushart, Susan. *The Winter of Our Disconnect: How Three Totally Wired Teenagers (And a Mother Who Slept with Her iphone) Pulled the Plug on Their Technology and Lived to Tell the Tale*. New York: Tarcher/Penguin, 2011.

Mohr, Joshua. *All This Life*. Berkeley: Soft Skull Press, 2015.

SECTION ONE

Outsider Characters and Other Oddities

"Why Spend Your Life Making Someone Else's Dreams?"

Ed Wood *Comes Out and Makes His Own Dreams in a Fluffy Pink Angora Sweater*

Gael Sweeney

> "We cannot keep this a secret any longer. Can your hearts stand the shocking facts of the true story of Edward D. Wood, Jr.?"
> —from Criswell's introductory speech in *Ed Wood*[1]

Johnny Depp infamously told a Disney executive who questioned the sexuality of his character in *Pirates of the Caribbean*, Captain Jack Sparrow, "But didn't you know that all my characters are gay?"[2] If that's so, then his gayest character—even if he's also "straight"—has to be Edward Wood, Jr., the subject of director Tim Burton's 1994 biopic *Ed Wood*. The cross-dressing, angora-loving Wood's journey to become the "Worst Director in the World" is also a coming out narrative. Initially afraid to reveal his penchant for women's clothes even to his girlfriend, Wood (played with gung-ho sincerity by Depp) seizes on the opportunity to direct the exploitation feature *I Changed My Sex* (eventually retitled *Glen or Glenda?*) by confessing that he's the perfect—in fact the only—director who could do it justice, because of his fetish for fluffy sweaters and ladies' lingerie. In a series of scenes in which he incrementally comes out to his producer, his girlfriend, his crew, even Orson Welles, Tim Burton marks the trajectory of Wood's creative process and his sexuality: for Wood, coming out as a transvestite and becoming a director are one and the same. Both reveal the "true self" that Wood offers to the world—whether or not the world is ready for it! As Orson Welles confides to Ed, director to director, "Why spend your life making someone else's dreams?" In Tim Burton's vision, Ed Wood's creative dreams come wrapped in pink angora.

In the introduction to their published screenplay for *Ed Wood*, Scott Alexander and Larry Karaszewski state that "In a perfect world, *Glen or Glenda?* would have been Ed Wood's final film—the man cranks out numerous silly monster movies, before learning his lesson, turning to personal honest film-making, and creating his autobiographical valedictory masterpiece. But unfortunately, *Glen or Glenda?* came first."[3]

With respect to the screenwriters, I would argue that they are exactly wrong—*Glen or Glenda?* had to be Wood's first film. It's the catalyst for his coming out, for revealing his true, angora-wearing nature. Without *Glen or Glenda?* he could not have directed *Bride of the Monster* or his anti-masterpiece, *Plan 9 from Outer Space*, because his creative self would never have emerged.

Ed Wood is a transvestite, a heterosexual cross-dresser, but he allies himself with the queer community of 1950s Hollywood. Wood is not gay, but he's undoubtedly queer—aligned with the sexually marginalized, like his friend and mentor, flamboyant former drag queen Bunny Breckinridge (Bill Murray), who wears heavy make-up, dreams of getting a sex change, and connects him to the drag queens and transgender people he will use in his first feature, *Glen or Glenda?*.

Like other queer characters in mainstream "coming out" narratives, Wood also has a secret: not his sexuality, which he affirms is solidly heterosexual, but his fetish for wearing women's clothes, especially fluffy pink angora sweaters. To be clear, the film, made in the mid–1990s, elides the terms gay, transvestite, transsexual, and transgender, but the assumption can be made that in the 1950s, when the narrative takes place, these categories would have been much more slippery and not as politically charged as they are in 2014. However, all of them would have been marginalized, pathologized, and criminalized in similar ways during the era of Edward D. Wood, Jr., and *Glen or Glenda?*, the key film in his coming out. As the real Ed Wood later told a friend, "If you want to know me, see *Glen or Glenda?*, that's me, that's my story. No question."[4]

Coming Out the First Time

> Being queer means fighting about these issues all the time, locally and piecemeal but always with consequences. It means being able, more or less articulately, to challenge the common understanding of what gender means.... Queers do a kind of practical social reflection just in finding ways of being queer.
> —Michael Warner, "Introduction: Fear of a Queer Planet"[5]

Ed Wood is not a gay movie, but it is a queer movie. A *very* queer movie. According to queer theorists like Michael Warner, what a society generally calls "normal" is what is "certified, approved"[6] by that society and its institutions: people, things, and ideas that conform and do not deviate from what the vast majority accepts. Heteronormativity is the rule of straightness, especially in America of the 1950s; if you aren't completely "normal" in your sexuality, your attitude, and your lifestyle, then you are condemned always to be an outsider and a misfit, which is exactly how Ed Wood is characterized throughout the film. Wood wants to break into the movies. He's a dreamer, a bad playwright, a wannabe filmmaker—and a closeted transvestite. But Ed is at the bottom of the Hollywood hierarchy, consigned to the z-grade dregs of the motion picture business. He aspires to be a triple-threat, a producer/director/writer like his idol, Orson Welles, whose film posters stare down from the walls of Ed's apartment and whose presence hovers over the film like the guardian angel hovers over the World War II battlefield in his terrible play that begins Burton's film. Instead, Ed's an errand boy, carrying potted palms around the backlot of a second-rate film studio (Universal is implied, although not named) and hanging out in a musty editing room where the only actual film he comes close to is unwanted stock footage of buffalo stampedes and explosions.

The truth is that while Wood had passion, determination, and a belief in himself as a visionary filmmaker like his idol Orson Welles, he lacked one thing he really needed to be a success in Hollywood: talent. The reality is that his movies were—are—bad: badly written, badly directed, and badly acted. Even the sets are ridiculous, with cardboard headstones that fall over at a touch, flying saucers made of pie tins dangling from fishing line, airplane cockpits created from office chairs and old shower curtains, and a "fearsome" rubber octopus that ends up being beaten up by a 72-year-old drug-addled Bela Lugosi (Martin Landau in an Oscar-winner performance).

But Wood perseveres, surrounding himself with a group of true believers, such as Lugosi, former drag queen Bunny Breckinridge, fake psychic Criswell (Jeffery Jones), behemoth wrestler Tor Johnson (real-life wrestler George "The Animal" Steele), and late night scary-movie hostess Vampira (Lisa Marie). They stay with him on film after bad film, infected with his enthusiasm for filmmaking, stealing for him, working for little money and less acclaim, and offering total acceptance when their fearless leader shows up on set in a blonde wig and pink angora sweater. As his first girlfriend, the skeptical Dolores Fuller (Sarah Jessica Parker) says as she walks onto one of Wood's sets, "I see the usual gang of misfits and dope addicts are here." Her words are not merely a description, but a prophecy.

Burton, through Depp's portrayal of Wood, seems to be making a statement about "coming out" as a director: the creative impulse is a fetish, something an artist *has to* do. Creative artists, even when seen as "misfits" and "weirdos," are attempting to negotiate a different reality for the norm, or the heteronormative, a liberating reality akin to coming out as queer. Ed's real "talent" is not for writing and directing films; that much is made clear in the narrative. His genius is in his bravery in embracing and liberating his true self, his unwavering belief in himself, and his enthusiasm for his own vision—an enthusiasm his true believers share ... with one important exception.

Girlfriend Dolores Fuller is Ed's link to the Fifties-style normality that keeps him in the closet about his transvestism. She's a sexy aspiring actress, blonde and toothy, if a bit horse-faced, but she's also a very 1950s woman. We see her in Ed's apartment, cooking and cleaning in a tight dress and high heels, encouraging his Hollywood dreams, even playing the angel in his failed play (the uniforms are the only thing that gets a good review), and generally standing by her man. Dolores is placed as the "voice of reason" in the narrative, which means she is also poised as the enemy of Ed's coming out and his connection with the sexual margins of Hollywood. At the beginning of the film, Dolores is completely unaware of her boyfriend's proclivities, her main complaint that her sweaters are always disappearing and then reappearing all stretched out. But at this point Ed lacks the courage and impetus to come out to her.

However, the game changes when an item appears in *Variety* that a pending film about early transsexual Christine Jorgensen is brought to Ed's attention. He immediately contacts the producer, George Weiss (Mike Starr), the president of Screen Classics, a z-grade exploitation company where the poster precedes the movie and the distribution rights are sold before there's a writer, a director, or a cast. But Ed catches Weiss's interest by claiming that "I'm more qualified to direct this than anyone else in town" and scores an interview, brushing off Dolores's curiosity about his special qualifications as typical Hollywood "hogwash." But Ed is determined to get this job even at a personal cost.

If the Universal backlot where Ed works is dream-like, Screen Classics is the grim reality of Hollywood's underbelly: a junky-stuffed office in a cinderblock building where deals rather than films are made. The slightly grainy, over-exposed texture of Burton's black and white film stock emphasizes this dreamy quality, but also the cheap and tawdry nature of Ed Wood's world. The ill-tempered George Weiss is a cynical businessman with no interest in the integrity of cinema or art. "I don't hire directors with burning desires to tell their stories," he tells Wood. All he wants is a picture about a she-male,

I Changed My Sex, that he can sell in Tulsa, where "those repressed Okies really go for that twisted pervert stuff"—a phrase that makes Wood wince. Later Weiss tries to level with Wood about the truth of the movie business: "Eddie, you must have me confused with David Selznick. I don't make major motion pictures—I make crap!"

To Weiss, movies are money and that's all. As he and Wood sit facing each other with the battered desk between them, the weary, loud-mouthed Weiss is the polar opposite of the young, idealistic Wood. Yet, Weiss is the first person to whom Wood comes out as a transvestite.[7] Weiss is the man who allows him to fulfill his dreams, but the price is his most closely guarded secret, the one he's never even told Dolores. When Weiss is dubious about the "special qualifications" that make him the only director who can do this project justice, Wood confesses: "I've never told anyone what I'm about to tell you ... but I really want this job. I like to dress in women's clothing." Of course, Weiss assumes that Wood is gay—"You a fruit?" But Wood insists that he loves women, that wearing their clothes makes him feel closer to them. Then, to prove his bona fide masculinity, he tells his backstory of wearing women's lingerie under his uniform during World War II: "I even para-trooped wearing a brassiere and panties.... I wasn't afraid of being killed, but I was terrified of getting wounded and having the medics discover my secret."

Weiss' reaction is surprisingly low key, given the sexual attitudes of the 1950s, even in Hollywood. But he comes across as a man who has seen everything in show business and can't really be shocked. In other words, he's the perfect person for Wood to come out to: dispassionate, non-judgmental, and interested only in what Wood can do for him. Weiss has no interest in Wood's personal life or angora fetish: if he can deliver *I Changed My Sex* as cheaply (under $20,000) and quickly (a four-day shoot) as possible, he can have the job.

Coming Out to Dolores

> Movies were his passion. Women were his inspiration. Angora sweaters were his weakness.
> —*Ed Wood* poster tagline

Once George Weiss gives him the job of writing, directing, and also starring in *Glen or Glenda?*—Wood's reimagining of *I Changed My Sex*—we see Ed furiously typing as he pounds out the deeply autobiographical screenplay. The "writer at work" trope in classic films is a familiar one, but in this iteration the look in Ed's eye is particularly intense. As he tells his friend Bunny, who is busy gathering transvestites and transsexuals for the projected film: "I don't care if they're not actors. I want realism! I want this film to tell the truth! I've waited my whole life for this shot and I'm not gonna blow it."

For Wood, *Glen or Glenda?* is more than just a job opportunity: it's a reflection of his own life and experience as a cross-dresser. The fact that the real Wood made this film in 1953 and, under the pseudonym Daniel Davis, played the title role is mind-boggling. Johnny Depp's sincerity makes Ed's dilemma not only sympathetic, but revolutionary, especially considering that, as the actual film makes explicit, cross-dressing was not only considered perverted, it was illegal. But this is Wood's personal statement about his two selves, about, as he tells his putative star, Bela Lugosi, "how people have two personalities: the side they show to the world and then the secret person they hide inside." In the 1950s coming out was not an option for most queer people, but Wood takes that step nevertheless because otherwise he'll never fulfill his dream of emulating his idol, Orson Welles. But the person he next needs to come out to proves the hardest: Ed's girlfriend, Dolores Fuller.

Hints have been dropped about Wood's "secret" all through the beginning of the film, but Dolores, although aware of her boyfriend's penchant for friends on the margins of society, has failed to put the pieces together. "Why are you the most qualified director for *The Christine Jorgensen Story*?" she asks innocently. But Wood evades the question. And when Dolores searches their closet (where else?) for her angora and asks, "Where's my pink sweater? I can never seem to find my clothes anymore," the camera pans across his guilty face. But now that he's finished the screenplay, he can't keep Dolores in the dark any longer, especially since he expects her to play Barbara, a character based on herself, just as he is planning to play Glen, his own doppelgänger, making for a nesting of narrative within narrative.

Wood gives Dolores the finished screenplay and insists that she read it immediately while he waits in the other room. Burton trains the camera on Sarah Jessica Parker's face as she reads with a dawning awareness of the truth. She looks up at the door, knowing he's behind it, and also knowing but not quite believing what she's about to see. Dolores opens the door, revealing Wood in full drag, with blonde wig, high heels, and fluffy angora sweater. She blinks and states the obvious, her voice deadpan: "So that's where my sweater's been."

Unlike George Weiss, however, Dolores is completely freaked out by Wood's revelation. She is, after all, not one of Ed's marginal misfits, but a "normal" woman who assumed she had a "normal" boyfriend. When she demands to know why he didn't tell her about his fetish, he replies that this is his way of telling her—or of coming out to her. But she won't be appeased. "By putting it in a fucking script for everyone to see?" she screams. "What kind of sick mind operates like that?" She loves Ed, but can't conceive of his transvestism as anything but sick and perverse, especially when he now plans to reveal it not merely in public, but on film.

Coming Out on the Street and in the Studio

> Everybody, we're about to embark on quite a journey ... but when it's over we'll have a picture that'll entertain, enlighten, and maybe even move millions of people.
> —Ed Wood's pep talk to his *Glen or Glenda?* film crew, delivered in drag

Tim Burton continually demonstrates how Wood's fetish for angora is bound to his creative impulse. But once he begins shooting *Glen or Glenda?*, the secret he was afraid to share with anyone becomes something he parades on the street. The first shot of Wood's first feature becomes a sight-gag as the crew gathers on a Hollywood sidewalk to hear their director's words—and the camera reveals Ed, in blonde wig, angora sweater, and megaphone, in full director's mode. This incongruous image is Ed Wood's "real self"—director and transvestite—finally and irrevocably out of the heteronormative closet. The crew takes the situation in stride and Ed, playing Glen as Glenda, strolls down the street, gazing into store windows. "Cut! Print it," Wood exclaims, instructing the crew to get ready for the next shot.

But his triumph is interrupted by the arrival of a patrol car. With no permit to film, they have to run for it. The illegal shoot underlines another reality of Wood's fetish: not only do his desires make him an outlaw, his is filming outside of the law. Men wearing women's clothing was a criminal offense everywhere in the 1950s and would continue to be for decades to come. Although Wood affirms that he's straight (as did the real Wood, who was married a number of times and had numerous girlfriends), in the eyes of the law he's a sexual deviant and now that he's out, he is at constant risk of arrest. Although Burton doesn't press this point in his film, in Wood's *Glen or Glenda* it is a major part of the narrative, driving another transsexual character, Patrick/Patricia, to suicide.

As Wood becomes more confident in his ability as a writer and director, he also becomes more open about his cross-dressing, much to the dismay of soon-to-be-ex-girlfriend Dolores. At the wrap party for *Bride of the Monster*, he does a faux-striptease—once again, in full drag including an angora shrug—to the lusty cheers of cast and crew. Dolores is appalled. This spectacle ends when Ed pulls away the veil covering his face to show the gap where his front teeth were knocked out in World War II—the same war in which, as a Marine in the Pacific, he went into combat with bra and panties under his uniform. For Dolores, this is the final indignity: "You people are insane!" she cries. "You're wasting your lives making shit! Nobody cares! These movies are terrible!" Dolores may be telling the truth, but she's cast here as the one who stifles the creative process, taking on an almost villainous role in a film that is too ridiculously sunny to have any actual villains. But for Ed Wood's gang of misfits, their leader can do no wrong: his "genius" is not only self-evident, for them it's inspiring and liberating.

Coming Out to His Idol

> Why spend your life making someone else's dreams?
> —Orson Welles to Ed Wood, in *Ed Wood*

Ed Wood's final coming out moment is also the moment that seals his legacy as a director. Bela Lugosi, his dope-addicted star, is dead, and the Baptist congregation backing the shoot[8] are meddling with the making of *Grave Robbers from Outer Space*[9]: the title seems un-Christian and they question Ed's basic ability as a director when the cast, especially the unwieldy 300-plus-pound Tor Johnson, keep knocking over the flimsy cardboard scenery. "Mr. Wood," they question. "Do you know anything about the art of film production?" "*I'm* the director!" Ed insists. "Nobody will ever notice that. Filmmaking isn't about the little details, it's about the big picture!" Stressed and depressed by people who obviously don't share his creative vision, Ed retreats to the dressing room, where an angora sweater hangs on a rack. He touches it sensuously. This, as always, is the answer. Since Dolores left, he's been holding back his true self. Angora is the emblem of his creativity and the only way he can feel comfortable and get the job done. But Wood needs one final affirmation before he can embrace his destiny.

If Bela Lugosi was Ed Wood's father figure, his creative idol was Hollywood maverick Orson Welles, who, in the mid 1950s, was himself in a creative downward spiral. Unable to secure funding, Welles scrambled for money for his own projects by taking thankless acting and directing jobs for the major studios he despised. In the film, Wood openly worships Welles: a poster of *Citizen Kane* owns a place of honor on his apartment wall and he often cites him as his role model. In this key scene in the final segment of the film, the

Baptists are horrified when Ed emerges from the dressing room ready to direct in his favorite ensemble: blonde wig, heels, pencil skirt, pink angora sweater—and mustache.

Wood flees the set and ends up at the legendary Hollywood dive bar, Musso and Frank, where he plans to drink himself into oblivion. Of course, in Tim Burton's 1950s Hollywood no one looks twice at a mustached man in pink angora. But then Wood has a moment of pure epiphany: sitting in the corner, also drinking his cares away, is Orson Welles. Ed approaches reverently, removing his blonde wig as if it's a hat. Welles (played by the uncanny Vincent D'Onofrio and voiced by Maurice *"Pinky and The Brain"* LeMarche), recognizes Wood as a kindred spirit and tells him the troubles he's having getting financing for *Don Quixote*, a film he worked on for twenty years without finishing. "I can't believe it!" cries Wood. "These sound like *my* problems!" Discouraged, Wood asks his idol if it's all worth it. But Welles gives him the word from on high: "It is when it works. You know the one film of mine where I had total control? *Kane*. The studio hated it ... but they didn't get to touch a frame. Ed, visions are worth fighting for. Why spend your life making other people's dreams?"

Scott Alexander and Larry Karaszewski's screenplay indicates that Wood returns to the set "a changed man."[10] He has found common cause with his idol: in the "normal" world, the world run by businessmen and fueled by money, both Wood and Welles are Hollywood misfits, Don Quixotes forever tilting at impossible windmills, never content with making other people's dreams. As Wood tells his interfering backers: "We are gonna finish this film just the way I want it! Because you can't compromise an artist's vision!" He plunges ahead with new enthusiasm to make the picture: the infamous *Plan 9 from Outer Space* (1959).

Comfortable and self-assured in angora and blessed by his idol, Ed Wood finishes his "masterpiece." "*Plan 9* is my pride and joy,"[11] the real Wood later told a friend, while Johnny Depp, watching the picture unfold, says, "This is the one I'll be remembered for"—and he's right for all the wrong reasons. Not only is *Plan 9* the acme of Wood's off-kilter vision, it also showcases his merry gang of misfits, including Bunny (as the Ruler of the Universe!), Tor Johnson, Vampira, the beautifully stage-named Dudley Manlove, and, in his final screen appearance, Bela Lugosi. *Plan 9* would also finally deliver the accolades that were denied Wood while he was alive. The film became a cult favorite and not long after his death in 1978, it would be crowned as the "Worst Film,"[12] with Ed himself taking the honor of "Worst Director" two years later.[13]

The rapturous scene at the "premiere" of *Plan 9* that ends the film serves as Ed Wood's symbolic coming out as the "Worst Director in the World." Unfortunately, it's a moment of fantasy (*Plan 9* barely had a release, let alone a premiere), a parody of the happy ending of the traditional Fifties biopic. As the gang cheers and waves, Ed and new girlfriend Kathy drive off to get married, secure in their dreams. The camera pans up over the Pantages Theater to an obvious model of the Hollywood Sign, illuminated, as it was at the beginning of the film, by flashes of lightning as the rain pours down. The picture has come to an end. But the last images are of what really became of the merry band of misfits, a litany of failure, obscurity, and ridiculous outcomes, including Wood's descent into porn movies and alcoholism. The final irony is that the most successful of the group turned out to be the only realist, the only one who was not a true believer: Dolores Fuller went on to a career as a songwriter for Elvis Presley's ignominious 1960s films, writing such non-hits as "Rock-a-Hula, Baby" from *Blue Hawaii* (1961) and "Do the Clam," from *Girl Happy* (1965).

Ed Wood, while critically well-received,[14] was a financial failure.[15] Since then, like Wood's movies, it has become a cult success, although one that is rarely considered a key moment in the careers of Burton or Johnny Depp, who have since earned hundreds of millions. But its message of the place of the creative process in the revelation of a creator's true self is more valid than ever, especially in the context of queer subjectivity and outsider status. Even today, *Ed Wood* reads like a dream narrative of wish fulfillment. I first watched it years ago in the grip of a fever that, undoubtedly, skewed my initial perception. But perhaps that is the only way to contemplate the young triumvirate responsible for *Ed Wood*: Tim Burton, Johnny Depp, and Edward Davis Wood, Jr., himself. From the heights of their current achievements, Burton and Depp might stop to remember that their small creation still endures on the queer margins of Hollywood industry and art, where to come out as an artist is to declare yourself an outlaw, proudly one of the usual gang of misfits and dope addicts. In *Ed Wood*, there, in a pink angora sweater, you can find your own beautiful, fevered dream.

Notes

1. The 1994 Tim Burton movie version and the Alexander/Karaszewski 1995 published screenplay differ substantially, so unless otherwise indicated all *Ed Wood* quotes are from the 2004 DVD release.

2. "Johnny Depp talks to Patti Smith," *Vanity Fair*, November 30, 2010.

3. Scott Alexander, and Larry Karaszewski, *Ed Wood Screenplay*, London: Faber & Faber, 1995, ix.

4. Rudolph Grey, *Nightmare of Ecstasy: The Life and Art of Edward D. Wood, Jr.*, revised edition. Portland, OR: Feral House, 1994, 86.

5. Michael Warner, "Introduction: Fear of a Queer Planet," *Social Text* 29 (1991).

6. Michael Warner, *The Trouble with Normal: Sex, Politics, and the Ethics of Queer Life*, Cambridge, MA: Harvard University Press, 2000, 56.

7. There's a disconnect here that the film (and the screenplay) glosses over, which is Wood's friendship with Bunny Breckinridge. Ed tells George Weiss that he's never told anyone about his transvestism, yet his best friend is Bunny, a very camp and knowing gay man who seems to know every drag queen, transvestite, and transsexual in Los Angeles. Bunny shows no surprise at all when Ed asks him to round up as many as he can to appear in *Glen or Glenda?*, or when he plays the part of Glen himself, so if Ed has not told Bunny his secret, Bunny certainly has long before surmised it.

8. One of the conditions of the Baptists' funding is that Ed and his cast all get baptized, including the dubious Bunny. While this scene has been used as an example of a ludicrous plot point, it, like many of the other insane details in Ed Wood, is completely true.

9. The original title of *Plan 9 from Outer Space*.

10. Alexander and Karaszewski, 163.

11. Grey, 86.

12. Harry Medved, and Randy Dreyfuss, *The Fifty Worst Films of All Time (And How They Got That Way)*, New York: Warner Books, 1978.

13. Michael Medved, and Harry Medved, *The Golden Turkey Awards*, New York: Putnam, 1980.

14. Martin Landau won the 1994 Academy Award for Best Supporting Actor, while Rick Baker won for Best Make-up.

15. *Ed Wood* made less than $6 million at the box office from a budget of $18 million. Its release on DVD was also held up for ten years (until 2004) under murky circumstances, undermining its ability to break even.

Bibliography

Aleksandrovic, Dimitri. "The Friendship of Tim Burton and Vincent Price." *Suite 101.Com*. http://suite101.com/article/the-friendship-of-tim-burton-and-vincent-price-a262043.

Alexander, Scott, and Larry Karaszewski. *Ed Wood Screenplay*. London: Faber & Faber, 1995.

_____."The Johnny Depp Interview." *Film Threat*, December 1994. http://www.johnnydeppfan.com/interviews/9412FilmThreat.htm.

Bérubé, Allan. *Coming Out Under Fire: The History of Gay Men and Women in World War Two*. New York: Plume, 1991.

Bronski, Michael. *A Queer History of the United States*. Boston: Beacon Press, 2011.

Butler, Judith. *Gender Trouble: Feminism and the Subversion of Identity*. New York: Routledge, 1990.

Chen, Joyce. "Johnny Depp Inspired by an 'Incredibly Stoned' George W. Bush for Willie Wonka Character." *The New York Daily News*, May 9, 2012. http://www.nydailynews.com/entertainment/tv-movies/johnny-depp-inspired-incredibly-stoned-george-w-bush-willy-wonka-character-article-1.1075100.

Clark, James. "That Was Perfect: Tim Burton's *Ed Wood*." *Wonders in the Dark*, November 24, 2010. http://wondersinthedark.wordpress.com/2010/11/24/that-was-perfect-tim-burtons-ed-wood.

Cortez, Joe. "Burton Influences." *The Tim Burton Collective*, 1994. http://lkolyada.narod.ru/2007/221MM/Ulia/infl.html.

Del Valle, David. "Savior of Lost Boogeymen: *Ed Wood*." *Academic Journal of Film and Media* #8, 2012. http://www.acidemic.com/id162.html.

Ebert, Roger. "Review of *Ed Wood* (1994)." RogerEbert.com, October 7, 1994. http://www.rogerebert.com/reviews/ed-wood-1994.
Edwards, Bruce V. "The Ed Wood Pages." *The Bad Cinema Diary*, 6th Edition, July 2009.
Ehrlich, David. "Their Best Role: Johnny Depp in Ed Wood." *The Moviephone Blog*, March 2, 2011. http://blog.moviefone.com/2011/03/02/johnny-depp-ed-wood-best-role.
Emin-Tunc, Tanfer, and Nichole Prescott. "*Glen or Glenda?*: Psychiatry, Sexuality, and the Silver Screen." *Bright Lights Film Journal* 41, August 2003.
Everitt, David. "Wood If He Could: Two Videos Celebrate Ed Wood's Eccentric Career." *Entertainment Weekly*, April 21, 1995.
Ferenczi, Aurélien. *Masters of Cinema: Tim Burton*. Paris: Cahiers du Cinéma, 2010.
Garber, Marjorie. *Vested Interests: Cross-Dressing and Cultural Anxiety*. New York: Routledge, 1992.
Galindo, Reverend Steve. "The Church of Ed Wood Homepage." Last Updated August 24, 2012. www.edwood.org/index-main.html.
_____. "The Life of Edward D. Wood, Jr." *The Church of Ed Wood*. www.edwood.org/bio.html.
Gore, Chris, and Jeremy Berg. "Ed or Johnny: The Strange Case of Ed Wood." *Film Threat*, December 1994.
Grey, Rudolph. *Nightmare of Ecstasy: The Life and Art of Edward D. Wood, Jr*. Revised Edition. Portland, OR: Feral House, 1994.
Healed1337. "Movie Review: *Glen or Glenda?*" *Healed1337's Blog of Doom*, February 5, 2011. http://healed1337.blogspot.com/2011/02/movie-review-glen-or-glenda.html.
Hilson, Hal. "*Ed Wood* Review." *The Washington Post*, October 7, 1994.
Jay, Sarah. "How Is the 1950s Re-Imagined Through the Lens of Tim Burton's Films?" *1950s Film, Perfection and Propaganda*, May 20, 2008. http://sarahjay.wordpress.com.
"Johnny Depp: Disney Bosses Hated Jack Sparrow Character ... and Asked If He Was 'Gay.'" *Mail Online*, November 30, 2010. http://www.dailymail.co.uk/tvshowbiz/article-1334428/Johnny-Depp-Disney-bosses-stand-Jack-Sparrow-thought-character-gay.html.
"Johnny Depp #1: The 100 Hundred Sexiest Movie Stars, 2009." *Empire Online*, 2009. http://www.empireonline.com/100sexiest2009/men/default.asp?star=1.
"Johnny Depp Talks to Patti Smith." *Vanity Fair*, November 30, 2010. http://www.vanityfair.com/online/daily/2010/11/johnny-depp-talks-to-p...king-with-angelina-jolie-jack-sparrow-and-his-own-musical-aspirations.
Lafrance, J. D. "Ed Wood Retrospective." *The Tim Burton Collective*. http://www.timburtoncollective.com/edwood2.html.
Latham, Rob. "Tim Burton's Trash Cinema Roots: *Ed Wood* and *Mars Attacks!*" In *The Works of Tim Burton: Margins to Mainstream*, ed. Jeffrey Weinstock. New York: Palgrave Macmillan, 2013.
Maslin, Janet. "Review of Tim Burton's *Ed Wood*." *The New York Times*, September 23, 1994.
Medved, Harry, and Randy Dreyfuss. *The Fifty Worst Films of All Time (And How They Got That Way)*. New York: Warner Books. 1978.
Medved, Michael, and Harry Medved. *The Golden Turkey Awards*. New York: Putnam, 1980.
Mellamphy, Deborah. "The Paradox of Transvestism in Tim Burton's *Ed Wood*." *Wide Screen*, Vol. 1, No. 1 (2009). http://widescreenjournal.org/index.php/journal/article/view/59/97.
miles e. "*Glen or Glenda* (1953)." *Plastic Exploding Blog*, January 28, 2011. http://plasticexploding.blogspot.com/2011/01/glen-or-glenda-1953.html.

Morris, Gary. "It's an Ed Wood World After All!" *Bright Lights Film Journal* 16, April 1996.

Muir, John Kenneth. "Cult Movie Review: *Ed Wood*." *John Kenneth Muir's Reflections on Cult Movies and Classic TV,* October 14, 2011. http://reflectionsonfilmandtelevision.blogspot.com/2011/10/cult-movie-review-ed-wood-1994.html.

Rosenblaum, Jonathan. "Allusion Profusion: *Ed Wood* and *Pulp Fiction*." *The Chicago Reader,* October 21, 1994.

Salisbury, Mark. *Burton on Burton*. London: Faber & Faber, 2000.

Sedgwick, Eve Kosofsky. *The Epistemology of the Closet*. Berkeley: University of California Press, 1990.

Siegel, Robert. "The Making of Tim Burton's *Ed Wood*." Blu-Ray.com, August 31, 2012. http://www.blu-ray.com/news/?id=9393.

Smith, Gavin. "Tim Burton Interviewed. "*Tim Burton Dream Site,* 1994. http://minadream.com/timburton/EdWoodInterview.htm.

Sontag, Susan. "Notes on Camp (1964)." *A Susan Sontag Reader*. New York: Vintage, 1983: 105–19. (Reprinted from *Against Interpretation*.)

Tauchert, Carley. "Revisiting Tim Burton's *Ed Wood*." *Den of Geek,* October 7, 2009. http://www.denofgeek.com/movies/14932/revisiting-tim-burton's-ed-wood.

Travers, Peter. "*Ed Wood* Review." *Rolling Stone,* September 28, 1994.

Vary, Adam. "Johnny Depp Says 'All My Characters Are Gay.' Yes, but HOW Gay?" *PopWatch,* December 1, 2010. http://popwatch.ew.com/2010/12/01/johnny-depp-all-my-characters-are-gay.

Vera, Veronica. "Homepage for Miss Vera's Finishing School for Boys Who Want to Be Girls." http://www.missvera.com.

Von Tunzelmann, Alex. "Reel History: Rating the Historical Accuracy of Films: Is *Ed Wood* a Cardboard Cutout?" *The Guardian,* November 17, 2011. http://www.guardian.co.uk/film/2011/nov/17/johnny-depp-sarah-jessica-parker.

Warner, Michael. *The Trouble with Normal: Sex, Politics, and the Ethics of Queer Life*. Cambridge, MA: Harvard University Press, 2000.

_____. "Introduction: Fear of a Queer Planet." *Social Text* 29 (1991).

Weinstock, Jeffrey Andrew, ed. *The Works of Tim Burton: Margins to Mainstream*. New York: Palgrave Macmillan, 2013.

Wreckme. "Most Successful Movies of Tim Burton." Listal.com, November 1, 2010. http://www.listal.com/list/most-successful-movies-tim-burton.

Yojimbo_5. "Don't Make a Scene: *Ed Wood*." *Let's Not Talk About Movies,* October 18, 2009. http://letsnottalkaboutmovies.blogspot.com/2009/10/I-make-scene-ed-wood.html.

An Odd Quest Continued
The Heroes of Tim Burton

RACHEL S. McCOPPIN

Innumerable texts and films have centered on the quest of the hero. Popular culture identifies a hero as someone who fulfills a specific mission, usually saves lives, and brings society back to familiar safety, oftentimes wearing a guise to mask his or her identity. Joseph Campbell[1] points out in *The Hero with a Thousand Faces*[2] that the mythic hero's journey is a process of introspection into unknown realms of the symbolic psyche. In myth, missions of the hero are murky and often unfulfilled; few are physically saved; societal codes are rejected, thus making the hero fit into the role of the "other."[3] The mythic hero strips off psychic masks to reveal his or her true self and partakes on a spiritual journey towards self-actualization.[4]

Campbell has been criticized for his lack of detailed understanding about the nuances of the global myths he explores, but Doty in his *Myth: A Handbook,* states "Contemporary approaches emphasize the need to look for the ways in which traditional myths can be resources for 'thinking outside of the box' today, rather than merely limiting consciousness to classical models of values,"[5] and though he criticizes such use of mythology, his statement still points out the value of Campbell to popular culture. Campbell's popularity, spurred much by his televised interview series with Bill Moyers, influenced a vast audience of contemporary viewers. Burton, as a contemporary director, therefore, is a good representation of the effect of the popularity of Campbell's vision of the monomyth.

Tim Burton, in repeated interviews, talks about the process of his filmmaking being, for him, a form of self-discovery.[6] Helena Bassil-Morozow contends that "Tim Burton is an essentially archetypal director in the sense that he works with basic mythological motifs,"[7] and this is certainly true of his *Pee-wee's Big Adventure* (1985), *Edward Scissorhands* (1990), and *Charlie and the Chocolate Factory* (2005). All three films are contemporary adaptations of the hero's journey: Burton's protagonists are called to leave their comfortable surroundings, encounter archetypal helpers and hindrances along their journeys, and bravely face unknown realms, but what is unique in Burton is that the crucial element of the hero becoming transformed by his journey is downplayed. Burton's heroes remain constant in their journeys and are left largely unchanged, enabling other characters to change. It is precisely the lack of grand transformation in the hero that reveals important meanings in Burton films.

Burton revitalizes the heroic myth narrative, as he instead focuses on the characters who generally go unnoticed in the adventures of the classic hero, because they may be assumed to be too weak or too odd to be deemed worthwhile, capable heroes. In fact, Burton's heroes may be mistaken as antiheroes; they appear to contrast the archetypal expectations of heroism, but it is precisely their contradictory nature that defines them as heroic. Burton's heroes represent the "other" in a society weighed down by stagnancy; their willingness to change the society in which they are part of, so that it may be improved, simply by maintaining their "otherness," marks them as heroes. Therefore, Burton's films show the importance of embracing difference towards achieving an inclusive and dynamic society, thus allowing the community to reach a state of apotheosis.

Pee-wee's Big Adventure follows the archetypes of the hero's journey. Burton identifies Pee-wee (Paul Reubens) as the "other"; the hero is often the "other," as the heroic quest serves to separate the hero from the norms of established society. Pee-wee's home is portrayed as an environment of extreme oddity with his numerous invented gadgets propelling him through his daily morning routine, but this opening scene also gives audiences a colorful glimpse into the character of Pee-wee. Pee-wee is innocent; his first introduction shows him smiling as he wakes up, and laughing as he starts playing with his fire truck on his Bambi rug. This scene also establishes Pee-wee as the "other"; he is a character who defies expectations of "normalcy"; his toothbrush is oversized; his window is actually a fish tank. In addition, this scene serves to show another important element of the Burton hero—Pee-wee is comfortable with his oddity; he chooses to be an anomaly; his Rube Goldberg gadgets that crack eggs and make pancakes are not exactly time effective, but serve their main purpose of delighting him. This opening scene of the hero in his element is similar to many of Burton's opening scenes. His heroes start off as solitary geniuses; their domains reveal a world of color that contrasts the monochromatic portrayal of Burton's society.

Pee-wee launches the first Campbell archetype of the hero leaving his familiar territory and entering into unknown realms the moment he leaves home. Pee-wee encountering Francis (Mark Holton) further establishes his call to begin a journey. Francis is rich and spoiled; he uses his father's money to buy anything from anyone, but then he encounters the oddity of Pee-Wee, who defies Francis' traditional societal operations by refusing to accept any amount of money for his prized bike. Francis becomes a villain in the film because he is threatened by Pee-wee and steals the bike. This theft spurs Pee-wee to fully embark on his quest.

Following the format of the hero's journey, Pee-wee finds many helpers along the way. Pee-wee first encounters Mickey (Judd Omen) fleeing authorities because he cut a label off a mattress. Although the offense is clearly laughable, he is still portrayed as a criminal who has broken societal laws, but Pee-wee does not label him as threatening. This encounter with a stranger is also important in revealing who Pee-wee is. He does not stiffen or recoil after hearing Mickey's confession—he does not judge others. Pee-wee supports Mickey in evading the police by dressing as a woman in an impromptu shawl and charming the officers by batting his eyelashes at them. Mickey's dumbfounded facial expression shows that he reluctantly enjoys this odd, new experience that undeniably would have turned out different had he picked up another passenger. From this first heroic encounter, Burton has revealed that Pee-wee is on a different journey than the typical hero's quest. Pee-wee transforms those who would normally be hindrances into helpers. It becomes clear that the real goal of Pee-wee's journey is to help others redefine themselves.

The next stage of Campbell's heroic journey is entitled the "Belly of Whale" because it describes a situation where the hero is immersed in an entirely unfamiliar experience. When Pee-wee and Mickey have lost control of their car and fall towards death, Pee-wee enters this next chapter. Although Mickey is terrified at facing an imposing death, Pee-wee laughs, revealing that he has faced his own mortality, and this is an important part of self-actualization. Pee-wee shows that he starts his journey already transformed; he is not changed by this experience with death. His experience in the realms of the unknown continues as he is dropped off by Mickey. Alone again, Pee-wee is picked up by semi-truck driver Large Marge (Alice Nunn), or rather her ghost, in the middle of the night. The scene is shot to show that Pee-wee's surroundings are changing to become reflections of the unconscious self; the road is deserted; he is alone with the late Large Marge, and only the beams of the truck's head lights illuminate the path ahead. Marge reveals her demented face of death to Pee-wee, her giant, white eyeballs sticking out of their sockets, seemingly demanding an acknowledgment of mortality from Pee-wee. Pee-wee is scared enough to ask to be dropped off; traditional heroic myths would show a transformation happening to its protagonist, but again,

Pee-wee only tells Marge to "have a nice day," and enters a diner as the predictable and unchanged Pee-wee there to transform another—now the waitress Simone (Diane Salinger).

Simone, with the exception of possibly Francis, is the most transformed within the film because of her encounter with Pee-wee. Pee-wee befriends her easily and talks with her about everyone in life having a "big but." Of course this conversation is comical, but it serves to reveal the message of Burton's take on the hero's journey. Pee-wee's advice to Simone reveals Pee-wee's own sense of selfhood. He tells Simone to be who she dreams of being, not allowing anything in life to keep her from realizing this. It becomes clear that Pee-wee lives by this proclaimed stance; thus far he has remained constant in his oddity, but in this scene it is revealed that he is conscious of his choice to act in accordance to his "otherness." Simone, as shown at the end of the film, was profoundly transformed by her encounter with Pee-wee; she meets him again after having fulfilled her lifelong dream of going to Paris because Pee-wee helped her find the courage within herself. The quality of being open-minded is an essential element of Burton films; those who are open-minded towards the Burton hero become heroes themselves because the quality of compassion towards others is often a key element of the heroic ideal. Heroes are often identified as such because they care about the well-being of others; Burton magnifies this heroic archetype by allowing this tenet to be one of central importance.

Burton then showcases Pee-wee's nightmare of hell, a portrayal which signals that Pee-wee is entering his archetypal journey into the underworld of his unconscious. Dark and dancing with flames, the scene portrays quintessential underworld imagery; clowns and devils are dissect Pee-wee's bike, directed by the archfiend, Francis. This is Pee-wee's conception of the horrific.[8] The facing of one's fears allows the hero to move on towards self-actualization, but again, Pee-wee merely awakens from the dream, and audiences see the same Pee-wee. This is not to say, though, that this aspect of facing fear to reach self-knowledge is gone in Burton. Burton provides many cases where the characters Pee-wee encounters must face and reconcile with his oddity, identifying themselves as either righteous or villainous people.

When Pee-wee enters the dingy biker bar, the Satan's Helpers motorcycle gang harass him for his odd appearance and force him to leave. After accidently knocking down all of their motorcycles, the gang decided to kill Pee-wee, but grants him a last request—to dance. His colorful dance, as an embrace of life, wins over the bikers who accept Pee-wee as part of the gang. Pee-wee's steadfast assertion of his identity allows the bikers and others in the film, like Mickey and Simone, to put aside their preconceived notions in regard to the "otherness" Pee-wee embodies and embrace his uniqueness instead, thus revealing themselves as unique as well as kind. There are no characters in the film who utterly fail to embrace Pee-wee. The main antagonist, Francis, is not a villain at all; he gets rid of the bike out of fear, and at the end of the film wants to be liked by Pee-wee. There is no real villain in this film because no one can change Pee-wee; he enjoys his epic journey just as enjoys his morning routine.

The focus at the end of the film is on the large crowd assembled at the drive-in to watch Pee-wee's movie of his adventure. Individuals, like Mickey, Simone, and Francis, and groups, like the truck drivers and bikers, who probably never would have otherwise interacted, are brought together as a lively community because of their interaction with Pee-wee. Pee-wee no longer is required to remain solitary. Burton shows the success of the other characters' heroic journey based on this last element of his films; if the odd hero is embraced and need not return to his isolated existence, then heroes abound in a new atmosphere of inclusion, and thus society is rejuvenated. In this film, Burton achieves a heroic ideal as a communal apotheosis, where the environment shifts from one of exclusion to one of inclusion, resulting in the betterment of all.

Oftentimes, the classic hero is portrayed as one who must be sacrificed for the greater good of the people, but Burton films do not promote this traditional archetype, as the requirement of this would counter the Burton idea of openness and acceptance to those who are different. Pee-wee forces those he encounters to face themselves—either they can go with society's view and label him as weird, or they can embrace his odd purity.[9] Those who are open-minded and can lay aside prejudice end up renewed by knowing Pee-wee; they become more like him and value the quirky uniqueness of their own personalities, receiving the final transformation of the hero's journey.

Burton's *Edward Scissorhands* follows a similar archetypal format to *Pee-wee's Big Adventure*. Peg (Dianne Wiest), the kind and motherly Avon seller, enters alone into Edward's realm, and again, Burton immediately visually contrasts the monotone world of Peg's society with the stunningly colorful domain of Edward as "other." Inside she finds that she has entered an immediate otherworld; her senses are dazzled as Burton captures her face lighting up at each massive lawn sculpture. This otherworld that she has stepped into is purposely shot to be lush and verdant, making Peg gasp in awe; Burton uses this technique of zooming in on the faces of characters as they experience the intense pleasure of a sensory overload in later scenes when people first encounter Edward's talents, showing Edward (Johnny Depp) and his talents as a needed interjection into a stagnant suburbia. Inside the castle, Edward creeps out from the shadows and into the light, fully facing Peg in his odd and scary form, a scene set up to meet traditional expectations of horror films, but Peg chooses another option than the expected scene where she might flee the castle screaming; instead, Burton shows Peg gasp, look fully at his gigantic scissor hands, and then immediately smile and walk towards him. Burton has laid down the foundation of the film—that Peg, in defying traditional expectations, has not rejected the man before her, labeling him a monster, but has instantaneously embraced him, showing the audience a new way of becoming a hero—open-minded kindness in the face of the "other."

Like Pee-wee's home, Edward's castle is also portrayed as odd and filled with vibrant inventions. Edward's appearance also solidifies him as odd; he is quite pale, with unruly hair, scars all over his face, and most notably has gigantic scissors for hands. Edward is distinctive in his artistic ability shown through landscaping. Audiences see tenderness in the connection between Edward and his creator and the kind purity they saw in Pee-wee. Audiences also see something that marks Edward as different from Pee-wee; Pee-wee is outwardly unique and confident, and those that know him become stronger because of this, but Edward is more subdued. His isolation, after the death of his inventor, shows a harsher side of existence. Though isolated, he has become an artist, which suggests a willingness to embrace the pleasure of life despite myriad challenges. Edward's portrayal as artistic, gentle, and sensitive to the feelings of others will provide a framework for Edward becoming a spiritual hero, thus, like Pee-wee, encouraging those who know him to also find their own spirituality.

Edward begins the first archetype of the hero's journey by leaving his comfortable surroundings to venture into what is, for him, the unknown of Burton's suburbia. Edward's fearful face shows that everything he encounters is foreign to him. Burton's portrayal of suburbia also makes this film darker than *Pee-wee's Big Adventure*; it focuses a great deal on the often grotesque side of society. Burton stated of his conception of "suburbia":

> I think the atmosphere that I grew up in, yes, there was a subtext of normalcy. I don't even know what the word means, but it's stuck in my brain. It's weird. I don't know if it's specifically American, or American in the time I grew up, but there's a very strong sense of categorization and conformity. I remember being forced to go to Sunday school for a number of years, even though my parents were not religious. No one was really religious; it was just the framework. There was no passion for it. No passion for anything. Just a quiet, kind of floaty, kind of semi-oppressive, blank palette that you're living in.[10]

True to Burton's conception of suburbia, he portrays the world in which Edward arrives as a representation of societal expectation for "normalcy";

each house as exactly the same, only painted a different pastel shade, he is identifying society in its demand for conformity as what is in need of transformation. Edward's entrance into this suburbia serves to start a process of growth for the residents of this community.

Edward encounters helpers and hindrances along his journey. The people of suburbia are immediately intrigued by Edward's "otherness." When they meet him, they seem to accept him, but Burton soon ends this and reveals that they are only treating him like a spectacle, wanting him to landscape their shrubs, groom their pets, and give them artistic haircuts. Burton plays with the effect Edward has on people; Joyce (Kathy Baker) and the women getting new hairstyles from Edward, are portrayed as experiencing the height of their sensual awareness. Their facial expressions and body language show that they thoroughly enjoy the release of a pent-up desire for change and nonconformity that Edward brings to them; even Joyce's toes suggestively curl with pleasure. Many state that they know someone who can "fix" Edward. Joyce tries to seduce Edward, and his reaction, of wide-eyed terror and shock as he sits frozen, and then flees from her, once again shows Edward's purity. His character is not in the film to be transformed by society; he is there to call out the quest in others. When Joyce is denied by Edward, she misunderstands his purity, and instead of choosing to embrace him on a platonic, even spiritual level, she decides to turn against him, getting the neighbors to support her disdain. Contrasting their earlier scene, the women of the neighborhood shift from embracing Edward to whispering about the danger he embodies; their intrigue of his uniqueness turns them from helpers into hindrances.

Edward enters the next heroic archetype because of the actions of the people of the community. The archetypal underworld forms when society shows its worst state. After breaking into Jim's (Anthony Michael Hall) home, because Kim (Winona Ryder) wanted him to, he becomes wanted by the police. It is at this stage that a clear villain emerges in Jim; he sets Edward up to be caught by the police for breaking and entering. Jim also witnessed Edward accidentally cut Kim and later Kevin (Robert Oliveri), Kim's brother, and he convinces people that Edward is violent. Burton presents the judgmental and negative aspects of society as creating a dark underworld, portrayed here, with again blatant Frankenstein overtones; shot in low light with grey overtones, the mob of suburban citizens seek to kill Edward. As Campbell states of his underworld archetype, "the cave you fear to enter holds the treasure you seek," meaning that the mythic underworld is the symbolic facing of one's worst fears in an effort to achieve physic betterment. Edward is forced to face his worst fear in an atmosphere that is now utterly different than the purity he embodies.

Far more than Pee-wee, Edward is viewed as a threat to society. Many who see him fear him when they see his giant scissors. His scissors keep him from having human contact; he oftentimes accidentally cuts anyone who gets too close. The scissors also make Edward appear disabled, but he repeatedly shows that the scissors are what make him an artist in a community of monotony, and again this attention to difference is undoubtedly a part of Burton's message. Because of the reaction of the community to his apparent disability, he is isolated from them and labeled a monster.

Martin Norden in his *The Cinema of Isolation* identifies a stereotype in film of, as he terms it, the "saintly sage," characters who are often portrayed as wise, asexual, disabled, usually afflicted with blindness, and serve to point out truth in a film.[11] Although Edward comes close to this filmic stereotype, Burton pushes the character of Edward beyond this role. Edward represents difference; those who encounter him are faced with an opportunity, much like the characters that encounter the "saintly sage," but Burton adds another spin here—to reject Edward, or members of one's own community who may be different, is wrong, and the rejection of diversity will only cause a society to stagnate and fail. Edward is portrayed as an embodiment of the necessary process of change society needs to endure in order to grow. His artistic hairstyles and landscape designs shows that he offers revitalization, but the duality of the same scissors that create causing friction, even pain, symbolizes the necessary challenges that come with change. His scissorhands force audiences to cut to the core of this issue—just because someone is different or even fearful, the rejection of him or her may abort necessary communal growth. Similar to Thomas More's utopia, where a disabled person becomes a "burden to themselves and all about them ... [and] should ... choose to die,"[12] the society of the film tries to symbolically euthanize Edward; they try to make him expendable, deeming his talents no longer useful to the community, and attempt to rid themselves of him, but in turn only succeed in euthanizing themselves as they succumb back into stagnation.

Edward has remained innocent throughout the film. Edward is kind and accepting, when much of society is judgmental and violent. The film closes with Edward's underworld experience extending to the safety of his home; there he faces the fear that accompanies the underworld archetype. Edward's one fear that dominates his psyche is another loss of someone he loves; the prospect of losing Kim allows him to take hold of the situation that he could not control when his creator suddenly died. Edward stabs and kills Jim to save Kim. At the end of his heroic journey, Edward also does not undergo the expected archetypal transformation. He closes just as he was at the start of the film, alone. Again, this lack of clear transformation shows Burton's twist on the journey of a hero. Edward, like Pee-wee, does not to need to change; he is already the self-actualized product of the heroic journey; his spirituality that was suggested in the beginning of the movie was actualized in his behavior towards others throughout the film. That Edward is forced to retreat back into isolation is Burton's testament of societal failure; at the end of *Pee-wee* a new and better vibrant community gathers; at the end of this film, the characters shuffle back to their monochromatic homes.

This film ends with a crowd assembled to demand the uniformity and monotony they embraced at the start of the film. The characters who participate in the mob resist and fear Edward, and so they are spiritual failures. Jim closes the film as a villain because he vilifies himself. He, like the mob, identified Edward as a threat to the community and labeled him as dangerous, not transformative. Jim dies at the close of the film because he is a character who resists change; he is threatened by Edward, and in this rejection, he has stagnated and is spiritually dead. The film closes with the opportunities Edward embodied lost forever to the majority of characters, but just as was discussed with Pee-wee, Burton does not allow Edward to be cast in a sacrificial role. Burton pointedly directs audiences away from accepting the hero archetype of sacrifice. Society's treatment of Edward is unacceptable; society should not sacrifice Edward because he is different. If one is sacrificed in a Burton film, like Edward seems to be, no one is saved, and the last scene of onlookers, is shot to only show disappointed faces with nothing left to offer themselves or their communities; they simply go back to the mundane lives they lived before.

Though Edward is the "other," and his presence forces people into uncomfortable realms, the characters who embrace him, thus supporting an atmosphere of inclusion, reach the final heroic archetype of transformation and apotheosis; which is the surpassing of "the delusions of [the hero's] formerly self-assertive, self-defensive, self-concerned ego," so that the hero "is filled with compassion for the self-terrorized beings who live in fright of their own nightmare.... 'Gift waves' go out from such a one for the liberation of all".[13] Peg never falters in her role as hero; from the moment she sees Edward, she chooses not to be afraid and fully supports him by taking him into her family. She treats him with the kindness he deserves, and at the end of the film, she is portrayed as heroically spiritual for knowing the worth of Edward and realizing that her society is not ready for his uniqueness, so she states that he should return home.

Kim is the most spiritually transformed at the close of the film. In the beginning she is portrayed as a young follower of the crowd and remains undecided about Edward throughout much of the film, but by the end, she falls in love with him. Kim physically embraces Edward, who has spent most of life not being able to touch anyone. It is also Kim who saves Edward's life at the end of the film and carries the lesson of his story on to the next generation in her telling of Edward to her granddaughter. Peg's and Kim's lives are filled with more beauty for having known Edward. Burton consistently shoots the scenes between first Peg and Edward, and then Kim and Edward, in close-up shots to show the full connection between the characters. The facial expressions of these actors when paired are only serene; each person looks directly into the other's eyes, and it is clear that spiritual the opportunity that Joyce missed when she attempted to seduce Edward, is understood by Peg and Kim. They love Edward, and it is this love for him, that allows them to love themselves. Inclusion and love of Edward offers an opportunity into the enlightenment of Campbell's final stage for the hero; if all the characters embraced Edward, as was done with Pee-wee, then a state of apotheosis for the community would have been reached, but this is distinctly not the case in this film.

Lennard Davis in *Enforcing Normalcy: Disability, Deafness, and the Body* advocates a reexamination of what society deems normal.[14] Burton's heroes, like Edward, allow those who encounter them an opportunity to assess societal definitions of what is "normal" and "abnormal"; these terms must be scrutinized and ultimately cast aside if Burton's characters can ever become heroes themselves.

Burton's *Charlie and the Chocolate Factory* also details heroic archetypes, but presents a twist to the expected format. Pee-wee and Edward both left behind their comfortable, odd surroundings to embark on a journey into the unknown, a heroic requirement. In this film, however, the hero brings society into his realm, and because of this twist, the supporting characters go on the heroic journey, and the hero stays in his element, but ends up spiritually transformed.

In this film, society is again in need of transformation. From the initial scenes, Burton shows an environment of degradation with myriad factories being the focus of this deprivation, and again, Burton's use of monochromatic colors signals to audiences the societal need for a colorful Burton hero. Early in the film, Burton also contrasts the rich and powerful with the poor. Charlie Bucket (Freddie Highmore) is portrayed as "neither rich nor powerful"; he lives with his parents and four grandparents in squalid conditions of extreme poverty, shot by Burton in an extreme dark, grey color schematic. Almost all of the other characters portrayed are only concerned with money and prestige, but Charlie, though undeniably poor, is kind and happy.

From the first glimpse of Willy Wonka, he is identified as the Burton hero prototype. His flamboyant appearance stands in stark contrast to all of society. Whereas audiences were forced to quickly leave Pee-wee's and Edward's home environment, this film brings society intimately inside Wonka's realm with the entrance of the five ticket winners and their chaperones. Wonka is the most grandiose inventor audiences have yet seen in Burton films, signaling again his originality and "otherness." Wonka is comfortable in his odd, solitary realm, and appears confident in his unique personality.

The moment the five kids and their caretakers step through the gates into Wonka's environment, they start the hero's journey, leaving behind their comfortable homes and immediately entering the "Belly of the Whale" archetype: Wonka's candy oasis, gum factory, squirrel room, etc. The unknown experiences these characters encounter still give them the familiar Burton opportunity to be transformed by the presence of the Burton hero. Most brought within fail this opportunity and are cast out.

The kids and their parents represent different facets of society.[15] The four children and parents do not listen to Wonka; they do not interact with him; they are much like the community members of *Edward Scissorhand's* suburbia. As accurately connected to Dahl's book, Burton portrays the children as mere representations of the parents, who are representations of society as Wonka sees it, and they all are shown as spiritual failures, with the exception of Charlie and his Grandpa Joe (David Kelly).

Wonka is a nebulous character. He is original, inventing a world based only on his whims, but he is also portrayed as having a dark side. He knows the outcomes of his experiment before the children get there, as evidenced by the rehearsed songs and actions of the Oompa Loompas (Deep Roy). Wonka watches with delight as the children succumb to their predetermined fates, whispering his warnings, and purposely not saving any of them. The character of Wonka follows the stereotype of a genius thriving in isolation, but as with Pee-wee and Edward, Burton requires that the protagonist enter society to allow others a chance to act heroically. Pee-wee and Edward came forward into the world of others fully self-actualized, but attainment of self-knowledge is lacking in Wonka; thus, the people, specifically Charlie and his Grandpa Joe, must switch Burton's formula and enter Wonka's realm in order to allow him the opportunity to act heroically when faced with the "other." Wonka is forced out of isolation and into spiritual self-actualization.

Charlie reverses Wonka's experiment, thus reversing the expected Burton heroic journey. Charlie will help Wonka to attain the final goal of Campbell's hero's journey. Charlie repeatedly takes the time to connect with Wonka; he is the only character who asks Wonka personal questions about his childhood. These scenes of Wonka as a child tie the film into Campbell's quest of the hero because Wonka's journey is revealed as taking place within his own psyche. Charlie helps Wonka revisit areas of his life that left him unfulfilled. As Burton's addition to the plot, audiences glimpse Wonka's childhood, a place he hasn't thought about for forty years, to find that Wonka's father (Christopher Lee) infringed on Wonka's sense of identity and freedom out of fear; never letting him eat candy for fear of allergies, or never allowing him travel for fear of losing him. As the children proceed on their heroic journeys, Wonka falls into more and more flashbacks of his past, and it is clear that Wonka, by the lost look in his eye, has fallen into melancholy, as he quickly skirts over his hurtful memories with commands for the children to "move along." Through his memories, Wonka must psychically face the same unknown places that the children are facing in their odd experiences in his factory, so that he too will have access to gaining Campbell's state of apotheosis.

Charlie is portrayed as spiritually heroic. He is kind and sincere and remains consistent in sharing a trait that Wonka, and other Burton heroes, value—enjoyment of life. He wins Wonka's game because he understands that the factory and candy are about embracing the goodness and pleasure of life. At the end of the film, Charlie and his family are shown to have been transformed in small ways; visually they have brought color into their existences by fixing their home and taking initiative in work, but just as Pee-wee and Edward never transformed far from their original selves, neither does Charlie after his heroic experience. Audiences also see that all of the outcast children are transformed in small ways as well; some are a bit odd now; Violet (Anna-Sophie Robb) is violet, but they appear happy in their oddity. Though, because the format of this film has switched, Wonka transforms more than Charlie and the other members of society.

As Wonka and Charlie ascend out of the factory, Wonka now physically begins his heroic journey. Wonka enters the archetype of the unknown as he arrives at Charlie's home. He further enters this state when he presents Charlie the gift of his factory, only if Charlie agrees to go there alone. When Charlie refuses to go without his family, Wonka states that this is "unexpected and weird," showing that even conceiving of this kind of human attachment is Wonka's "Belly of the Whale" stage. Wonka's isolation within his factory has only actualized his father's definition of him; Wonka has made himself an outcast who travels nowhere; the Oompa Loompas are all identical, and so no diversity is valued within what was meant to be a pronouncement of the importance of difference. Charlie encourages Wonka to confront his actual father, which is again another quintessential heroic archetype—the "atonement with the father," and this he must do in order to fully embrace his own selfhood.

Wonka enters his underworld, the home of his father. Inside, Wonka and his father are reconciled, and now Wonka is ready to present his odd, actualized self back into the world again. The film concludes as flipped from the format of the other two—Wonka has undergone the heroic transformation because of his encounter with an inclusive society, through his experience with Charlie's family. Charlie and his family showed Wonka that society was not all he labeled it to be; their consistent inclusion of Wonka transformed him spiritually and allowed him to heal the scars left by his own childhood, thus enabling him to reach the final stage of the heroic journey—self-actualization. Wonka in this flipped format shows that the hero in his oddity can be a part of the outside world; by coexisting, and not being forced to retreat like Edward had to, they transform each other. After all, Wonka created candy for people to experience moments of the sublime, and when he could not connect with others, he could no longer create. Burton renews Campbell's heroic quest by allowing the once solitary transformed hero to reconnect with the others, and out of this union of Charlie with Wonka, marvelous new creations can emerge because there is at least the possibility for a state of communal apotheosis at the close of the film.

Though Burton's films appear fanciful, the message behind them is one of stark societal criticism; Burton repeatedly showcases that the flaws of society come from a resistance to embrace difference. His films promote the necessity of the "other"; those who are different are heroes because they can revitalize and provide meaning to a stagnant society. Burton's heroes present their complete, and odd, selves to the world, and enable society to embark on their own journeys by either embracing them, thus embracing the unique components of themselves, or shunning them, and imprisoning themselves within stagnant monotony. Because of the encounter with the odd Burton hero, communities of rowdy bikers, lonely housewives, selfish factory owners, and audience members have been given an opportunity to partake on the journey of the hero with its promise of an inclusive, vibrant communal transformation.

Notes

1. Joseph Campbell, famous modern mythologist (1904–1987), though renowned in popular culture, has often been criticized within academic circles (Alan Dundes, *Sacred Narratives*, 1984; Walter Gulick, "The Thousand and First Face," *Noel*, 1990; Marc Manganaro, *Myth, Rhetoric, and the Voice of Authority*, 1992; Robert Ellwood, *The Politics of Myth*, 1999) for not displaying a deeper understanding of the myths he referenced in their entirety; Bob Trubshaw, "An Overview of Mythological Theory," *Mythology, Cultural Studies and Related Disciplines*, 1–17. Rosemary Zumwalt notes "Joseph Campbell ... was certainly the most popular of those who studied pattern. Campbell divides the

hero's adventures into the formula of separation, initiation, and return. He truncates the hero's biographies, never examining the life of one person in its entirety. His major conclusion, in keeping with the tenor of the myth-ritual school, denies historicity to the heroes of tradition"; cited in Magoulik.

2. Joseph Campbell, *Hero with a Thousand Faces* (Princeton: Princeton University Press, 1949), 49–68. The adventure of the hero, according to Campbell, continuously holds a set of predictable patterns: first the hero is called to leave the comfort of his or her familiar surroundings. Next, the heroes often encounter helpers along the way that guide them towards a heroic outcome; it is also common for the heroes to encounter hindrances in the form of people, possibly villainous, monsters, or simply obstacles to overcome. The heroes also face a stage that Campbell terms the "Belly of the Whale" where they find themselves in a realm that is completely unfamiliar to them; this experience of the unknown can take many forms, but often it culminates to a journey to the underworld or otherworld. Here, the hero faces his or her fears, coined by Campbell as "Atonement with the Father." After leaving this realm, the hero is usually transformed and has gained a sense of inner enlightenment.

3. Heroic Gilgamesh in the Sumerian "Epic of Gilgamesh" does not save anyone and does not achieve his mission to find immortality, but still Gilgamesh concludes his journey transformed; the boon of his journey was self-knowledge. Hercules works to eradicate his shame of killing his wife and children by overcoming twelve impossible tasks and finishes his journey healed and transformed, achieving immortality.

4. Carl Jung used myth to represent "the process of individual development," stating that an individual's unconscious contains both personal and collective elements, and that the "collective unconscious contains archetypal patterns of human experience of more than a million years"; they represent "the symbolic process that … is fundamental to the development of the mind" to allow one to attain self-actualization. Carol Leader, "The Odyssey: A Jungian Perspective," *British Journal of Psychotherapy* 25.4 (2009), 507–508.

5. William Doty, *Mythography: The Study of Myths and Rituals* (University of Alabama Press, 2000), 175; Mythology scholar Doty, citing Manganaro (1992), also criticizes Campbell's often inadequate understating of the entirety of the myths background; "Campbell's 'synthetic' master-myth ignores cultural holism in the colossal authorial effort of fitting together a piecework universalism—precisely part of the modernist 'finding an answer to everything' project, but it deconstructs as 'an ethnocentric valorization of Western power mechanisms.'"

6. Tim Burton, *Tim Burton: Interviews* (Jackson: University of Mississippi Press, 2005), 3.

7. Helena Bassil-Morozow, *Tim Burton: The Monster and the Crowd* (New York: Routledge, 2010), 22.

8. Campbell's archetype of the hero entering an underworld presents the hero with an opportunity to face his worst fears.

9. There is a difference here between childlike purity and the purity embodied by Pee-wee and other Burton heroes. The "purity" of the Burton hero is directly tied to their own self-actualization; they are "pure" because they are full themselves. They are not naïve heroes; they choose a pure innocence that comes directly from their experiences.

10. David Breskin, "Tim Burton: The Rolling Stone Interview," *Rolling Stone*, July 1992.

11. Martin F. Norden, *The Cinema of Isolation: A History of Physical Disability in the Movies* (New York: Rutgers University Press, 1994), 131.

12. Thomas More, *Utopia* (London: Cadell Davis, 1808), 102.

13. Campbell, *Hero*, 165–6.
14. Lennard Davis, *Enforcing Normalcy: Disability, Deafness, and the Body* (New York: Verso Publishing, 1995).
15. Augustus Gloop fails first because he is gluttonous and "infantile," as the Oompa Loompas state, and this quality within society is something Wonka rejects. Violet Beauregarde and her mother fail because they are perfectionists and only care about prestige. Veruca Salt and her father are obviously greedy, so they are sent out with the rotten garbage. Mike Teavee represents the side of society that is unconcerned with human connection, preferring technology and violence, so he is shrunk down to a level of unimportance.

Bibliography

Bassil-Morozow, Helena. *Tim Burton: The Monster and the Crowd*. New York: Routledge, 2010.
Breskin, David. "Tim Burton: The Rolling Stone Interview." *Rolling Stone*, July 1992.
Burton, Tim. *Tim Burton: Interviews*. Jackson: University of Mississippi Press, 2005.
Campbell, Joseph. *The Hero with a Thousand Faces*. Princeton University Press, 1949.
Davis, Lennard. *Enforcing Normalcy: Disability, Deafness, and the Body*. New York: Verso Publishing, 1995.
Doty, William G. *Myth: A Handbook*. Westport, CA: Greenwood Press, 2004.
_____. *Mythography: The Study of Myths and Rituals*. University of Alabama Press (2nd ed.), 2000.
Downing, Christine. "Journeys to the Underworld." *Mythosphere* 1.2 (1999): 175–193.
Leader, Carol. "The Odyssey: A Jungian Perspective." *British Journal of Psychotherapy* 25.4 (2009): 506–519.
Lefkowitz, Mary. "The Myth of Joseph Campbell." *American Scholar* 59.3 (1990): 429–434.
Magoulik, Mary. "Quotes from Scholars of Myths On Heroism and Myth throughout History and in Today's World," 2000. https://faculty.gcsu.edu/custom-website/mary-magoulick/hero_quotes.htm.
Norden, Martin F. *The Cinema of Isolation: A History of Physical Disability in the Movies*. New York: Rutgers University Press, 1994.
Potter, Russell A. "Edward Schizohands: The Postmodern Gothic Body." *Postmodern Culture* 2.3 (1992): 1–11.
Trubshaw, Bob. "An Overview of Mythological Theory." *Mythology, Cultural Studies and Related Disciplines* (2003). http://www.indigogroup.co.uk/foamycustard/fc047.htm.

Mixed Assortment
The Typical and Atypical Body
in Charlie and the Chocolate Factory

Elizabeth Leigh Scherman

> MIKE TEAVEE: "Why is everything here completely pointless?"
> CHARLIE BUCKET: "Candy doesn't have to have a point. That's why it's candy."
> —*Charlie and the Chocolate Factory*, 2005

In Roald Dahl's 1964 children's book *Charlie and the Chocolate Factory*, the eccentric chocolatier Willy Wonka creates just what he pleases, and doesn't particularly care what others think. In like manner, director Tim Burton creates films to please himself.[1] He lurches merrily forward creating worlds populated by deviant and atypical bodies, and apparently never worries about the "point." He has said that he abhors political correctness, and his films certainly seem to underscore that belief.[2] Yet in his very denial of what is acceptable and non-acceptable, Burton offers us a glimpse into a world where atypicality is neither forbidden nor patronized. It is a world where the outward form may offer little clue as to the soul within.

The atypical body in Burton's films may, then, be both celebrated and pitied—and often at the same time. It depends upon the story, the setting, and the characters themselves—and in this, films such as *Charlie and the Chocolate Factory* (2005) may be seen to present what is called a social model of disability.[3] Regardless of whether an individual experiences his or her body as impaired, society can *disable* that individual by attitude, law, politics, medical acts, and lack of access. It is society which ultimately assigns certain bodies value and others less value, and thus what we call "disability" changes with time and differs from culture to culture; it is not a fixed characteristic of any one body or behavior. Burton's Charlie (Freddie Highmore) argues that candy doesn't have to have a meaning or a "point"; it exists in a myriad of varieties simply to be enjoyed. In like fashion, we humans inhabit the earth in a myriad of embodiments, and certainly our bodies are real and meaningful to us—not simply constructed by society.

Unlike candy, however, our bodies are often assigned a meaning or moral value by society—and particularly by media. In film, for example, a conspicuously disabled body is rarely, if ever, incidental. The disabled character is commonly evil or inspirational—virtually never neutral. Yet if we extend the analogy, we are indeed a "mixed assortment" of humanity, delicious in all of our flavors and incarnations, and any "meaning" that is externally conferred upon our bodies or behaviors is not inherent, but rather given to that body by society.

In *Charlie*, we see three common ways in which meaning is assigned to our bodies. First, we are valuable if we can be commodified—if we can contribute economically to society. Second, we are valuable if we can be "cured" or "fixed"—if for example our appearance, health, or body particularities can be altered to meet society's expectations. Finally, we are valuable if we can be "redeemed" from what society perceives as unnatural thought or behavior, brought back into the fold, and "normalized." But because this is a Burton film, such homogenization does not go unchallenged. There remains, at the end of *Charlie and the Chocolate Factory*, a certain gleeful refusal of certain characters to be "fixed" and subsequently assimilated into typical, homogenized society. That they are able to do so speaks to their agency—their ability to *act upon* society rather than merely be *acted upon*—and thus presents an intriguing, if idealistic, illustration of the critical nature of socioeconomic power in the lives of disabled people.

"Are They Real People?" They Are If They Can Earn a Living!

There is not a sign of humanity in the first minutes of Burton's *Charlie and the Chocolate Factory*. The film opens with a view of the foreboding smokestacks of Willy Wonka's factory, which towers over the snow-covered village below. Composer Danny Elfman's score plays in an apprehensive minor key as we enter the dark world of the factory, where chocolate bars whirl and ascend without the touch of human hands. Mechanical, spider-like machines wrap them and send them on their way. The only touch of color in the monochromatic landscape is that of the bright red trucks moving through the factory gates, which automatically open before them.[4] However, there are—as far as we can see—no drivers. It is a world without emotion—

a phenomenon that foreshadows Burton's Willy Wonka (Johnny Depp) himself.

It is telling that the first human being that we see is Charlie Bucket himself. Burton has selected Charlie to act as the initial juxtaposition to a sterile and mechanical world—he is the antithesis to the depersonalized, industrialized world of the factory.[5] He is, as the narrator tells us, an "ordinary" little boy, who is "not faster, stronger, or more clever than other children." In other words, Charlie Bucket is Everyman, the most "average" of children—if poorer than most. In a word, *normal*.

Burton wanted the actor who played Charlie to appear underfed, rather than a "rosy-cheeked guy who looks like he's just had a good lunch"—an apparent reference to the young actor who portrayed Charlie in the 1971 film version of the book.[6] He is joined by an equally believable cast of half-starved Buckets: Mr. and Mrs. Bucket (Noah Taylor and Helena Bonham Carter), Grandpa Joe and Grandma Josephine (David Kelly and Eileen Essell), and Grandpa George and Grandma Georgina (David Morris and Liz Smith). "They're old," writes Burton. "So make them look old, like they can't get out of bed."[7] Burton has identified as a person who thinks in pictures, who (is) "much more into the visual aspect of things."[8] Morozow observes in the film Burton's trademark "dialecticity of design" using color, size, and contrast.[9] The visual elements to which we are introduced in *Charlie* are never random, never done merely for art's sake. Thus the monochromatic palate of the homogenous "normal" world outside of the factory will give way to riotous color once we enter the marvelously "deviant" world within its walls.[10]

While Charlie himself is a perfectly "ordinary" boy, the shack where he lives with his family is not. It leans precariously to one side, its chimney toppling, its roof torn open with a gaping hole. It stands in stark contrast to the cookie-cutter rows of other houses in the village, which line the gloomy street that leads downhill from the immense factory. It sits, as though quarantined, an aberration—a misfit among the other houses; outcast, disabled. Yet within its broken and fragile body lives a most loving and functional family.

Mr. Bucket works at a toothpaste factory, screwing the tops on toothpaste tubes. His paycheck is secure as long as Willy Wonka's factory churns out the cavity-causing chocolates, but when Wonka suddenly closes the factory, Mr. Bucket's job is eliminated. His ability to provide for his family and to function as an economically valuable member of society is dependent on the whims of the corporate owner up the hill. Even the family's ultimate salvation—Charlie's winning a visit to the newly-reopened factory by his purchase of a candy bar with a golden ticket—is due to the largesse of the wealthy factory owner, Willy Wonka. Had Wonka chosen to keep his factory closed, the Buckets may have lived on cabbage soup forever.

Like the Buckets, the workers who have made the renaissance of the factory possible have also been "rescued" by the magnanimous Willy Wonka. Burton's version of the commodification of these workers, the Oompa-Loompas (all portrayed by actor Deep Roy), might be seen as an absurdist parody of the colonialist's attitude toward a "primitive" people, with the Oompa-Loompas surviving on green caterpillars and worshipping the cocoa bean. Enter chocolatier Willy Wonka. Wonka believes that he knows what's best for the diminutive people, transports them away from their home to what is the equivalent of a sheltered workshop, and pays them—not in peanuts, but in cocoa beans.

The story's implications of colonialism did not go unnoticed. Author Roald Dahl's book met with harsh criticism for its portrayal as the Oompa-Loompas as simple-minded jungle people,[11] living "where no white man had ever been before,"[12] shipped over in "packing cases with holes in them," as animals are shipped,[13] but by the release of the 1971 film version, they were "no longer alcoholic immigrants dressed in leaves as they are in the book."[14] The publishers released a revised version of the book in which the Oompa-Loompas are illustrated as bearded, white-skinned munchkins. By the 2005 film adaptation, they are "kitted out like operatives in the lair of a 1970s James Bond villain."[15] However, they are still portrayed as objects of curiosity, both to the young visitors as well as to the spectatorial audience. They could not pass for "normal" in the village, and they need special provision—warm temperatures—in order to function in the Wonka factory. They are miniature in size, hardly recognized as human.

In addition, they have morphed from individuals to The Oompa-Loompa. Unlike in the 1971 film, where the Oompa-Loompas were portrayed by actors who were little people, people with unique faces, bodies, and ways of moving—the 2005 version reduces all Oompa Loompas to a homogenous aggregate. All Oompa-Loompas look alike. They have no names—at least no names that matter to Wonka or to non–Oompa-Loompas. As Wonka stated in response to Augustus Gloop's question of whether Wonka wanted to learn the children's names, "Can't imagine why it would matter." The children are only a means to an end—his selection of an heir. In like fashion, the Oompa-Loompas—for all Wonka's bragging of how he saved them—are but a means to an economically beneficial end. All Oompa-Loompas can be asked to perform any task, and they are happy to do so. They are atypical, "abnormal" workers, but they are "good" workers because they serve the larger industrial purpose uncomplainingly.

"What is it?" asks Veruca Salt (Julia Winter), seeing an Oompa-Loompa for the first time. The little person she spies in the factory is not yet a person, he is an "it." Then she looks closer and declares, "It's a little person." "Are they real people?" asks Mike Teavee (Jordan Fry). It is Charlie who changes the question from whether the Oompa-Loompas are an "it" or "real people" to their identity. "Who are they?" he asks. "Of course they're real people," replies Wonka. "They're Oompa-Loompas. Imported direct from Loompaland."

Wonka's choice of the word "imported" rather than "immigrated" is notable: these diminutive people are a product, an import, valuable despite the fact that they are an aberration in a taller world. The Oompa Loompas are "real" because their economic contribution to the factory is real. Their differences are tolerated, as differences in physically disabled veterans were tolerated even in the climate leading to the Third Reich—as long as the disabled citizens could earn a living and contribute to the tax base.[16] They are jacks-of-all-trades, interchangeable, serving uncomplainingly as factory grunts, hairdressers, psychiatrists, and entertainers. They are compliant and grateful for their position in the factory. They serve the factory, as others of us serve society, as good workers. In racial terms, they are what has been historically described as a "good negro"; a servant who does not question nor complain about his or her subservient position in society.[17]

This framing of a population of less entitled individuals as "good" if they serve the more highly entitled members of that society without complaint has also been applied to disabled people. The "good crip" ("good cripple"— a reclaimed pejorative used by many who identify as disabled) does not expect to have the same rights, access, and respect that the "normal" citizen enjoys. He or she is tolerated and even appreciated if this is understood.[18] Both the Oompa-Loompas and Mr. Bucket are grateful for the generosity of their benefactors, never questioning their position in life or the fairness of the economic system. Were they to fail in either of these tasks—the ability to contribute to the economy,[19] or the gratitude of "knowing their place," they would, as so many disabled people are today—be frowned upon and devalued.

Of Teeth and Touching: Willy Wonka as Disabled

"Destroy all beauty!" commands a teenaged Tim Burton, speaking to the monster he's created in *Doctor of Doom*, an indie short he produced in 1979.[20] Burton knew well a society which rewarded external beauty and excluded those who were different. He describes suffering through an adolescence marked by orthodontic headgear, which was not only unattractive, but which also prevented him from sleeping at night.[21] Burton describes the "cure" for his orthodontic transgressions as "painful, isolating," and "symbolic, when you have this ugly-looking thing on your head and you already feel like an outsider … that brace was really a symbol of the lack of being able to connect with people."[22] His later films set out to challenge audiences to identify with bodies that have been historically responded to as undesirable, films that were intended "to skewer conformist attitudes and affirm alternative ways of life,"[23] including skeletons, stitched-together bodies, and bodies with unusual parts, such as scissors.

Often described as an "outsider,"[24] Burton has been described as dark and brooding. Yet he has repudiated that notion. "People [who] really know me know that I'm not dark at all," he has insisted.[25] Instead, it is the genre of fantasy—including horror—that is itself dark, he asserts. Fairy tales, he observes, are "amazingly horrific."[26] The fantastical world of *Charlie and the Chocolate Factory* is no exception. Dahl himself refused to tidy up his stories for his young audiences, writing of greedy, nasty people—including children—who were often chillingly punished for their misbehavior.[27] His unflinching portrayal of the cruelty in life came from his own experiences at an English boarding school, as detailed in his novel, *Boy*.[28] "I never got over it," he later recounted, referring to his mistreatment at the hands of older boys.[29]

Like Dahl, Burton himself never "got over" his childhood isolation, but rather than mourn his atypicality, he embraced it. The monsters[30] and outcasts in his films are much more likely to be celebrated as the protagonists than demonized as the other. However, their difficulty in communicating to others mirrors Burton's own difficulty as a child who found verbal communication difficult.[31] "Your image and how people perceive you are at odds with what is inside you," he explained. "You are taught at an early age to conform to certain things … this person's weird, this person's normal. From day one you're categorized. …[p]eople are categorized very easily."[32]

Burton's observation is confirmed by our society's taxonomical reduction or categorization of people labeled "disabled." This one is "hearing impaired," that one is "sight impaired," this one is "cognitively impaired"—the list goes on. Individuals are pigeonholed into neat little cubbies for the sake of medical treatment, "therapy," and funding. In disability studies research as well, the temptation to categorize is difficult to escape. For example, there are the ubiquitous content analyses of texts that are little more than head counts of types of "differences" or "impairments," the largely unquestioned dichotomization of "physical" versus "mental" disabilities (as if the brain were not a physical organ), and the careless conflation of very different life experiences into one convenient category.

It is as if we are one gigantic Sears catalog of genotypes, a catalog broadly divided into "normal" and "abnormal" sections, with the "abnormal" section fastidiously divided into types of aberrations and undesirable characteristics. Into this pottage of human variation steps Burton—for make no mistake, his creatures are human—refusing to play the label game. Dahl's Charlie may serve as the über-normal sun around which all of the deviant characters spin, but the goodness and grace assigned to Charlie are also the defining characteristics of many of Burton's decidedly "abnormal" protagonists, who lack skin, hands, eyes, or good manners. It is these characters that Burton champions and with whom he holds affinity.[33] For example, he describes the character of Edward Scissorhands (Johnny Depp) as a cross between "a newborn and a dog I'd had—unconditional love and purity."[34] The character of Willy Wonka is complex, yet Wonka is not portrayed without sympathy.

The inspiration for Burton's variation on the eccentric chocolatier is debatable. Burton explains that he was influenced by children's television hosts such as Captain Kangaroo and Mr. Rogers.[35] Johnny Depp, who portrays Wonka, has described him as "what I imagined George Bush would look like incredibly stoned."[36] Burton's Wonka has been called "creepy"[37]; "like Dustin Hoffman in *Tootsie*"[38]; as a campy and infantile Pee-wee Herman,[39] and as Michael Jackson.[40] It is Burton himself, however, that may be seen most clearly in Wonka. Wonka is a genius, a rich eccentric who can afford the luxury of isolation from an often unaccepting society. Burton has described a childhood deprived of physical touch and intimacy,[41] much like the motherless childhood of little Willy Wonka. This inability to make human contact is symbolized by the purple rubber gloves worn by elder and younger Wonka, a prop which is also seen in *The Nightmare Before Christmas* (1993), *Edward Scissorhands* (1990), and in *Stalk of the Celery Monster* (1979), a film Burton made while a student at CalArts.

In Burton's version, young Willy (Blair Dunlop) is also imprisoned and disfigured by a medieval-looking set of orthodontic headgear, inflicted upon him by his cold, clinical dentist father (Christopher Lee).[42] In the father's view—ostensibly that of the medical profession, as the older Wonka is described as "the city's most famous dentist"—Willy needs "fixing" because his teeth are not perfect. A disabling and absurd construction is placed upon his head, wrenching his teeth into an artificial smile and rendering eating difficult. Yet the boy Willy does manage to force a piece of clandestine Halloween candy between the prison bars of his headgear, at once swooning over the delicious taste. He is determined to become the maker of the world's most delicious chocolates. Ironically, once he has achieved this goal, he still bears the stigma of the artificial smile—this time as a set of denture-perfect teeth, proffered in an insincere grimace as he attempts to interact with other humans. When he first meets the children, his eyes are wide and terrified as he bares his absurdly "corrected" teeth in what is more like a wince than a smile. In addition, like his creator, Burton's Wonka finds verbal communication difficult. In a failed bid toward "normalcy," he reads platitudes from index cards, grimaces, and glances anxiously at his audience, trying to exhibit the behavior that he believes is expected of him—and it is an utter failure. Like his singing animatronic greeters, he desperately attempts to meet some bizarre standard of chipper cordiality—only to melt down from the effort.

Burton's invention of the backstory of Wonka's childhood might be seen to reflect his own adolescent experience with being "fixed." The final product, however, does not necessarily serve the "abnormal" person, but rather the society. Those whose eyes, faces, speech, or way of behaving or moving are disturbing to the greater community must be made to conform, whether this means physical modification of their body or placing constraints on their behavior. At the very least, their offending characteristics must be made more palatable, even if doing so renders their appearance to that of a store mannequin.

When translated into the real world, the implications of enforced conformity are psychologically and economically sobering. For example, the monocular individual should use a (useless) prosthetic eye rather than inflict upon society the vision of a person with an eye patch; those who are missing a limb should employ a prosthetic limb that looks as "normal" as possible (a prejudice now changing with the development and use of running blades and other prosthetic limbs, in part due to the funding of rehabilitation technology following war), and a wheelchair user should grow excited at the prospect of using a robotic exoskeleton at monumental cost rather than dare to expect society to offer accessible design, such as curb cuts and basic public transportation.[43]

Wonka, however, has the advantage of being extremely wealthy. He grows up to be the designer of a world into which he is not only accepted, but which he controls. How many of us, as children, have desired such a world? In reality, few of us who are treated as outcasts have the luxury of escaping from a society which disables and stigmatizes us. If we attempt reentry into the society, we must meet its standards. Wonka largely escapes this enforced conformity due to his elevated position in society, but the majority of "deviant" or "different" individuals may not indulge themselves in this manner.

For example, Edward Scissorhands—the titular character of Burton's 1990 film—does in fact inhabit an imposing castle which, like the chocolate factory, towers over the village below. However, once he is introduced into the "normal" society by the "harmless as apple pie" Avon lady, Peg Boggs (Dianne Wiest), his need to conform or be banished unfolds at heartbreaking pace. The innocent, naïve Edward (Johnny Depp) lacks hands and is left to fend for himself as an incomplete creature, although his creator had the best of intentions. Edward's scissor-like appendages come from a drawing Burton did in his youth, "a character who wants to touch but can't touch."[44] In fact, to touch another is to wound them, Edward discovers. He is driven out of a town by a mob reminiscent of another intolerant kill-the-creature story, Mary Shelley's *Frankenstein*. Yet like the creature in that classic novel, Edward—and the spectator realizes this[45]—is "human" inside. Burton again uses the deviant body to suggest that all is not as it appears; the outer body may lead to "someone being perceived to be the opposite of who he is."[46]

Edward begins his integration into society as a harmless and even adorable "misfit," earning a place in the neighborhood by—in true Oompa-Loompa fashion—being cute and nonthreatening, and by gratefully performing all of the tasks that he is asked to do, from hair-cutting to topiary creation. However, unlike the diminutive and one-dimensional Oompa-Loompas, Edward has desires of his own, and he is ultimately dangerous—drawing blood and showing his anger by lopping off sections of his topiaries. He has become, in the eyes of the "normals," a "bad crip." He must be returned to the institution from which he came. After all, concedes even his gentlest supporter, Peg, "You know, I think that maybe it might be best if he goes back up there. Because at least there it's safe, and we'd just go back to being normal." Better that Edward is kept safe from society and that society is kept "safe" from him. Both Wonka and Edward remain, in the end, in a self-imposed institution. Wonka, however, experiences twinges of "redemption," while Edward, like Charlie Bucket, has remained pure and blameless from the beginning.

The soul within, as Burton has expressed, may bear little resemblance to either the beauty or monstrosity of the body in which it resides. Children's book author Jane Yolen describes this phenomenon as what we may see as a moral model of disability, where outer form signifies inner character; where "a loving heart [can] be encysted in a horrible form."[47] Alternately, as we shall see, Burton shows us that an outwardly "normal" form can mask an inwardly ugly heart.[48]

You're a Blueberry: Redemption and Punishment *in* Charlie and the Chocolate Factory

In the book *Charlie and the Chocolate Factory*, Willie Wonka invites children to his factory to select a successor to his chocolate kingdom. "The one I liked best at the end of the day would be the winner," he explains. "I want a good sensible loving child, one to whom I can tell all my most precious candy-making secrets."[49] In contrast, Burton's Wonka is merely looking for "the one who is least rotten." Burton may construct Wonka as lowering his standards, but his Charlie is Boy Scout perfect: "modest, cheerful, helpful, creative, generous, and polite."[50] In short, everything that society desires in a productive individual. In contrast, the naughty children—fiercely competitive Violet Beauregarde (AnnaSophia Robb), gluttonous Augustus Gloop (Philip Wiegratz), violent Mike Teavee, and spoilt rotten Veruca Salt—are "monsters" who are from the beginning shown as well deserving of punishment.[51]

Dahl himself experienced a life in which good people were not always saved from injustice. He was no stranger to tragedy, losing a father and sister within two months of each other, and suffering through his own son's disabling accident.[52] In the worlds of his own creation, however, justice is perfectly meted out. Dahl's targets are those whose vices may or may not be apparent on the outside, but inescapably, the nastiness inside of the "bad" children will come to be manifest in their bodies. While the decent, "normal" child, Charlie, does not personally seek vengeance on the others, he displays revulsion at their behavior.[53] "Bullies, nerds, fatsoes, spoiled rich overachievers—all can become objects of hatred for the child who considers himself both normal and victimized," writes Dahl biographer William Schultz. "…[t]he 'revenge' is directed almost exclusively against other children, and mostly for what they are, rather than for some specific harm they have done the hero."[54] Charlie has watched as privileged but horrible children purchase and devour chocolate bars in search of the Golden Ticket, while he and his family starve.

More importantly, Charlie is the avatar of Roald Dahl, who wrote of cruel treatment at the hands of wicked classmates. Thus Charlie is the only child to remain unchanged, both internally and externally—that which is "normal" does not need cure. In contrast, the otherwise typical bodies of the bad children (with the possible exception of the corpulent Augustus Gloop) do not "match" their inner ugliness, and thus must be changed. At the end of the film, the violent Mike Teavee is stretched to an almost one-dimensional figure, most suitable for one who is addicted to the flat screens of television and video games. The competitive gum-chewer gymnast, Violet Beauregarde, is justifiably turned into a giant blueberry after she purloins a forbidden stick of gum. Although she is "de-juiced" down to her normal size, she remains purple, and she is hideously flexible. Veruca Salt covets a trained squirrel and ends up being dragged by a pack of them down the garbage chute, as Augustus covets the chocolate river and ends up being sucked up in a suction tube. Both emerge in disgrace: Veruca covered with reeking garbage and Augustus covered in fecal-like chocolate—a symbolic, if temporary, reflection of their greed. None of the children repent.

Thus they are marked by "assaults on their body shapes"[55] and are deserving, as Schultz observes, of "enduring stigmata."[56] Such stigmata, or embodied marks, have since antiquity been understood to indicate inner moral character. What is referred to as the "moral model" of disability reflects some of the first recorded attempts to explain why a baby is born impaired (or perceived to be impaired) or why people acquire impairments or disfigurements.[57] These explanations commonly associate disability with morality of character, ascribing meanings to the disabled body that go beyond mere biological incidence. In other words, the atypical body is not neutral; it is a signifier of morality.

In the case of the young visitors to Wonka's factory, the physical or outward signifiers are acquired, but the implications are the same: a deviant body is suspected of harboring a deviant soul. Joseph Shapiro argues that children especially learn early on to equate physical wholeness and attractiveness with quality of character, and that "youngsters learn to assume that people with disabilities are more 'different from' than 'similar to' persons without them, and those differences set them apart. The consequences of such beliefs result in segregation and isolation."[58] For example, the beast in the fairy tale "Beauty and the Beast" (and its many cinematic adaptations) is ugly and isolated because his inner character is selfish and ugly; when he repents, he is redeemed by being offered an outwardly beautiful body, which now "matches" his inner person. In contrast, the movie *Shrek*[59] challenges the audience's expectations of redemption as "cure" when Fiona does not achieve "love's true form" as they anticipate. That is, Fiona is inwardly changed for the better, but her outer body does not reflect this by being magically changed into a "normal" and beautiful woman, but rather she remains an ogre. *Shrek* is critically useful as the exception that may prove the rule, as it may be seen to break the rules of the beautiful body/beautiful soul trope.

In *Charlie and the Chocolate Factory*, we move in the opposite direction: the "normal" and even attractive characters are punished by being transformed into hideous monstrosities.[60] At first consideration, then, the message to society, seems to remains the same: the outward body signifies inward morality. As Schultz observes, "Only Charlie escapes doom.... Charlie wins the prize just by being himself."[61] Charlie is "normal" to begin with, a sentiment expressed in Karen O's song "Strange Love" from the *Frankenweenie* soundtrack which champions a persons inner beauty over their outer appearance.[62]

As accommodating as this sentiment may seem in regard to inviting tolerance of different bodies, its premise still runs along a morally modeled vein: that a disabled person must have a "beautiful" or inspirational inner soul to compensate for the sin of inhabiting a deviant body. Certainly Burton himself felt trapped in his outwardly geeky teenage body, and many of his outwardly creepy cinematic characters—including the sweet but stitched-up Sally from *The Nightmare Before Christmas* (1993), Karl the gentle giant in *Big Fish* (1993), and Edward from *Scissorhands*—are not inwardly creepy. However, it is worth remembering that Burton above all resisted categorization of people, and it is difficult to reduce each and every one of his menagerie of misfit characters to "good" or "bad." Burton's films champion the individual standing up for his or her eccentricities and differences, and the punishment falls upon those who would try to force the hero to conform. Like Roald Dahl himself, Burton has expressed a strong sense of justice springing from his boyhood years—and make no mistake, those nasties in Burton's films will not escape unpunished. That the punishment sometimes comes in the form of bodily alteration, as in the case of the naughty children in *Charlie*, or that the nasties may inhabit an outwardly distasteful body (though as often they do not) does not mean that Burton equates outward deviance with inward deviance.

In fact, Burton creates a surprising twist on the story that offers a resistive reading to the outer beauty/inward beauty correlation. At the end of the film, there remains more than one "character" who remains deviant and who offers the audience the scandalous option that one may actually choose to inhabit an atypical body or lifestyle.

Not Quite Homogenized

Wonka's chocolate may be "homogenized" by being mixed in a giant waterfall, but not everyone or everything in his world fits neatly into a standardized wrapper. The first of the characters to defy assimilation or "normalization" is Burton's Willy Wonka himself. To an extent, one could argue that he is "redeemed." He is reconciled with his estranged father and he allows the Bucket family to adopt him—a concession that nevertheless hints at his pleasure at being brought "back into the fold." In the ending scene, he is shown being invited to join the Buckets at dinner, a chance to join a family, something which he obviously welcomes. When Grandma Georgina leans over to him and whispers, "You smell like peanuts," Wonka hesitates only a moment to collect himself. Then he leans in return toward her and whispers, "You smell like old people. And soap. I like it." When Mrs. Bucket scolds Wonka and Charlie for "talking business" at the dinner table, they exchange one last conspiratorial whisper, for all the world like young brothers.

Yet it is in the closing frames of the film that we learn that the joke is on us: Burton's Wonka hasn't been assimilated into society after all. Rather, he has remained true to his deviant self and required that society adapt to him. We see the Buckets' tumbledown, outcast shack, complete with leaky roof and precarious tilt. It is snowing, and the Buckets are seated around the supper table. As the camera pulls out, however, we realize that the entire house is contained within the chocolate factory, surrounded by candy trees, and that the "snow" is sugar being sprinkled from giant machines. The house itself, as a character, has refused to be "cured."[63] It has remained its magnificently crippled self, apparently with the blessing of both Wonka and Buckets. Like Charlie, it had inner beauty, even though it's exterior is still dull and monochromatic, but rather than assimilating itself into the "normal" outside world, it has now been assimilated into the marvelously colorful, rule-breaking world of the chocolate factory. It is over the rainbow, in Wonderland, now celebrated for its oddness and brokenness, and filled with a whole, loving family. The image is entrancing: if only we could create our own world, our own home, our own rules. Yet the sugar-coated province of Wonka's world is not all fantasy. The reality is that the misfits, Buckets and Wonkas of our world—including Burton—are able to make their own rules because they have the money to do so. They are producing a lucrative commodity, and thus they themselves can escape the economically marginalized lives in which many "deviant" or disabled members of society are imprisoned.

Burton offers a film that may be read as both enforcing and challenging the concept that the atypical body reflects a devalued or disabled inner character, although the atypical body may be commodified or the character morally "redeemed." He treats both outwardly beautiful and outwardly unusual bodies with equal lack of sentimentality. In the clincher, however, he tips his hand to the outcast and the deviant; that which in our society may find its parallel in disabled or disfigured individuals. The Bucket house is uncompromised; "whole" in its incompleteness. It does not need to be redeemed, for it was "normal" to begin with. Burton reflects, "Sometimes people say, 'Are you going to do a real film with real people?' But to me the words 'normal' and 'real' have a thousand different meanings. What's real? What's normal?"[64] Burton's *Charlie and the Chocolate Factory* invites us into a world where the variations of humanity are as diverse as the candies rolling off the conveyer belt.

Notes

1. Tim Burton, *Burton on Burton*, ed. Mark Salisbury (London: Faber & Faber, 2006).

2. Alison McMahan observes that Burton appears to make choices that "jeopardize the broadest possible acceptance of his films." See Alison McMahan, *The Films of Tim Burton: Animating Live Action in Contemporary Hollywood*. (New York: Continuum, 2005). See also Burton, *Burton on Burton*, 223, and Christopher Lee, "Tim Burton," *Interview* 35, no. 7 (August 2005), 78–80.

3. There are actually many social models of disability—models which focus on society's role in disabling its members—thus I resist using the term "*the* social model of disability."

4. This gloomy and monochromatic landscape is trademark of sorts of Burton's films; for example, *The Nightmare Before Christmas* and *Edward Scissorhands*, where a gray palate serves as the backdrop for riotous and carefully placed color. Contrast this with the 1971 version of Dahl's book, which opens with chipper music and a bright, sun-drenched vision of Charlie's village. In Burton's film, the drab outer façade of the Bucket home belies its bright "inner character" of love, belonging, and joy. It is a literal embodiment of the adage "it's what on the inside that counts."

5. Roger Clarke writes that Burton's vision of the factory reflects a relatively new anxiety about factory mechanization. He notes that in 1964, the year the book was published, "a sizeable number of people were working in factories." Roger Clarke, "An Improper Charlie," *Sight & Sound* 15, no. 8 (November 9, 2012), 22–25.

6. Burton, 226.

7. Ibid.

8. Christopher Lee, "Tim Burton." *Interview* 35, no. 7 (August 2005), 78–80.

9. Helena Bassil-Morozow, Tim Burton: The Monster in the Crowd, A Post-Jungian Perspective. (London: Routledge, 2010), 131.

10. The term *deviant* may be appreciated for its many layers of meaning. In its purest form it is a reference to a statistical deviation from the norm, with no moral value implied. In this sense I would feel comfortable using it without scare quotes to describe characters or situations in the film. However, the term is also used to assign perverted or suspect morality to a character or situation, and as this is a subjective description, I put the term in scare quotes. In contrast, the term *monster* is largely inseparable from its negative connotation as an aberrant variation, one that is not to be desired or valued.

11. Paul Heins, ed., *Crosscurrents of Criticism: Horn Book Essays, 1968–1977*, (Boston: Horn Book, 1977).

12. Donnarae McCann, and Gloria Woodard, *The Black American in Books for Children: Readings in Racism* (Metuchen, N.J.: Scarecrow Press, 1972), 112.

13. Roald Dahl, *Charlie and the Chocolate Factory*. (New York: Knopf, 1964), 76.

14. Clarke, "An Improper Charlie."

15. Ibid.
16. See Carol Poore, *Disability in Twentieth-Century German Culture* (Ann Arbor: University of Michigan Press, 2007).
17. See Ed Guerrero, *Filming Blackness: The African American Image in Film.* (Philadelphia: Temple University Press, 1993), 77.
18. Ibid.
19. According to the Bureau of Labor Statistics, only 17.8 percent of persons with a disability were employed in the previous year, compared to 63.9 percent employment of persons without a disability. "Persons with a Disability: Labor Force Characteristics Summary," Bureau of Labor Statistics: June 12, 2013. Accessed January 24, 2014. http://www.bls.gov/news.release/disabl.nr0.htm.
20. Ronald S. Magliozzi, and Jenny He, *Tim Burton* (New York: Museum of Modern Art, 2009).
21. Burton, 229.
22. Ibid., 229–230.
23. Ibid., 13.
24. Thomas Caldwell, "Tim Burton: The Exhibition—into the Weird and Wonderful Mind of Cinema's Most Popular Outsider," *Screen Education* 59 (November 9, 2012), 6–12.
25. Ibid.
26. Lee, 2005.
27. Dahl's approach to storytelling was not universally applauded; for example, a scathing review of *Charlie and the Chocolate Factory* appeared in the esteemed Horn Book essays, to which Dahl wrote an equally scathing rebuttal. See Paul, Heins, ed. *Crosscurrents of Criticism: Horn Book Essays, 1968–1977.* (Boston: Horn Book, 1977), 97–125.
28. Roald Dahl, *Boy: Tales of Childhood.* (New York: Farrar, Straus, Giroux, 1984).
29. Benjamen Bergery, "American Cinematographer: July 2005." American Cinematographer: July 2005. Accessed January 20, 2013. http://www.theasc.com/magazine/july05/charlie/index.html.
30. That is, those who are seen as monsters, or monstrous beings, although they may not see themselves in that manner. This includes corpses, skeletons, reanimated dogs, scissor-handed men, and the like. Burton's films also feature those who are outsiders or who exist on the fringes of society, whether due to their beliefs and practices, such as the inventor of Edward Scissorhands, or because of their bodies, such as the largely benign circus "freaks" in the film *Big Fish*.
31. Caldwell, 8.
32. Tim Burton, *Burton on Burton*, ed. Mark Salisbury (London: Faber & Faber, 2006), 87.
33. Caldwell, 8
34. *The Ellen Show*, NBC Universal, May 7, 2012.
35. Burton, 223–345.
36. Ibid.
37. Leah Rozen, "Charlie and the Chocolate Factory," *People*, November 15, 2012, 31.
38. Roger Clarke, "An Improper Charlie," *Sight & Sound* 15, no. 8 (November 9, 2012), 22–25.
39. Ibid.
40. Helena Victor Bassil-Morozow, *Tim Burton: The Monster and the Crowd: A Post-Jungian Perspective.* (London: Routledge, 2010).
41. Caldwell: 8, and Josh Tyrangiel, "Big Fish in His Own Pond." *Time*, (November 9, 2012), 88.

42. The fear of dentists was also an early theme in Burton's works, notably his Cal Arts student production of *The Stalk of the Celery Monster*, 1979.

43. See for example the discussion of the ethical and medical complications of exoskeletons at https://sites.google.com/a/cortland.edu/exoskeletons-for-paraplegics/ethics). A major point that this discussion highlights is the narrow range of wheelchair users that would physically or economically qualify for such technology. The health advantages of such a device are worthy; however, few can afford such a luxury—just as few can afford to create their own Wonka-esque world to suit their needs. See Ciara Byrne, "VentureBeat Paraplegics Walk Again with Bionic Exoskeleton ReWalk," *VentureBeat | News About Tech, Money and Innovation*," comments, December 24, 2012. Accessed January 29, 2013. http://venturebeat.com/2012/12/24/paraplegics-can-walk-again-with-bionic-exoskeleton-rewalk/ for a discussion of the benefits of such robotic exoskeletons as the ReWalk, as well as the cost. The prohibitive economic factor of such devices are particularly heightened for individuals in less prosperous countries.

44. Burton, 87.

45. The character of Edward Scissorhands has continued to meet with affection from those of all ages. The magical (and oft purloined) theme song that plays at the end of the movie is the music of the snow falling down from the hill where the banished Edward still creates his ice sculptures. The audience is clearly positioned to sympathize with the character. See for example Jordan S. Mattos, "*Edward Scissorhands*—Movie Review," August 7, 2005. Accessed January 26, 2013. http://www.commonsensemedia.org/movie-reviews/edward-scissorhands. Mattos writes, "Depp's deer-in-headlights self-consciousness is adoring [sic] enough to soften the sharpest of pointed appendages. The pastel-colored township cuts a drastic figure against Edward's looming mansion in the distance.... The film exposes the cynical underbelly of front porch Americana, forcing us to find beauty and truth in the grotesque when we allow what is 'good' to run more than skin-deep."

46. Burton, 92.

47. Jane Yolen, *Touch Magic: Fantasy, Faerie and Folklore in the Literature of Childhood* (New York: Philomel Books, 1981).

48. Burton is not the first to offer this trope of the outwardly normal or desirable body masking inner moral decay; it is as old as the lovely but wicked queen in the tale of Snow White; more recently, the unrepentant and selfish princess Fiona of *Shrek* and *Shrek 2* inhabits an outwardly beautiful body, and it is in fact a signifier of her redemption that she ultimately chooses to inhabit the body of an ogre.

49. Roald Dahl, *Charlie and the Chocolate Factory* (New York: Knopf, 1964), 157.

50. Bernard Beck. "It Takes an Exorcist: Charlie and the Chocolate Factory, Brat Camp, and the War Against Children." *Multicultural Perspectives* 8, no. 2 (November 1, 2006), 25–28. doi:10.1207/s15327892mcp0802_5: 27.

51. Ibid.

52. William T. Schultz, "Finding Fate's Father: Some Life History Influences on Roald Dahl's Charlie and the Chocolate Factory." *Biography* 21, no. 4 (Fall 1998), 463–81. doi:10.1353/bio.2010.0270.

53. For example, not only does Violet call him a loser, but Augustus mocks him by asking "Would you like some chocolate?" When Charlie replies, "Sure," Augustus sneers, "Then you should have brought some!" The look in Charlie's eyes says it all.

54. Schultz, "Finding Fate's Father."

55. Clarke, "An Improper Charlie."

56. Schultz, 466.

57. Susan School Eberly, for example, writes that "congenital disorders" and "birth defects ... have produced feelings of fear and awe since earliest times ... [and] have

evoked a religious response," and describes Assyrian clay tablets from 2000 BC as one of the earliest written records where a society has recorded and categorized disability; the tablets detail the description by soothsayers of 62 babies who were considered deformed or abnormal (p. 58).

    58. Arthur H. Shapiro, *Everybody Belongs: Changing Negative Attitudes toward Classmates with Disabilities* (New York: Garland, 1999).

    59. *Shrek*, [Roma], Paramount Home Entertainment, 2007.

    60. Bernard Beck, "It Takes an Exorcist: Charlie and the Chocolate Factory, Brat Camp, and the War Against Children." *Multicultural Perspectives* 8, no. 2 (November 1, 2006), 25–28. doi:10.1207/s15327892mcp0802_5

    61. Schultz, "Finding Fate's Father."

    62. Karen O. "Strange Love." In *Frankenweenie Unleashed*. Walt Disney Records, 2012, CD.

    63. In like manner, Dr. Willy Wonka's house has refused to be "cured" as well, existing in its latter days as a lonely, isolated building in the middle of a snowy field that all of its neighboring houses have abandoned—obstinate to the end.

    64. *Burton on Burton*, 94.

Bibliography

Bassil-Morozow, Helena Victor. *Tim Burton: The Monster and the Crowd: A Post-Jungian Perspective*. London: Routledge, 2010.

Beck, Bernard. "It Takes an Exorcist: Charlie and the Chocolate Factory, Brat Camp, and the War Against Children." *Multicultural Perspectives* 8, No. 2 (November 1, 2006): 25–28. Doi:10.1207/S15327892mcp0802_5.

Bergery, Benjamen. "American Cinematographer: July 2005." *American Cinematographer*: July 2005. Accessed January 20, 2013. http://www.theasc.com/magazine/july05/charlie/index.html.

Burton, Tim. *Burton on Burton*. Mark Salisbury, ed. London: Faber & Faber, 2006.

Burton, Tim, Caroline Thompson, Stan Winston, Johnny Depp, Winona Ryder, and Dianne Wiest. 2005. *Edward Scissorhands*. Beverly Hills, CA: 20th Century Fox Home Entertainment.

Caldwell, Thomas. "Tim Burton: The Exhibition—Into the Weird and Wonderful Mind of Cinema's Most Popular Outsider." *Screen Education* 59 (November 9, 2012): 6–12.

Clarke, Roger. "An Improper Charlie." *Sight & Sound* 15, No. 8 (November 9, 2012): 22–25.

Dahl, Roald. *Charlie and the Chocolate Factory*. New York: Knopf, 1964.

_____. *Boy: Tales of Childhood*. New York: Farrar, Strauss, Giroux, 1984.

Depp, Johnny, Tim Burton, Freddie Highmore, David Kelly, Helena Bonham Carter, Noah Taylor, Philippe Rousselot, Danny Elfman, and Roald Dahl. 2005. *Charlie and the Chocolate Factory*. Burbank, CA: Warner Home Video.

Eberly, Susan Schoon. "Fairies and the Folklore of Disability: Changlings, Hybrids, and the Solitary Fairy." *Folklore* 99, No. 1 (1988): 58–77.

The Ellen Show. NBC Universal. May 7, 2012.

Guerrero, ed. *Framing Blackness: The African American Image in Film*. Philadelphia: Temple University Press, 1993.

Heins, Paul, ed. *Crosscurrents of Criticism: Horn Book Essays, 1968–1977*. Boston: Horn Book, 1977.

Karen O. "Strange Love." In *Frankenweenie Unleashed*. Walt Disney Records, 2012, CD.

Lee, Christopher. "Tim Burton." *Interview* 35, No. 7 (August 2005): 78–80.

Magliozzi, Ronald S., and Jenny He. *Tim Burton*. New York, NY: Museum of Modern Art, 2009.

Mattos, Jordan S. "*Edward Scissorhands*—Movie Review." August 7, 2005. Accessed January 26, 2013. http://www.commonsensemedia.org/movie-reviews/edward-scissorhands.
McCann, Donnarae, and Gloria Woodard. *The Black American in Books for Children: Readings in Racism*. Metuchen, NJ: Scarecrow Press, 1972.
McMahan, Alison. *The Films of Tim Burton: Animating Live Action in Contemporary Hollywood*. New York: Continuum, 2005.
Poore, Carol. *Disability in Twentieth-Century German Culture*. Ann Arbor: University of Michigan Press, 2007.
Rozen, Leah. "Charlie and the Chocolate Factory." *People*, November 15, 2012, 31.
Schultz, William T. "Fiding Fate's Father: Some Life History Influences on Roald Dahl's Charlie and the Chocolate Factory." *Biography* 21, No. 4 (Fall 1998): 463–81. Doi:10.1353/Bio.2010.0270.
Shapiro, Arthur A. *Everybody Belongs: Changing Negative Attitudes Toward Classmates with Disabilities*. New York: Garland, 1999.
Shelley, Mary Wollstonecraft, and Maurice Hindle. *Frankenstein; Or, the Modern Prometheus*. London: Penguin Books, 2003.
Sugden, Angela. "Inadepptrance Scripts: Charlie and the Chocolate Factory." Inadepptrance Scripts: Charlie and the Chocolate Factory. Accessed December 29, 2012. http://www.inadepptrance.com/Scripts-AA-CATCF.htm.
Tyrangiel, Josh. "Big Fish in His Own Pond." *Time*, November 9, 2012, 88.
Yolen, Jane. *Touch Magic: Fantasy, Faerie and Folklore in the Literature of Childhood*. New York: Philomel Books, 1981.

Corporeal Mediation and Visibility in *Sleepy Hollow*

Lori Parks

In *Sleepy Hollow* (1999), Tim Burton transforms the character of Ichabod Crane from the superstitious schoolmaster of the original short story by Washington Irving (1820) to an eccentric investigator (Constable Crane, played by Johnny Depp) determined to apply new (though not accepted) theories in science and forensics to a series of grisly murders believed to be carried out by the supernatural being the Headless Horseman (Christopher Walkin).[1] The film is set in 1799, when major scientific and technological changes are beginning to accelerate.

My analysis stems from the perspective that Burton's characters represent an intriguing site of corporeal, psychological and social conflict. Burton is an expert at presenting ideas and characters in the visual form that are often outsiders or "othered" and subject to mediations within their given world that go beyond the explicit subject that is being presented. The body is, in a sense, the composite of all of our experiences both individual and collective. As a body we are creators and participants in the various forms of consumption available within our society. To offer visual representation is to select both consciously and unconsciously rather than merely reflect a pre-given world. No longer is the body viewed as simply a natural entity; it is instead understood as a cultural representation, constructed and inscribed by our world, our values and our language.[2] This is further complicated when one considers the body within the context of the medical gaze. Corporeal objectivity is achieved through direct observation, poking and prodding, and dissection creating a disjuncture between the individual self as a cohesive entity and a material object.

My interest herein lies in the mediation and eventual transformation of Constable Crane during the course of the film and his murder investigation.

Crane is not just attempting to solve a case that has remained "unsolvable" but his methods and beliefs are also on trial as the Burgomaster (Christopher Lee, of Hammer Studios' *Dracula*) states as much as he sends him to Sleepy Hollow.

> BURGOMASTER: [...] So you take your experimentations to Sleepy Hollow and deduce, er detect the murderer. Bring him here to face our good justice. Will you do this?
> ICHABOD (swallowing doubt): I shall, gladly.
> BURGOMASTER: And remember—it is you, Ichabod Crane, who is now put to the test.[3]

The detection and punishment of crime and murder speak to fundamental human problems: the themes and nature of violence, sin, guilt and redemption. Burton seamlessly mixes genres of horror, mystery/detective and fairy tale specifically with the Headless Horseman for there is never any doubt for the viewer that this supernatural being is very real. In this context, mediation is used as a flexible and general term which alerts the viewer to the overlapping and complex meanings that are being represented. This is especially the case for Constable Crane who must navigate the roles of gender, social community and conformity within the context of his investigation.

During the course of this essay I will consider a number of issues as they pertain to the film *Sleepy Hollow*. I will begin by examining the theme of the head and its beheading as an emblem of identity and as it pertains to the traditional binary (and gendered) oppositions of reason/emotion, male/female and spirit/flesh that Constable Crane must attempt to resolve during the course of the film. In the section "Seeing is Knowing," I will locate Constable Crane's interest and practice of forensics of the body within a medico-historical context of late Eighteenth century America. Constable Crane is an amalgamation of Enlightenment ideas regarding the body as a site of knowledge and the impact and practice of dissection within the context of burgeoning ideas of penology. Finally, in the section "Material as Metaphor," I will continue to develop and discuss the various ways the film textualizes and contextualizes the visual act of gaining knowledge and how sight as a highly valued sense in Western tradition is associated with ideas of power and control, and yet, cannot be separated from the flesh.

Tim Burton relies on a number of tropes in his films that are informed by his childhood predilection for Hammer Films horror movies (produced by the English studio from the 1950s–70s).[4] *Sleepy Hollow* has a mysterious and gothic atmosphere, shot in sepia tones with little saturated color, and a lot of fog. Like much of Burton's work the audience is presented with a blond *ingénue*, a hero as an outcast, the use of flashbacks to reveal the origin of the hero's "otherness" and a sense of transition often in the form of innocence/knowing, child/adult and life/death.

"Their heads weren't found severed. Their heads were not found at all"

Western culture places importance on the head as the seat of reason and the "self" as it represents the principal site for identity, and communication. As Crane attempts to debunk the myth of the Headless Horseman, the head becomes an interesting symbol of Crane's dependence on his analytical powers of reason in contrast to the Headless Horseman's base desires for violence both in his past life during the Revolutionary War and in his death as he continues to inspire fear as he lops off the towns people's heads. The mouth is an important aspect of the head, both literally and symbolically. The mouth is an opening that allows for the incorporation of food and fluid; as a cavity it occupies a prominent part of the face and is the source of sound and speech (or denial of speech through selective or non-selective muteness). As the point of entry for the digestive tract, the mouth begins the process that breaks down food while retaining the nutrients and energy it supplies for the body before expelling the waste. Burton's "head to head" between Crane and the Headless Horseman call forth images of Mikhail Bakhtin's grotesque body as a disruptive force against the *status quo* of society.

For Bakhtin, The grotesque image reflects a phenomenon in transformation, an as yet unfinished metamorphosis, of death and birth, growth and becoming. The relation to time is one determining trait of the grotesque image. The other indispensable trait is ambivalence. For in this image we find both poles of transformation, the old and the new, the dying and the procreating, the beginning and the end of the metamorphosis.[5]

In *The Body & Society*,[6] Bryan Turner implicitly picks up on Bakhtin's grotesque body (which is characterized by its "openness" and flexible boundaries) as he describes the function of the mouth and its importance as an orifice located on the head and connection to identity and community.

We appropriate the world through the mouth, as our original social link with our mothers, as an organ of speech and articulation, as an organ of consumption and animal violence. Eating is the origin of community, where festivals are celebrations of belonging and membership through a sharing of food.[7]

Crane's introduction to the Van Tassel was during a social event that was being held for prominent people of Sleepy Hollow. It is during this party

Crane first lays eyes on the beautiful and blindfolded Katrina Van Tassel (Christina Ricci) as she recites a rhyme on witches and bestows a kiss upon him. This first meeting reveals Crane's reliance on sight and observation in contrast to Katrina's ("blind") reliance on intuition, emotion and belief. This reflects a traditionally gendered paradigm that Crane will struggle against throughout the film.

The mouth exemplifies the problems of safety, communication, control and taste. The mouth physically takes in and gives forth: it can speak and eat, but it may also vomit both ideas and food. In *A Thousand Plateaus: Capitalism and Schizophrenia* (1980), Deleuze and Guattari contend that the face is not really a part of the body, but rather a specific organization of human society. In the beginning of their text on faciality, they state that the face is a "horror story"; its skin or "façade" conceals a monstrous "horror" of bloody tissue, muscle and bone. Without skin, the face gives way to the concave spaces and ghoulish grin of the death's head.[8] The Headless Horseman is without his head for the majority of the film only to be depicted with an intact head with sharply pointed teeth through a flashback and later when Constable Crane returns his head the viewer witnesses a re-integration rather than disintegration of flesh. Yet throughout the film the Horseman does not utter a word. He becomes a symbol of emotion without discipline in contrast to Crane's reliance on his analytical reasoning powers through scientific method detached from emotion. The Horseman is the weapon of a real flesh-and-blood murderer and a symbol of death both physically as on a dissection table and in terms of Constable Crane's dependence on and pursuit of knowledge through reason. He represents the monster concealed behind the veneer of society.

The head as a site of reason has a long history that is best exemplified by Descartes' (1596–1650) text *Discourse on Method* (1637), where he envisions the body as a machine, along with his *Cogito ergo sum* "I think, therefore I am."[9] This focus on reason reflects a general sentiment within Christian mythology, where emphasis was placed on the rational mind over the physical body. Architectural, pedagogical and medical practices have manipulated the body by generating and enforcing the Cartesian image of an individual as a separate and isolated machine whose ultimate goal is self-mastery. Such a viewpoint places value on the rational, objective human mind as the seat of knowledge, truth and wisdom, putting it at odds with the body's fleshy, instinctually driven and emotional side. This dualistic methodology has also been applied to issues of gender, where men have historically been connected to the mind, its reasoning powers and perceived as creators of culture, while women have been relegated to their bodies, reproduction and nature.[10] The word "gender" implies that the masculine and feminine attributes are always defined in relation to one another. Gender for society is one way of establishing notions of identity.[11]

Such a legacy has sought to essentially divorce the mind from its body, nature from culture and reason from emotion. This is limiting, especially to the question of human embodiment. While it is established early on in the film that Crane is a follower of scientific process and order through analytical reasoning, his faith in its practice is tested during the course of his investigation. Not only must he contend with a potential love interest in the form of blond *ingénue* Katrina Van Tassel who represents the emotional side that Crane has so vehemently denied. Crane steadfastly refuses to believe in the supernatural, until he literally comes upon the horseman for himself (seeing is believing). Crane's obsession with logic and science as a method of gaining knowledge and thus controlling and distancing himself from emotion is symbolically exposed through the crime he is investigating and the physical act of removing the head.

In a series of dream sequences shown intermittently throughout the film in brighter and more saturated color, it is revealed that Ichabod's reliance on logic has its roots in a traumatic childhood event between his father, a Puritan minister and mother, a white magic practitioner and as Crane describes a "child of nature." This leads to a horrific and torturous confrontation between his mother and father. After the Horseman kills Katrina's suitor Brom Van Brunt (Casper Van Dien) Crane is injured and in his delirium dreams of his mother's murder which reveals the origin for his obsessive reliance on reason and logic.

> KATRINA: [...] Tell me what you dreamed.
> ICHABOD: How I found my mother dead ... how good and evil sometimes wear each other's clothes. She was an innocent, a child of nature, condemned ... murdered ... by my father...
> KATRINA: Murdered by...?
> ICHABOD: Yes—murdered to save her soul! By a Bible-Black tyrant behind a mask of righteousness. I was seven when I lost my faith.
> KATRINA: What do you believe in, Ichabod?
> ICHABOD: Sense and reason, cause and consequence, an ordered universe.... Oh lord, I should not have come to this place where my rational mind has been so controverted by the spirit world...[12]

The dualisms of the past have been influential though limiting in the definition of the body. In *Embodying the Monster* (2002), Margrit Shildrick discusses the idea of identity, especially as it pertains to the Western imagination. "To be a self is above all to be distinguished from the other, to be ordered and discrete, secure *within* the well-defined boundaries of the body rather than actually being the body."¹³ The body is always socially formed and located. What it is to be man or woman is a social definition, since even physiology is always mediated by culture. Crane's sense of self is not secure. He is an outsider, an interloper who does not fit in with his colleagues back in New York City, nor can he easily navigate the community of Sleepy Hollow. In *Between Monsters, Goddesses and Cyborgs* (1996), Nina Lykke observes that, "over the centuries monsters have acted as 'boundary phenomena' between the viewable and unviewable, between the human and the animal, between socially acceptable and abject bodies."¹⁴ Rosi Braidotti attempts to deconstruct the historical understanding of the monster as radical other. She argues "the peculiarity of the organic monster is that s/he is both Same and other. The monster is neither a total stranger nor completely familiar; s/he exists in an in-between zone."¹⁵ By removing the head one is removing the identity or individuality of the person; they are symbolically and physically reduced to an object that is both reminiscent of the previous person and yet unrecognizable in its new inception of flesh. Thus the body has become monstrous as it has come to occupy the "in-between zone" that Braidotti alludes to.

In the film, death is being brought down upon the people of Sleepy Hollow by a supernatural "monster." He enters the world of living through a gateway in the form of a large dead tree located deep within the woods. Part of the horror that can be provoked within the viewer when confronted with visual depictions of murder and gore is the "othering" of the dead body through its reduction to simply flesh. For William Ian Miller:

> There are few things that are more unnerving and disgust evoking than our partibility. Consider the horror motif of severed hands, ears, heads, gouged eyes. These do not strike me as so many stand-ins for castration. Castration is merely a particular instance of severability that has been fetishized in psychoanalysis and the literary theoretical enterprises that draw on it.¹⁶

Death and knowledge, or rather, knowledge of death is problematic for a character like Crane. Death throws into relief the precarious nature of the body and the difficulty for any person, let alone Crane, to reconcile the ephemerality of the fleshy casing. As J. Lofland astutely describes it death is both the "possibility of impossibility and the impossibility of possibility, [which] cannot be 'believed,' 'magicked' or 'scienced' away."¹⁷ The horror of death is the splitting of the body and soul. The Horseman is a supernatural entity that occupies the in-between as it literally and figuratively splits the body and head, death and life, emotion and reason. Burton's use of real effects rather than a reliance on computer animation is apparent when viewing the film. There is a greater sensation of the visceral along with an overwhelming presence of foreboding that permeates the landscape. The muted colors and murky atmosphere works to make the supernatural feel very tangible and in contrast Crane's intense focus and reliance on reason seems even more at odds with the community. Burton's reflection on the photographic value of the film echoes this sentiment: "I feel like we got a good dream-like quality. I also felt good when I was on some of those sets—even though this is much more stylized, it felt good, it felt like that haunted feeling I get when I go upstate in New York."[18]

Seeing Is Knowing...

The root meaning of "autopsy" is essentially to look or see (*psy*), with one's own eyes (*auto*). One could extrapolate it further to mean: to look *into* one's self. Crane is a proponent of forensics as a way to *see* or gain knowledge about a crime. His trip to Sleepy Hollow is a test of his knowledge and detection methods, yet it also becomes a journey of self-discovery that ultimately transforms him as he recalls events from his childhood previously blocked from his conscious self. As Constable Crane searches for the killer he asserts: "the assassin is a man of flesh and blood, and I will discover him." The emphasis on visibility—and the premise of "seeing is knowing" raises the complex question of what is the body, understood as an entity that is both material and metaphorical, and considered from a medico-scientific viewpoint and from the viewpoint of the individual's experience of their own body? The corpse is the farthest a body can change and yet still be a "body." The dead body is the ultimate state of marginality, fraught with the possibility potential of for dangerous pollutants. Death leads to the dissolution of the physical body as it begins to decompose; it is no longer a coherent being with emotional attachments or reasoning capabilities. Death will be the end for everybody, and this reinforces the fear that ultimately undermines the cultural ideal which views the living body as controllable and whole.

Films help shape ones perceptions on crime, as viewers we are focused on the detection and "why" of the crime. Crimes are considered crimes because they violate the norms within a society, thus the punishment is also a reflection of the values within a society. In *Crime Films* (2002) Thomas Leitch points out "from their beginnings, then, American crime films have been less interested in winning viewers' sympathies for innocent victims than in exploring the possibilities of action available to those victims, the more apparently hopeless the better."[19]

Crane is presented to the viewer as a Constable that is ahead of his time with regards to his methods of detection. This is evident when he is in New York City before being sent off to the hamlet of Sleepy Hollow. Yet historically at this point there were no full-time professional police forces present in America. It wasn't until 1838 that Boston created the first police force with New York City following suit in 1845.[20] The viewer also learns that part of Constable Crane's method of detection includes post-mortems of bodies. Again, it is interesting and illuminating to situate this within a medico-historical context. Crane's reliance on forensic methods for detection reflects his general systematic outlook and provides an interesting analogy to the general conception of autopsy and dissection within the Eighteenth century. In *Body Criticism: Imaging the Unseen in Enlightenment*, Barbara Maria Stafford states,

> The Galenic conception of anatomy as an "opening up in order to see deeper or hidden parts" drives to the heart of a master problem for the Enlightenment. How does one attain the interior of things? Anatomy and its inseparable practice of dissection were the Eighteenth-century paradigms for any forced, artful, contrived, and violent study of depths.[21]

Crane has transferred his own insecurities and loss into an intense study of the body that focuses on the minute and (potentially) the interior. It is both manual probing and cerebral grasping. Critical thinking is an aspect of the Enlightenment period where the powers of reason and intelligence should be able to "cut" through superstition. Crane's "why" in his "science"-based inquiry is also a "why" to his past. Burton discusses the character of Constable Crane:

> I think I've always responded to characters who have conflicts of interest within themselves, and Ichabod's a character who's pretty fucked up, in the sense that he's smart but sometimes there's a kind of tunnel vision. If you think too much, sometimes you can think yourself into a corner. Reading the script, what I liked about Ichabod, which is different from the cartoon, is that he was written very much as somebody who's just living too much up here—inside of his own head—and not relating to what's happening in the rest of the world. And that, juxtaposed against a character with no head, was a really good dynamic.[22]

Curiously Crane's strong reliance on forensics has an interesting connection with the history of medicine, again bringing the theme of belief vividly into play. Initially dissection was used as an additional punishment that might be applied to a sentence of death. This practice led to the fear as to whether one could have an afterlife if the body was cut up through dissection. Public execution (as well as public dissection) could easily become less about punishment or social order and more about a kind of Dionysian spectacle where the body is deconstructed.[23] The idea of an established and ethical protocol in post-mortem examination for medico-legal purposes does not come into play until later in the nineteenth century although the wounded or dead body as evidence has roots in the *Ancien Régime* of France (16th–18th centuries). Scientific collecting and the subsequent trial had the goal of "finding and punishing the murderer—[which] was more powerful than the ethical concerns, such as the deceased's bodily integrity or the feelings of grieving relatives."[24]

Katherine Young discusses the grotesque or monstrous body in conjunction with medicine. Here, the gruesome act of removing the face during a dissection is an interesting reference to the beheading in Sleepy Hollow:

> He lifts the head and tugs the scalp down over the forehead, holding it by the hair. It folds down, inside out, over the brown face, which crumples underneath like an old leather mask. He continues to cut away scalp along both edges of the incision with a scalpel. The face is now covered with tissue, hair inside, forming a ball of whitish integument, its protruding chin rimmed with gray furze.[25]

Body fluids are a marker for a private territory of the body and intimate "proof" of our existence, as well as public sites where regulation (via the cultural majority) and penetration through the medical and technological gaze occur.[26] Science and medicine claim a special "truth" status along with the capacity for unimpeded vision if one only looks beyond the surface. The act of dissection has one overriding goal: to discover the cause of death. This would be carried out by a medical person—which Crane is not. The difference would be the purpose—whether it was for science or for justice. For Matthew Sorrento, "with crime stories, the character abandons the ordinary world once a crime casts its shadow, either before him (if he is a criminal) or upon him (if he is the victim). A crime is surefire storytelling fodder—it demands a change in the character, since it alters his universe in a flash."[27]

In one particularly vivid scene, after a gruesome postmortem, Crane emerges from the building covered in blood and addresses a group of horrified onlookers. "We are dealing with a madman," he states. The irony here is that although Crane is referring to his pursuit of the perpetrator, his own actions would have also been labeled as such. Embalming was not practiced during the early Republic thus a funeral would have been conducted rather quickly especially during the summer months. What would Crane actually be able to discover by exhuming the bodies given the state of decomposition? Moreover, this act of discovery would have further branded him as an "other" within the close-knit community of Sleepy Hollow given the 18th century ideas regarding death and a need for an intact body (as much as possible) for the afterlife.

Alison Bashford discusses the close connection between dissection and punishment as "a legacy of the longstanding Western practice of public disemboweling and flaying. Hanging and dissection was the most severe sentence in the Eighteenth century; the ultimate corporal punishment. For a considerable time medical men, scientists and anatomists received their bodies from the gallows."[28] Crane is a Constable and in the context of the film, sent to solve and bring to justice the murderer. He has also taken on the role of a medical practitioner with his theories that the flesh provides the answers. The autopsy and thus Crane's need to exhume the victims of the Horseman would have represented an additional assault upon the dead both physically and more importantly spiritually, "since it condemned them to wander, mutilated and with identity lost, through eternity."[29] In one scene Crane stops to investigate a headless corpse. He pulls out mysterious chemicals and his eyeglasses jut out from his face magnifying his eyes and distorting his appearance. His contraptions are meant to enhance his ability to see and to detect. It is classic Burton, both whimsical and ghoulish.

Crane is not alone in his quest for answers. He is accompanied by Katrina and the young Masbath (Marc Pickering), who has lost his father to the Headless Horseman. Both of whom contribute to the transformation of Constable Crane and a subject I will discuss further in the following section. In Constable Crane's search for the Tree of the Dead or transitional gateway between the worlds of the living and dead, he discovers forensic traces that not only indicate that it is the Horseman's grave but physical evidence that reveals that the dark rider does not murder at random. It stands to reason, then, that Crane's use of scientific methodology in this investigation is not, in fact, entirely misplaced, because the true culprit is of "flesh and blood." Still, Ichabod laments "I should not have come to this place, where my rational mind has been so controverted by the spirit world."

Material and Metaphor

> Every body is a book of blood;
> Wherever we're opened, we're red.
> —Clive Barker, *The Books of Blood*

The opening scene of the film provides clues to the viewer through the preparation of a document. A light brown expanse becomes a backdrop in which a deep, viscous red fluid is dripped upon. As the scene unfolds the viewer is relieved to learn that it is not a pooling of blood but warm wax used to seal a legal Last Will and Testament. Burton communicates through color—or the general lack thereof. The visual aesthetic of the film is a *grisaille* or mostly monochromatic shades of grey. The exception is the color red—it focuses the viewer's attention on blood and flesh and its metaphorical connections. As the epigram above suggests, blood, with its histories, symbolism and rituals, is a flesh bound text about bodies. Blood is quite literally the fluid of life and death for it (like skin) is a physical necessity and thus imbued with intense emotions and meaning.

The textual theme present within the film functions in various interrelated ways. The decapitation of the heads raises a number of textual and contextual issues. The lack of head symbolically speaks of the inability to rely on one's sight. The action of searching or inquiry is directly linked to the eyes. Crane makes assumptions based on his powers of observation and upon occasion relies on fantastical contraptions to "help" him see more, or more closely. The focus on the head continues when he first sets his eyes upon Katrina and she bestows a kiss upon him while blindfolded—thus without the power and information provided by sight. She represents a different kind of knowledge and knowing. Katrina's appropriation of knowledge does not rely on only sight; it is instead based on intuition and feelings, areas that Crane finds foreign and unreliable. She is belief to Crane's need for proof.

As an outsider who must discover the killer, Constable Crane must be able to deduce through the interview process the dynamics of the community. Seeing and being seen also speaks of a social encounter and the information that can be transmitted verbally and non-verbally. Historically, any problems would have been dealt with locally. As a member of a community one was expected to be aware of their neighbors and report suspicious activities to the local church. Only in especially severe cases would a public official become involved. More often than not crimes would have been dealt with by the churches and resolved in some form of public display of punishment.[30]

One major thrust of Enlightenment thinking was in the questioning and condemnation of traditional, i.e., supernatural beliefs. Witchcraft and other mystical entities were dismissed as superstitious. Crane's investigation leads to a complex web regarding the community and heritage of Sleepy Hollow. The creation of the Last Will and Testament at the beginning of the film, we later learn was for the Widow Winship, the pregnant woman killed by the horseman. The elaborate family tree within the Bible, the shifting of property and thus family status within the community all become signs that Crane must navigate and attempt to make sense of. His investigation leads him to Katrina's stepmother, Lady Van Tassel (Miranda Richardson), whom he discovers had as a child, witnessed the beheading of the horseman and, later, in exchange for her soul, uses the head to command the Horseman in order to avenge her family, who had lost their land to Katrina's father.

Crane's interaction with the living and investigations of the dead are often awkward and there are several occasions where he attempts to investigate the body only to be liberally squirted with blood. At one point he gives up and begins to leave Sleepy Hollow because the investigation seemed to (unreasonably) point to Katrina whom he has feelings for. It is only at the last moment that he opens the book given to him by Katrina and learns that the symbols she had been making (much like his mother had made) where for the protection of loved ones. Her presence is a catalyst for his own repressed memories of his mother and his cautious acceptance of a world beyond reason. Crane's scars on his hands are another physical and psychic symbol of his childhood. Katrina's use of spells to protect her loved ones are impotent in comparison to her step mother Lady Van Tassel and her sister a crone that Crane visits in the forest.

The dramatic confrontation between the Horseman, Katrina, young Masbath and Crane leads to a climactic scene on a burning windmill recalling a similar scene in James Whale's *Frankenstein* (1931).[31] The windmill is a large manmade structure that stands in contrast to the Tree of Dead where the viewer witnesses the Horseman finally get his head back and bestow a bloody kiss upon Lady Van Tassel which bookends with the blindfolded kiss given to Crane by Katrina early in the film. Lady Van Tassel is taken by the Horseman as they are swallowed by the gaping wound of the gateway tree.

The symbol of the red cardinal connects Crane to his past, present and future. The *trompe l'oeil* effect of this childhood toy showing the bird both caged and free reflects both the burden of reason and his past. It is an interesting choice of a symbol (and nod to cinematic history): a seemingly simplistic "toy" that connects Crane to his past and causes "magical" delight when he demonstrates it for Katrina. This illusionary device is called a Thaumatrope and is viewed as one of the many "philosophical" toys created in the first quarter of the nineteenth century that are viewed as ancestors of cinema. Tom Gunning describes how the inclusion of the term "philosophical" "expresses their dual purposes of enlightenment and entertainment—with the primary purpose of using the entertaining aspect of toys to instruct children in scientific principles, thereby making education enjoyable and entertaining."[32] The whole point of this object was to demonstrate the process of manipulating human perception. Thus it encompasses elements of astonishment and scientific explanation of optics. That Crane carried one of these around with him as a tangible link to his past also makes a statement against the multiple dualisms that have been presented to the viewer throughout the film. Crane could never really fully deny the other senses present sensory organs on the head. What good is analytic reasoning and logic based on inspection without intuition and an awareness of human fallacies and perceptions? This is Burton at his best, quirky characters who display their struggles as "others."

Art and film can challenge a viewer to consider one's own narratives of past, present and future in the context of the presented subject. It can also throw into critical relief the relationship between reality and representation and how it is typically enacted within one's society and upon the body. The element of sight is central to the process of viewing a film. Sight is further reinforced through Crane's confrontation with the Headless Horseman, his attempt to acquire knowledge through science and medicine and the signs that those fields promote as a form of visual acuteness. Crane's quest for knowledge as it pertains to the murders and ultimately self-knowledge is situated between the blind kiss of Katrina and the bloody encompassing of the Horseman. Between life and death, spiritual and material and most importantly for Crane: "other" and belonging. Meaning is always culturally imposed and then coopted or internalized. Thus, the enduring desire to transcend the body whether through fantasy or technology inevitably also reinforces our embodiment as still very connected to our flesh. Tim Burton's vision of *Sleepy Hollow* communicates visually and symbolically. It is a moody and expressive fairy tale that poses intriguing dilemmas about knowledge and belief, alienation and belonging, the body and the mind.

Notes

1. There have been two previous film adaptations of the Sleepy Hollow story: an animated version called *The Adventures of Ichabod and Mr. Toad* (Algar & Geronimi, 1949), made by Disney and a made for TV movie starring Jeff Goldblum (Schellerup, 1980). In Mark Salisbury, Ed. *Burton on Burton* (London: Faber & Faber [1995], 2000), Burton discusses the original short story of which this film is based "it's a fascinating story, a story that a lot of people know about but that nobody's really read" 164. Burton's familiarity with the story reflects the animated version by Disney.
2. There is a well-established body of scholarship that focuses on corporality and its representation across the disciplines. Scholars such as Michel Foucault, Bryan Turner, Thomas Laqueur, Lynda Nead and Donna Haraway to name but a few, who focus on a longer trajectory of representation of the body in Western history.
3. *Sleepy Hollow* (1999) movie script. Screenplay by Andrew Kevin Walker and Tom Stoppard. Based on "The Legend of Sleepy Hollow" by Washington Irving. Shooting draft Sept. 29, 1998. http://www.dailyscript.com/scripts/sleepy-hollow_shooting.html (accessed Sept. 22, 2013)
4. Mark Salisbury, ed. *Burton on Burton* (London: Faber & Faber [1995], 2000), 170. Hammer Films began as a distribution company in the 1930s but has become best known for its reinterpretations of classic horror characters like Dracula or Frankenstein as well as making household names of stars like Christopher Lee.

5. Mikhail Bakhtin, *Rabelais and His World* (*Tvorchestvo Fransua Rable*, 1965), trans. Helene Iswolsky (Bloomington: Indiana Press, 1984), 24.
6. Bryan Turner. *The Body & Society* (London: Sage [1984] 1996).
7. Ibid., xiii.
8. Gilles Deleuze and Félix Guattari. *A Thousand Plateaus: Capitalism and Schizophrenia* (*Mille plateaux, v. 2 of Capitalisme et schizophrénie*, 1980) (Minneapolis: University of Minnesota Press, 2002), 167–68.
9. Descartes, *Discourse on Method* (*Discours de la method*,1637).
10. There has been a lengthy record of criticism focused on binary opposition with regard to gender. Hélène Cixous and Luce Irigaray have built upon the pioneering work of feminist Simone de Beauvoir in *The Second Sex*. Scholars like Donna Haraway, Elizabeth Grosz and Judith Butler to name but a few, have expanded upon these ideas of gender to critique the categories of identity.
11. Lori Parks, *The Bordered Body* (unpublished dissertation, The University of Reading, England, 2009), 19.
12. *Sleepy Hollow* (1999) movie script. Screenplay by Andrew Kevin Walker and Tom Stoppard. Based on "The Legend of Sleepy Hollow" by Washington Irving. Shooting draft Sept. 29, 1998.
13. Margrit Shildrick. Embodying the Monster: Encounters with the Vulnerable Self (London: Sage, 2002), 50.
14. Nina Lykke and Rosi Braidotti, Eds. Between Monsters, Goddesses and Cyborgs: Feminist Confrontation with Science, Medicine and Cyberspace (London: Zed Books, 1996), 14.
15. Rosi Braidotti. "Signs of Wonder and Traces of Doubt: On Teratology and Embodied Differences," in *Between Monsters, Goddesses and Cyborgs: Feminist Confrontation with Science, medicine and Cyberspace*. Nina Lykke and Rosi Braidotti, Eds. (London: Zed Books, 1996), 141.
16. William Ian Miller. *The Anatomy of Disgust* (Cambridge, MA: Harvard University Press), 27.
17. J. Lofland, *The Craft of Dying: The Modern Face of Death* (Beverly Hills: Sage, 1978).
18. Salisbury (2000), 175.
19. Thomas Leitch. *Crime Films* (Cambridge: Cambridge University Press, 2002), 86.
20. David B. Wolcott and Tom Head, *American Experience: Crime and Punishment in America* (New York: Infobase Publishing, 2010), xi. Wolcott and Head point out that during the 18th century "American cities would have been guarded by casual, part-time, ill-organized 'watches' (often composed of men moonlighting from their day jobs: or constables who served court orders in exchange for payment. Even with the creation of police forces, police functioned mainly as all-purpose guardians of public order rather than law enforcers."
21. Barbara Maria Stafford, *Body Criticism: Imaging the Unseen in Enlightenment Art and Medicine* (Cambridge: MIT Press [1991] 1993), 47.
22. Salisbury (2000), 167.
23. In her biography of the British surgeon John Hunter, *The Knife Man*, Wendy Moore discusses how: "most God-fearing Georgians were convinced that if their bodies were mutilated by anatomists and their remains scattered far afield, they would never be resurrected whole on judgment day" (New York: Broadway Books, 2005), 35.
24. Sandra Menenteau, "Stigmata of the Autopsy: Operative Liberties and Protocol in Forensic Examination of the Dead Body in Nineteenth-Century France" *Intertexts*, Vol. 15, No. 1, 2011, 20.

25. Katharine Young, "Still Life with Corpse: Management of the Grotesque Body in Medicine," *Bodylore*, Katharine Young, ed. (Knoxville: University of Tennessee Press, 1993), 119.

26. There is a growing trend focused on the study of digital practices and media. This area of study considers the use of digital information, how it is consumed and communicated and the aesthetics involved in the design and contents.

27. Matthew Sorrento, *The New American Crime Film* (Jefferson, NC: McFarland, 2012), 5.

28. Alison, Bashford. Purity and Pollution: Gender, Embodiment and Victorian Medicine (London: Macmillan Press, 1998), 109.

29. Roy Porter. *Flesh in the Age of Reason* (NY: W.W. Norton & Co., 2003), 223.

30. Wolcott and Head (2010)

31. Burton's films typically feature fantastical gadgets, see for example: *Edward Scissorhands* (1990), his *Batman* films (1989 and 1992), *Charlie and the Chocolate Factory* (2005). Many of his characters have orphan status: Bruce Wayne, Young Masbath of *Sleepy Hollow*, and Edward in *Edward Scissorhands*. Burton also relies on the use of the flashback to help establish the character and provide greater context as to why they have outsider status.

32. Tom Gunning, "Hand and Eye: Excavating a New Technology of the Image in the Victorian Era," *Victorian Studies* Vol. 54. No. 3, Spring 2012: 496.

Bibliography

Bakhtin, Mikhail. *Rabelais and His World* (*Tvorchestvo Fransua Rable*, 1965). Trans. Helene Iswolsky. Bloomington: Indiana Press, 1984.

Bashford, Alison. *Purity and Pollution: Gender, Embodiment and Victorian Medicine*. London: Macmillan Press, 1998.

Deleuze, Gilles and Felix Guattari. *A Thousand Plateaus: Capitalism and Schizophrenia* (*Mille Plateaux, V. 2 of Capitalisme Et Schizophrénie*, 1980). Translated by Brian Massumi. Minneapolis: University of Minnesota Press, 2002.

Gunning, Tom. "Hand and Eye: Excavating a New Technology of the Image in the Victorian Era." *Victorian Studies* Vol. 54. No. 3, Spring 2012: 495–515.

Jordanova, Ludmilla. *Sexual Visions: Images of Gender in Science and Medicine Between the Eighteenth and Twentieth Centuries*. Madison: University of Wisconsin Press, 1989.

Leitch, Thomas. *Crime Films*. Cambridge: Cambridge University Press, 2002.

Lofland, J. *The Craft of Dying: The Modern Face of Death*. Beverly Hills: Sage, 1978.

Lykke, Nina and Rosi Braidotti. Eds. Between Monsters, Goddesses and Cyborgs: Feminist Confrontation with Science, Medicine and Cyberspace. London: Zed Books, 1996.

Menenteau, Sandra. "Stigmata of the Autopsy: Operative Liberties and Protocol in Forensic Examination of the Dead Body in Nineteenth-Century France." *Intertexts*, Vol. 15, No. 1, 2011.

Miller, William Ian. *The Anatomy of Disgust*. Cambridge: Harvard University Press, 1997.

Porter, Roy. *Flesh in the Age of Reason*. New York: W. W. Norton, 2003.

Salisbury, Mark Ed. *Burton on Burton*. London: Faber & Faber [1995], 2000.

Shildrick, Margrit. *Embodying the Monster: Encounters with the Vulnerable Self*. London: Sage, 2002.

Sleepy Hollow (1999) Movie Script. Screenplay by Andrew Kevin Walker and Tom Stoppard. Based on "The Legend of Sleepy Hollow" by Washington Irving. Shooting Draft

9/29/98. http://www.dailyscript.com/scripts/sleepy-hollow_shooting.html (Accessed September 22, 2013)
Sorrento, Matthew. *The New American Crime Film*. Jefferson, NC: McFarland, 2012.
Stafford, Barbara Maria. *Body Criticism: Imaging the Unseen in Enlightenment Art and Medicine*. Cambridge: MIT Press [1991] 1993.
Sullivan, Larry E. *Forlorn Hope: The Prison Reform Movement*. Boston: Twayne Publishing, 1990.
Turner, Bryan. *The Body & Society*. London: Sage [1984] 1996.
Wolcott, David B., and Tom Head. *American Experience: Crime and Punishment in America*. New York: Infobase Publishing, 2010.
Young, Katharine. "Still Life with Corpse: Management of the Grotesque Body in Medicine." In *Bodylore*. Edited by Katharine Young. Knoxville: University of Tennessee Press, 1993.

Capitalism and Its Discontents
Gender, Property and Nature in *Batman Returns, Sleepy Hollow* and Corpse Bride

Susan M. Bernardo

> It is impossible to escape the impression that people commonly use false standards of measurement—that they seek power, success and wealth for themselves and admire it in others, and that they underestimate what is of true value in life.
> —Sigmund Freud *Civilization and Its Discontents*

In Tim Burton's *Batman Returns* (1992),[1] *Sleepy Hollow* (1999)[2] and *Corpse Bride* (2005),[3] women and men live, die and reanimate in worlds that clearly link villainy and wealth; however, this seemingly overwhelming combination of privilege (especially male privilege) and power unravels in the face of the joining of the sexes in pairings that create androgyny and empathy. In these three films, Tim Burton expands gender boundaries through crises, the transformation of characters and challenges to community. What is really rotten in each film is not so much the corpses, but the twisted living members of society who think they have control of their worlds and themselves. Burton's works expose this decay while involving his protagonists in the miserable worlds they initially do not understand, but later investigate and, consequently, reject.

Though each film has origins in a different genre (*Batman Returns*, the influential comic book hero, *Sleepy Hollow*, a literary antecedent in Washington Irving's story, and *Corpse Bride* with roots in the gothic and folklore about the mingling of the living and the dead) they share the concern with the corrupting potential of capital and property and how women and men who occupy the fringes of society manage to survive. These characters' positions as outsiders, often made clear by their relationships to nature, enable them to see and uncover the problems in their societies, yet? Their insights do not lead to their joining their communities in a meaningful way.

All three films feature the struggles of these outsiders against purported norms. For example, Batman (Michael Keaton) and Catwoman (Michelle Pfeiffer) complicate notions of masculinity, femininity and power as they battle both Shreck (Christopher Walken) and the Penguin (Danny DeVito), as do Ichabod (Johnny Depp) and Katrina (Christina Ricci) within the patriarchal web of Sleepy Hollow. The triad of Emily (Helena Bonham Carter), Victor (Johnny Depp) and Victoria (Emily Watson) who face materialistic parents and a predatory bride groom in *Corpse Bride* act as allies. On the way to resolving the strange conundrums that face them, the characters in these films destabilize gender and class categories and ultimately embrace their marginal status.

Patriarchy and Resistance

Tim Burton's films are firmly in the tradition of the Victorian gothic[4] in their treatment of instability of categories such as gender, the appearance of the supernatural, the overbearing dominance of morally blind men, and struggles over wealth. In his hands, however, the reestablishment of order requires transformations that do not completely reinstate the status quo. Neither women nor men go back to the positions and priorities of the overarching capitalist, patriarchal structures of the societies they have lived in and struggled against. The three films always link capitalism with patriarchal privilege: in *Batman Returns* Max Shreck, Oswald Cobblepot and Bruce Wayne either come from money or acquire great wealth over time through both business dealings and inheritances; in *Sleepy Hollow* Van Garrett owns most of the land in the area and Van Tassel succeeds to that position through his association with Van Garrett and his own work; the opening of *Corpse Bride* with its 19th century setting, juxtaposes the social rank and old money of the Everglots, to the nouveau riche social climbing fish mongers, the Van Dorts. Money, men and power drive the plots of all three films even though wealth and influence have their roots in different areas: land, inheritance and business profits. Women play complicated, and initially passive roles in each story since the men in their worlds are part of structures that either subjugate women or ignore the possibility of female agency.

Corpse Bride's opportunistic murderer, Lord Barkis (Richard E. Grant), clearly sees Victoria as he saw Emily, as a way to acquire wealth without working for it. To retain social status he murders women whose bodies and signatures on a marriage license are his tickets to those material goals. These women, from a Marxist view, are commodities and have sign-exchange value since Barkis's links to them grant him status and wealth. Lord Barkis is an overtly evil manifestation of the interloper in the class-conscious world of the film. Furthermore, he is clearly not content to just run through women's money and then dispose of them; he disposes of the woman as soon as he has her money and then enjoys the wealth, as we see in the case of the unfortunate Emily, and plans to do the same with Victoria. He focuses on himself as well as on lucre. This narcissism also characterizes powerful men in the other Burton films I am discussing.

In *Batman Returns*, Shreck declares that one can never have enough power when Bruce Wayne points out that Shreck's plan to build more power plants does not make sense since Gotham has plenty of power for the foreseeable future. Max cares only about his image, his power and passing that on to his son, the aptly named Chip. He not only pushes Selina Kyle out the window after which she becomes Catwoman, but also tells Chip that he is willing to push her out a higher window if she causes trouble after she unexpectedly shows up at work on the day he has a meeting with Bruce Wayne. When Penguin threatens Gotham's sons and tries to kidnap Chip, Max talks Penguin into taking him instead, clearly showing his affection for Chip. Max wants Chip to inherit so he can create the sort of dynasty he claims he despises. When he speaks with Bruce Wayne he alludes to Wayne's being born with a silver spoon in his mouth and sees himself as the superior capitalist since he is a self-made magnate.

Though Shreck is a business mogul and *Sleepy Hollow's* patriarchs' wealth comes from land ownership, they both have a work ethic born of greed and the desire to create dynasties. The figure of the hard worker who succeeds also inhabits Sleepy Hollow. From the first frames of the film that show the dripping red candle wax that prepares the seal of Van Garrett's will, with its visual play on blood and bloodlines, inheritance and power are central. Van Garrett was altering his will to leave his wealth to the widow Winship who was carrying his child. Had the widow inherited as Van Garrett intended, the Van Tassels could not lay claim to the estate and thus Baltus Van Tassel (Michael Gambon) would be cut out of the gains. This, of course, would thwart his second wife's plan to use Baltus (who remains ignorant of all the machinations that go on around him) to get to as much property and power in Sleepy Hollow as she can, so she commands the Horseman (Christopher Walken) to get rid of anyone who stands between her and the wealth she seeks. She is apparently working out revenge for her mother, herself and her sister who had been turned out of their house. After the Archer family's father's death Van Garrett evicted them to provide for the newly arrived Van Tassels.

The second Lady Van Tassel, née Archer (Miranda Richardson) is no defender of women, though she is a woman who seeks revenge as the result of patriarchal abuse and classism. She is an angry, self-serving feminist who acts on her own behalf and even kills her own sister because she gets in the way of the revenge agenda. Ironically, the plotting of the powerful men of Sleepy Hollow helps to divert Van Garrett's will since they did not want the Widow Winship to inherit, but Lady Van Tassel goes them all one better since she is willing to have people killed and to commit murder directly when necessary. While the men of Sleepy Hollow think that they are clever in manipulating a legal text, in other words, she destroys bodies and with them the power to have any will or desire that does not serve her own.

In contrast, both Ichabod and Katrina sympathize with women's plights.[5] We see this when each of them speaks of their mothers: Katrina about the inheritance of lore she has from her mother and Ichabod about how his father destroyed his mother, of whom he says "she was an innocent." Both Ichabod and Katrina do their best to be kind and caring. The dynasty they represent is one of affection inherited from their mothers and in Katrina's case, her father as well, since Baltus is a generous person who does not participate in the underhanded plots of the other men of the town. When Crane arrives in the town and goes to the Van Tassel house Baltus stands apart from the other men when they gather in the library to talk with the Constable. He stands in front of the fireplace with his hands at his sides while the rest of the men (the doctor, the notary, the minister, the magistrate) appear anxious and suspicious of the newcomer. Later in the film in the scene in the church as everyone flees from the Horseman, Baltus stands apart after the doctor tells him that his four friends have betrayed him. He stands in front of a large window with a red cross in its stained glass as he announces that there is a conspiracy that he will seek out. At that moment the Horsemen, who cannot enter the churchyard or the church, hurls a fence post through the window impaling Baltus and making clear his role as a sacrificial figure. None of the other conspirators meet ends that link them graphically with the cross, the church and sacrifice.

Though *Sleepy Hollow's* Baltus clearly loves his daughter and cares about his family, in *Corpse Bride* the parental generation is made up of cold caricatures, who see their offspring as pawns in the game of wealth of and social station. They seek not only to control their children Victor and Victoria, but also to use them as supports for their own goals. The opening song of the film shows us both sets of parents who emphasize that all must go, as the song title states, "According to plan." They have created a structure into which their children must obediently fit. The social orders in each of the three films rest on patriarchy, materialism, selfishness and corruption.

Individual material and sexual appetites are the drivers of the films, and act to preclude any broader sense of community or familial warmth. Though Katrina says that everyone is pretty much related to everyone else in Sleepy Hollow, that is no guarantee of compassion or concern for one's neighbor. The same is true in Shreck's Gotham and the 19th century town in *Corpse Bride*. Both settings are foreboding and dark. Gotham's streets create a sense of claustrophobia in the viewer, since buildings that seem to lean in dominate them, while *Corpse Bride's* grey Victorian houses and cobblestone streets convey coldness and monotony. The caring moments in *Corpse Bride* occur only when the worlds of the living and the dead converge at the wedding reception of Victoria and Barkis: a wife at first beats her dead husband, but recognizes him and relents, a small boy appears to be in danger of being attacked by a ghoul, but when he looks up, the ghoul embraces him and the child says "grandpa." The living beings we see in *Corpse Bride* have no such affection for each other, with the exception of the newly met Victor and Victoria. For example, Victor's mother chides Mayhew, the coachman, because he has a cough and its noise irritates her. The cough is a symptom of a serious illness that leads to his death. His demise is also a necessary device to bring the information that Victoria is marrying Barkis to Victor, who is trapped in the underworld. The coachman's declaration when he gets there that he feels much better dead also serves as an indictment of the cruel capitalists who employed him. Many of the denizens of this dead world led either violent or marginal lives—we see military men, servants and spinsters. Among the living, only Victoria exerts herself to help another. She attempts to help Victor when he escapes from Emily and tries to remain in the land of the living, but Pastor Galswells to whom she appeals for help returns her to her parents who thwart her efforts by locking her in her room. As Victoria pleads that Victor needs their help all her mother can think about is their reputation: "Will the mortification never cease? It'll be years before we can show ourselves in public again. What shall we do?" Her father replies "We shall continue as planned with or without Vincent [sic]." The name of her suitor does not matter since the primary goal is to see that she marries for money. They see her as a commodity as does her second intended, Lord Barkis, so everyone around Victoria agrees with the patriarchal view of her as an object. Horribly enough the wedding goes forward, but the powers of capitalism lose control when the dead disrupt the union at the reception dinner. Technically they head above ground in order for Victor to actually die so he and Emily can have a binding relationship, but the doubling of a wedding scene in the church instead furthers the contrast between the nefarious living Barkis and the justice minded dead wedding guests and their friend, Emily. Community among the dead, though helpful, cannot really settle Emily's woes. As she transforms into a flock of butterflies/moths and heads for the bright light of the moon, she is many, and she is one. The butterfly, of course, also indicates the possibility of transformation. In *Corpse Bride* there is hope for the community of the living since Victor and Victoria will get together, but the film does not provide a vision of that world for the audience.

Indeed, community in both *Sleepy Hollow* and *Batman Returns* appears as an ironic construct. In each society there are those who are powerful and those who are not, those who consume thoughtlessly (everything from goods at Shreck's department store to ideas about feminine beauty in *Batman Returns* to agrarian living and its attendant boredom in *Sleepy Hollow*) to those who barely get by. In the place of community, we see societies divided along class lines.

Transformations of Capitalism and Reshaping Gender

Each film apparently shows the defeat of the worst elements of capitalism such as greed and the lust for power over others. These victories take the shape not only of rejection of the society in which capitalism's abuses flourished, but in the case of *Sleepy Hollow*, also the abandonment of the locale itself. Though individuals grow strong and realign their lives, they do not bring about a shift in point of view in their societies. Especially in *Sleepy Hollow* the sense of the old versus the new world comes to the fore. The film emphasizes that the events occur as one century is ending (the events are set in the year 1799) and another beginning, and shows us Constable Crane, who relies on scientific methods of investigation. His scientific view and reliance on evidence both assist in his investigation, but that investigation also bears out the existence of the ghastly Horseman who roams the area seeking his head. Old superstitions, in the forms of the figure of the witch Lady Van Tassel and Katrina's belief in charms to protect those she loves, operate alongside the clever plot to gain wealth and power that entangles Sleepy Hollow's patriarchs. The presence of the supernatural certainly undergirds the film's gothic sensibility, but with the gothic comes destabilization. By the end of the film the men who had so much power and those associated with them are dead: Van Garrett, Magistrate Phillipse, Reverend Steenwyck, Notary Hardenbrook, Doctor Lancaster, Baltus Van Tassel, Widow Winship, Midwife Killian and her family, and Jonathan Masbath. The Horseman and the witch also disappear in a ghastly scene that features the Horseman "kissing" the second Lady Van Tassel as he draws blood from her bitten mouth and takes her to the underworld through a gap in the tree of the dead. Though all the forces of evil and greed that haunted Sleepy Hollow are gone, their absence is not enough to keep Katrina there. At the film's end we see her, Crane, and young Masbath, arriving in New York City as the new century begins. The rejection of the site of her woes and losses creates the acceptance of the possibility of a different society. The New York City of the film, however, is clearly no utopia, though Ichabod cites its apparent material and geographic stability when he says "the Bronx is up and the Battery's down."[6] Before Crane sets out for Sleepy Hollow to test his methods in solving the mystery there, we see a man's dead body dragged from the river and a court system that is clearly less concerned with solving mysterious cases of dead men than working to expedite cases and lock up anyone who steps out of line. It is unclear whether Crane's success in solving the Sleepy Hollow case will have any influence on the way the law operates in the city.

Batman Returns presents an equally bleak prospect. Though Selina, as Catwoman, manages to kill Shreck, Gotham is still a place of crime and grime. She rejects the idea that she and Bruce could be a happy couple because she does not want to endorse the roles that fairy tale happy endings support. Indeed the roles open to women in Gotham run the narrow gamut from beauty queen to secretary, mother or helpless old lady. Catwoman creates a new niche with which she is not yet completely comfortable, but her new rebellious role clearly means that she cannot and will not go back to older ideas that define male and female roles. Though as Petrie says, the film does not "offer a real understanding of female sexuality and desire,"[7] he misses the point that Selina is working through a transformation. The fact that her self is not completely settled and may never be, is not necessarily grounds for complaint. As Selina looks in a store window decorated for the Christmas holiday she says to herself "Why are you doing this?" and follows this up with a response to Bruce Wayne, who approaches her from behind and apologizes for scaring her, with "Scare me? No I was scaring myself, actually." Of course, all three protagonists, Catwoman, Penguin and Batman, are misfits, but her struggle against her vicious and overbearing boss supplies a central node of conflict. Shreck is the only one she kills as she works toward recreating herself. The film makes clear that as a secretary she is as invisible as furniture until she comes across a file that she should not have seen. She assumes that Max should not see her knowledge of his plans as a threat when she says, "How can you be so mean to someone so meaningless?" Her statement about meaninglessness works in more than one way: she certainly means nothing to him, she also lacks meaning in her life and she has no overall goal that would lead her to deploy the information she finds. What even the less empowered, pre–Catwoman Selina does not quite understand is that men do not like a woman who can show them up. This is true of her ex-boyfriend whom she had beaten at racquetball and of Max and Penguin. Batman, as a broader thinker, does not see Selina as a threat to his power or masculinity; instead he finds her complexity fascinating and attractive. As Catwoman she challenges the capitalist system directly when she goes "shopping" at Shreck's department store. She significantly looks with mischievous glee through the store's logo etched into a window—a cartoonish happy cat face—mocking consumer satisfaction and desire.[8] As she decapitates the mannequins she swings her whip playfully and uses it as a jump rope after she severs their heads. She is both whimsical and destructive as she uses the same whip to trash a display case. The security guards appear in the foreground of the shot as male viewers with Selina in the their sights, but they are confused. One says "Who is she?" and the other asks "What is she?" One of them follows this up with "I don't know whether to open fire or fall in love" as the shot shifts to focus face-on only on the two men. She has no part in their conversation or their ineffectiveness as guards of the goods. She accuses them of confusing their "pistols with their privates" and drives them off before she firebombs the store using a microwave and a gas line. She clearly sees the consumer culture that props up Shreck's power as essential to the abuse she has suffered. Her success begins to unravel at least part of Max's empire and makes the point that capitalists are vulnerable precisely because they rely on commodities and the money they generate to sustain their power. Though her methods are violent, she aims her ire at goods and at Max, since Gotham's normal channels cannot address the ongoing abuse of workers by bosses. Reed reminds us that part of the setting of Gotham features "colossal statues of men operating levers and cogs in homage to industry and technology,"[9] thus making the point that physical labor is embedded in Gotham's image and material success.

The mayor of Gotham, a seemingly decent person, is actually worse than ineffectual, so a man with the public good at heart cannot operate in the world that power brokers and madmen like Max and Penguin control. Max's attempt to repackage Penguin as a candidate for mayor, while it appeals to Penguin's need to commandeer the city, acts more as an exposé of the public's ignorance than it does as a way to manipulate Penguin. When Batman takes control of the public address system at Penguin's political speech to reveal the insults Penguin had leveled at the citizens of Gotham via a recording he made of Penguin's comments, the recreated candidate in his black and white Victorian gentleman's suit reacts violently to the crowd's disapproval. The camera angle shifts from candidate Cobblepot in front of the microphone speaking to an adoring audience, to angry listeners in the town square and back to a chaotic scene of unleashed violence as Penguin fires on the crowd against the backdrop of huge campaign banners. Penguin is willing to play the roles that the public will buy for as long as he can sell them—a male Madonna who saves the mayor's baby or an abandoned heir to a rich and callous family—but does so for his own reasons. He bends gender and class in order to manipulate rather than challenge the categories. Like Lady Van Tassel in *Sleepy Hollow*, Penguin wants revenge on the powerful of Gotham and wants to replace them in the corrupt society that helped produce both him and them. If either Max or Penguin had succeeded in taking over Gotham, the city would simply be its very worst self, rather than an evil construct that somehow replaced a good one. Equilibrium in this society means returning to more manageable levels of crime, abuse of workers and consumer rituals like Christmas shopping.

Similarly, in *Corpse Bride* the world of Victor and Victoria does not change in any deep way. As far as we know, the two of them go on to fulfill their parents' plans for them and marry. They do not even leave the town that has been the scene of all their pain, though they certainly reject the idea that marriage does not require that the people involved love each other. Justice here is simply the elimination of Barkis who drinks the poison that Victor would have taken when he had agreed to become the actual husband of Emily (thinking that he has lost Victoria to Barkis since that wedding went forward). The town, like Gotham, remains a dark and dull setting. As critics have pointed out, the land of the dead is far more colorful and lively than the world above ground.[10] The dead appear to have freedoms that the living lack, but can only have these freedoms without life and thus achieve no consolatory victory. This film's world shows that one cannot have wholeness since one can either be dead and free or be living and subject to bad choices. The dead deal with the decay of the body as we see most prominently in Emily's fleshless arm and leg and the worm that inhabits her eye, while they try to "live" in a way that includes consuming. For example, when one Napoleon-like figure drinks, the wine flows out of his ribbed chest and into the goblet of a waiting skeletal companion. They emblematize the futility of consumption while retaining its forms, since they have no other model to emulate. They do not change the world even underground except that they develop loyalties to one another. Since material goods and standing are no longer available to them, they manage to create a sense of community, but the world above cannot reach this state. The message is clearly that you cannot have a full material, capitalist cycle and meaningful community. While Victor and Victoria will have each other, there is no indication that their union portends anything better for their world.

Though the worlds they inhabit may not shift in major ways, the characters in all three films do offer wider possibilities for gender roles at the individual level. Selina's Catwoman transformation also has an affect on her identity. She not only looks different when she returns to the office, she also acts in a way that unbalances the men she addresses. Max is especially surprised by her confidence. Significantly, though, when Catwoman tries to intervene on behalf of women even as she scorns their weakness, these attempts do not completely succeed. For example, she thinks that Penguin is using the Ice Princess in order to lure and destroy Batman and that the Princess will not be harmed, but Penguin murders the Princess by releasing bats that frighten her so she loses her balance and plummets from a tower to the square below. When Catwoman rescues a woman from a would-be rapist, she adds a comment about how women like this would-have-been victim are always waiting for a man to rescue them. She has learned self-reliance, but still needs to navigate the patriarchal morass in which she lives. She does not become a political actor who seeks to liberate women, though she begins to shift her own position in society. Batman manages to live within Gotham's confines while he resists the criminals that threaten the day-to-day operations of society. Selina, on the other hand, is less sure about what is worth preserving. They clearly realize each other's identities as they dance at a party—ironically for them it is a costume party and the two of them lack physical disguises—but all this recognition achieves is trust between two people, rather than a broader shift in gender categories. In their earlier encounters she uses the stereotypes to trick Batman ("you'd hit a woman?") so she can hit him harder, thus showing him the stupidity of buying into traditional ideas about women and their capacity for physical violence. In the sense that they help each other see beyond limitations, they challenge norms, but Batman is not ready to act completely outside society's structures, since he is a capitalist, though apparently a benevolent one. As Walton says, "*Batman Returns* ... demonstrates disturbing tendencies to reinforce conventional power hierarchies."[11] Even with this limitation, Batman has a better understanding of the complexities of himself and others than Catwoman, Penguin or Shreck because "he knows he is a peripheral subject and ... accepts that status moreso than his antagonists."[12] Batman also does not fall victim to the mania for power that includes the desire for the accumulation of influence and position that drives Max and Penguin.

Nature(s), Freedoms and Capitalism

Just as society serves a capitalist structure in the three films, nature becomes a key index to concerns that surround consumption and commodification. The birds and bats that appear in Gotham, like workers and consumers, are manipulated. A bizarre example of this manipulation occurs when Penguin straps small missiles to the penguins he has lived with in his sewer kingdom and controls them remotely as though they are weapons in a video game. He commandeers the Batmobile the same way earlier in the film. These animals are as close as Penguin gets to a family—a group of emperor penguins attend his dead body as he slides down a ramp into the water in his underground lair—but he is willing to use them as walking bombs. His own hybrid nature does not give him sympathy for the oppressed, but makes him an oppressor.[13] The fact that his parents jettisoned him from the world of elegance and excess makes him an other in a different way from either Batman or Catwoman. After it becomes clear that he will not get elected mayor he rejects the humanity that he had so carefully worked to reclaim. He declares, "My name is not Oswald, it's Penguin. I am not a human being. I am an animal! Crank the a/c! Bring me my lists!"[14] In this declaration he also rejects his hybridity and ironically does so using human language. He rejoins with his animal self, but denies part of himself to do so. Unlike Catwoman and Batman he refuses to be a split being and authorizes himself to be a type of animal capitalist who uses his peers just as surely as Shreck uses his power. The obvious affinities that Catwoman and Batman have with the creatures that afford them their identities does not lead to their abuse of cats or bats. It is Penguin who uses bats (in trying to frame Batman) to scare the Ice Princess and Catwoman's relationship to felines initially contains a bit of envy, but the only non-human creature she threatens is a caged bird in Penguin's apartment. She puts it in her mouth, but does not consume it; Penguin threatens a cat and she releases it. In other words, she enacts the role of the feline predator, not the role of a megalomaniac.

Birds also appear prominently in *Sleepy Hollow* in both natural and artistically rendered forms. The obvious gesture of freeing a bird from its cage that Crane performs as he prepares to leave for Sleepy Hollow has its artistic analog in the *trompe l'oeil* spinning toy that his mother gave him and that he in turn gives to Katrina. The other creature we see is a bat that the crone,

Lady Van Tassel's sister, in the Western Woods uses in her trance spell as she replies to Ichabod's question about the location of the Horseman. She gets the bat from a basket where she keeps a few of them, tips one out, grabs it and, appropriately, severs its head. The bird figures clearly associate Crane with the idea of the cage, while Katrina declares that she would never have the heart to cage one, though she might like a tame bird. The cage or trap for Crane is not only the network of male power and the female supernatural in Sleepy Hollow, but also the cage of reason. He has more to overcome than his counterpart Katrina does since she is less bound by patriarchal ideologies that privilege logic, and more motivated by affection for others. Significantly, she joins him when he searches for the Horseman and this assistance that provokes his statement "I am now twice the man." Their bond helps him get over his limitations, while she already has qualities of strength and bravery that align her with traditional notions of masculinity. Katrina and Ichabod are androgynous characters whose joining makes each of them stronger. Both characters clearly link to the nonverbal worlds of images: he in his dreams about his mother and Katrina through the white magic symbols she uses. She, however, is more adept at reading these signs.

The Western Woods also play an important role in both the plot of the film and the identification of those who are on the margins of power. When Lady Van Tassel and her sister were children trying to survive, they saw the Horseman fleeing from his pursuers and the sister who became Lady van Tassel snapped a twig to signal his location. She uses the place and circumstances to get an advantage since her knowledge of where he is buried allows her to take his severed head and control him. She uses a violent man who enjoyed killing for the thrill of it, to undermine other men. She also has no sympathy for nature. The Tree of the Dead as the Horseman's portal to the living world clearly stands out as an emblem of pain. Even Irving's story highlights a tree that accents Crane's fear. It is a giant tulip tree in the text "which towered like a giant above all the other tress of the neighborhood" and whose "limbs were gnarled and fantastic, large enough to form trunks for ordinary trees, twisting down almost to the earth and rising again in the air."[15] In the film the tree bleeds when Ichabod hacks at in an attempt to find a way into the Horseman's lair. The tree bleeds in the film just as the corpses bleed since it contains all the heads the Horseman has collected in his quest to find his own. In the alignment of the world of nature with the supernatural and the criminal, the tree itself clearly suffers.

The woods in *Corpse Bride* also supply a place that is on the margins of society as Victor wanders there practicing his wedding vows. He has extraordinary difficulty remembering his lines when he is at the wedding rehearsal, but in the woods he gets them right and places the ring on a twig that sticks out of the ground. The twig is Emily's skeletal finger, and thus the film clearly links her with nature and marriage. Their "courtship" occurs not in the town or in the pretentious but run down Everglot mansion, but in the snowy woods under a moonlit sky. Emily, who transforms into a host of butterflies at the end of the film, also clearly echoes Victor, who releases a butterfly at its beginning. Other than the released animal, the town Victor lives in contains only dead fish (his family's wealth comes from their fish monger business), a tired carthorse and a sprig of flowers that looks forlorn in the dark rooms of Victoria's home. By contrast, when he is in the underworld, Emily finds and gives him back his dead dog, Scraps, and he sadly remembers that his parents never approved of his having a dog. Emily tries to help Victor see himself as she sees him: an appropriate suitor/husband in contrast to the man who victimized her, the pompous Lord Barkis. Her animal helpers (a spider and a worm) further emphasize her connection with the animal world. Though initially Victor and Victoria see Emily as an impediment to their happiness and Emily tries to trap Victor at the start of their acquaintance, she releases him from his promise just as he had released the butterfly, because she has wisdom and the strength of experience. Emily represents the best qualities of both Victor and Victoria: Victor's gentleness and sensitivity (Emily and Victor both play the piano, while Victoria does not) and Victoria's bravery and desire for independent will (Emily confronts Barkis and makes her own choices). The natural emblems of the butterfly and the forest help the viewer understand that the best relationships between men and women do not place limits on their roles or include domination of one by the other. A real partnership cannot involve hierarchy and a focus on material wealth and class standing though the Everglot and Van Dort parents are unable to see anything but capitalist imperatives.

The lens of the gothic opens the door to issues surrounding property, wealth and inheritance, but these three films present ways to maneuver and at least individually subvert the claustrophobic effects of hierarchy, patriarchy and capitalism. Together men and women claim their outsider status not as a sad default method of coping with an entrenched system, but as a path to recreating themselves and evoking a hope for their futures that they cannot share with their societies, but can potentially share with each other.

Notes

1. All citations to the film refer to the DVD version: *Batman Returns*, directed by Tim Burton (1992, Burbank, CA: Warner Home Video, 2005) DVD.
2. All citations to the film refer to the DVD version: *Sleepy Hollow*, directed by Tim Burton (1999, Hollywood, CA: Paramount Home Entertainment, 2006), DVD.

3. All citations to the film refer to the DVD version: *Corpse Bride*, directed by Tim Burton and Mike Johnson (2005, Burbank, CA: Warner Home Video, 2005), DVD.

4. As Killeen says of the gothic: "While an earlier generation of Gothic critics established the transgressive tendencies of much of this literature, a host of new studies have demonstrated that there are also profoundly conservative aspects to the Gothic, including its tendency towards hyperbolic and chauvinistic types of nationalism, extraordinarily reactionary views of sexual deviance, and rigid paranoid policing of the domestic space. Gothic is a mode of writing riven with ambivalence, articulating both disgust and desire." Jarlath Killeen, *History of the Gothic: Gothic Literature, 1825–1914* (Cardiff: University of Wales Press, 2009), 10.

5. David L.G. Arnold, "Fearful Pleasures or 'I am Twice the Man': The Re-Gendering of Ichabod Crane." *Literature/Film Quarterly*. 31, no.1 (2003), 38.

6. Susan Bernardo, "The Bloody Battle Between the Sexes in Tim Burton's *Sleepy Hollow*," *Literature/Film Quarterly*. 31, no. 1 (2003), 43.

7. Duncan Petrie, "But What if Beauty is a Beast? Doubles, Transformations and Fairy Tale Motifs in *Batman Returns*" in *Cinema and the Realms of Enchantment: Lectures, Seminars, and Essays*, ed. Duncan Petrie (London: British Film Institute, 1994), 109.

8. Susan Bernardo, "Recycling Victims and Villains in *Batman Returns*," *Literature/Film Quarterly*. 22, no. 1 (1994), 19.

9. Cory Reed, "*Batman Returns:* From the Comic(s) to the Grotesque," *PostScript*. 14, no. 3 (1995), 39.

10. Steven Allen, "Bringing the Dead to Life—Animation and the Horrific," *Fear Itself Reasoning the Unreasonable*, eds. S. Heppel and M. Huppert. (Amsterdam: Rodopi, 2009), 2. e-book. It is also worth noting that the underworld as a motif is powerful in Burton's films including *Batman Returns* and *Corpse Bride*, but that we do not see the Horseman's underworld in *Sleepy Hollow. Corpse Bride's* underworld does not represent the greed and corruption that it indicates in the other two films I am discussing

11. Priscilla L. Walton, "A Slippage of Masks: Dis-Guising Catwoman in Batman Returns," Canadian Journal of Film Studies/Revue canadienne d'études cinématographiques. 6, no. 1 (1997), 97.

12. Philip Orr, "The Anoedipal Mythos of Batman and Catwoman," *Journal of Popular Culture*. 27, no. 4 (1994), 175.

13. Peter Lehman, *Running Scared: Masculinity and the Representation of the Male Body* (Detroit: Wayne State University Press, 2007). See Lehman's chapter two, "I Will Suppress Nothing': Sexuality in Male Feral-Child Narratives" which discusses the intersection of the animal, the feral state and gender in Truffaut's and Herzog's films.

14. Susan Bernardo, "Recycling Victims and Villains in *Batman Returns*," *Literature/Film Quarterly*. 22, no. 1 (1994), 20.

15. Washington Irving, "The Legend of Sleepy Hollow" in *The Legend of Sleepy Hollow and Other Stories in the Sketch Book* (New York: Signet, 1981), 353.

Bibliography

Allen, Steven. "Bringing the Dead to Life—Animation and the Horrific." *Fear Itself Reasoning the Unreasonable*. Eds. S. Heppel and M. Huppert. Amsterdam: Rodopi, 2009. 9.Ebook.

Arnold, David L. G.. "Fearful Pleasures or 'I am Twice the Man': The Re-Gendering of Ichabod Crane." *Literature/Film Quarterly*. 31, no.1 (2003): 33–38.

Bernardo, Susan. "The Bloody Battle Between the Sexes in Tim Burton's *Sleepy Hollow*." *Literature/Film Quarterly*. 31, no. 1 (2003): 39–43.

_____. "Recycling Victims and Villains in Batman Returns." *Literature/Film Quarterly.* 22, no. 1 (1994): 16–20.

Freud, Sigmund. *Civilization and Its Discontents.* trans. and ed. James Strachey. New York: W.W. Norton and Company, 1961.

Irving, Washington. "The Legend of Sleepy Hollow." In *The Legend of Sleepy Hollow and Other Stories in the Sketch Book.* 329–360. New York: Signet, 1981.

Killeen, Jarlath. *History of the Gothic: Gothic Literature, 1825–1914.* Cardiff: University of Wales Press, 2009.

Lehman, Peter. *Running Scared: Masculinity and the Representation of the Male Body.* Detroit: Wayne State University Press, 2007.

Orr, Philip. "The Anoedipal Mythos of Batman and Catwoman." *Journal of Popular Culture.* 27, no. 4 (1994): 169–182.

Petrie, Duncan. "But What If Beauty Is a Beast? Doubles, Transformations and Fairy Tale Motifs in *Batman Returns.*" In *Cinema and the Realms of Enchantment: Lectures, Seminars, and Essays.* Ed. Duncan Petrie, 98–110 London: British Film Institute, 1994.

Reed, Cory. "Batman Returns: From the Comic(s) to the Grotesque." *PostScript.* 14, no. 3 (1995): 38–50.

Walton, Priscilla L. "A Slippage of Masks: Dis-Guising Catwoman in *Batman Returns.*" *Canadian Journal of Film Studies/Revue canadienne d'études cinématographiques.* 6, no. 1 (1997): 91–110.

SECTIONTWO

The Nature of Adaptations

Becoming the Stories
Indefinite Play in Big Fish

Lisa K. Perdigao

While Tim Burton's films share characteristics that reflect what critics and audience members have come to identify as the director's style, *Edward Scissorhands* (1990) epitomizes Burton's vision. Like Victor Frankenstein's famous creature, Edward Scissorhands (Johnny Depp) is born from science but, in the course of the film, Edward becomes more than his creator's (Vincent Price) work. The last scenes of the film reveal Edward as a creator who transforms the landscape with his art; his artistry in snow sculptures turns the neighborhood into a wonderland. In a metafictional turn, Edward can be read as Burton who transforms his cinematic world with the introduction of the fantastic. In his own history of filmmaking, Burton often turns to inherited texts and, like Edward, reshapes them to fit a new medium. Within and between his films, Burton suggests how he conceives and reconceives the space between the printed page, stage, and film screen. While *Edward Scissorhands* suggests Burton's idea of his art, it is in *Big Fish* (2003) that Burton zooms out to consider a larger picture. In *Big Fish*, Burton utilizes his source, Daniel Wallace's 1998 novel, to meditate not only on his own distinctive style of filmmaking but also on the medium of film itself.

In *Big Fish*, Burton self-consciously explores the significance and meaning of storytelling through the development of the character Will Bloom (Billy Crudup). Like *Edward Scissorhands* and *Alice in Wonderland* (2010), *Big Fish* presents a protagonist who struggles with the loss of his father and questions about his own identity. Yet, unlike Edward Scissorhands and Alice (Mia Wasikowska), Will Bloom does not romanticize his relationship with his father. Where Edward Scissorhands and Alice are inspired by their fathers' fantastic imaginations, Will has resented his father's fanciful stories since childhood. After a period of estrangement, an adult Will returns home to spend time with his father in his last days, trying to discover the "real" story of Edward Bloom (Albert Finney and Ewan McGregor), the facts instead of the fiction. Wallace's novel, designed with chapters as cinematic "takes," is a rich text for Burton's adaptation that allows the filmmaker to consider the possibilities of storytelling within and between different mediums—spoken word, page, and film screen. As Will grows to appreciate his father's stories and blossoms with this new understanding, the film depicts the inauguration of Will Bloom into Burton's cinematic world. Will matures into a man who not only remembers his father's stories and legacy but also becomes an artist, Burton's kind of storyteller.

Burton's use of metafiction can be traced throughout his filmography in instances where Burton the filmmaker is exposed. Michelle LeBlanc and Colin Odell write, "A common figure to see in a Burton film is that of Tim Burton, or rather an idealised version of himself."[1] For LeBlanc and Odell, *Big Fish*'s Edward Bloom fits within the Burton pantheon of outsider characters. While Edward is comparable to Edward Scissorhands, Richie (Lukas Haas) in *Mars Attacks!* (1996), and Willy Wonka (Johnny Depp), he is also reflective of Burton himself.[2] Molly Hite describes how the "postmodernist use of the authorial persona disrupts both realist and modernist strategies of reading" by "resist[ing] the reader's desire to assign a textual phenomenon to a particular ontological level, such as the level of real-world fact, fictional 'fact,' or fictional 'fiction.'"[3] She writes that this kind of "frame-breaking," "one of the most important features of postmodern writing," "aligns the postmodern novel with a kind of radical undecidability, a suspicion that the question 'What's the real story here?' cannot be answered in any satisfying way—satisfying, that is, in terms of the sorts of expectations bred by realist and modernist fiction."[4] Many of Burton's films share this postmodernist stamp; however, *Big Fish*, like its tall tales, offers an exaggeration of the idea. Expanding beyond the "authorial persona," *Big Fish* performs the work that Julie Levinson describes:

> Metafictions hold a mirror up to their own processes and turn their gaze back on themselves, giving us a double vision of both the product of the creator's endeavors (the story told) and the processes that go into creating that product (the storytelling). These narratives add one more ingredient to the Platonic recipe of mimesis (showing) and diegesis (telling) by also containing their own exegesis (explaining or analyzing). Indeed, they conflate all three modes, as interpretation and criticism become immanent with fiction.[5]

Recalling Will Bloom's line, *Big Fish* becomes what it was always meant to be: Burton's critical examination of the storyteller *and* his stories. *Big Fish* allows the director to reflect on the world that he has created in his career as a filmmaker.

Questioning the efficacy of stories and their transmission, *Big Fish* evidences the poststructuralist turn of the late twentieth century, most notably deconstruction.[6] Hite writes that "Both postmodern fictional practice and poststructuralist critical theory tend to question a commonsense view of language as simply the vehicle that relays the world to the mind, or as an ideally transparent medium guaranteeing the unequivocal presence of meaning in efficacious discourse."[7] *Big Fish* represents the "web of intertextual overlap" that Patricia Waugh says exists between postmodernist writing and poststructuralist theory.[8] That Burton focuses on the relationship between father Edward Bloom and his son William Bloom is significant. It recalls a particular aspect of deconstruction: Jacques Derrida's figuration of speech and writing as father and son.

Burton examines the divide between speech and writing in his presentation of a storyteller father and writer son. In her introduction to Derrida's *Dissemination*, Barbara Johnson writes, "Derrida's critique of Western metaphysics focuses on its privileging of the spoken word over the written word."[9] Privilege is given to the spoken word because "the speaker and listener are both present to the utterance simultaneously," which seems to "guarantee the notion that in the spoken word we know what we mean, mean what we say, say what we mean, and know what we have said."[10] Will can be seen, in a sense, as the deconstructionist critic. He refuses to privilege his father's stories and doubts their veracity. A reporter by trade, Will offers a competing discourse. For LeBlanc and Odell, "In many ways William is almost a cinematic critic of Burton and his works, a detractor who would consider elaborate fancies or fantasy as somehow unworthy of his attention as it is not based on real life."[11] Will's work within the film is the examination of the stories and the man behind them; the result is the deconstruction of Burton's cinematic world. Johnson describes how the writer "puts his thought on paper, distancing it from himself, transforming it into something that can be read by someone far away, even after the writer's death."[12] Her terms are suggestive for what is at work in *Big Fish*: Edward wants his story to be remembered after he passes and, ultimately, it is up to his son, the writer, to make use of the inherited stories, to find a medium for them. And, like Derrida, Burton does not privilege one over the other; he maps a new space between the two by the film's end.

Almost literalizing Derrida's theories, the relationships between fathers and sons are foregrounded in *Big Fish*'s diegesis and in extratextual materials. Both Wallace and Burton say that *Big Fish* is a personal story that is representative of their own relationships with their fathers. Burton has said, "I try to treat all [my films] personally, but this one ranks up there" and "I wasn't close to my father."[13] Edwin Page notes the uncanny timing of *Big Fish* in Burton's life: "[Burton's] father died not long before he received the script, and two months before the release of the film he became a father himself."[14] Further reflecting the intertextual loop between story-world and reality, Burton's son's name, Billy, offers another link back to the character Will Bloom (played by Billy Crudup). Of his own source material, Wallace says, "My own father was a charmer and a kind of rover, similar to Edward Bloom in many respects.... The emotions William experiences in the book are ones I experienced in my own life, and so in this way at least *Big Fish* is a reflection of reality, and thus somewhat autobiographical. But at the same time there's not a factual word in it: I made up everything."[15] Again, in the space outside of the film, the "real story" is eluded and evaded. Burton's and Wallace's statements offer rich contexts for analyzing how *Big Fish* experiments with the divide between fathers and sons, reality and fiction, and, ultimately, speech and writing, conceived in and as the space of the film.

Wallace's *Big Fish: A Novel of Mythic Proportions*, is, as its title suggests, about the tall tale and Burton's film adapts the tall tale to cinematic proportions. Chapter titles in Wallace's novel announce its fit within the genre, for example, "How He Tamed the Giant," "His Three Labors," and "His Immortality." As William Bloom faces his father's death, he attempts to discover the truth of the man that his father was, beyond the extraordinary stories that he told his son throughout his life. At the beginning of the novel, William and Edward are on one of their last car trips when they stop by the river. As William watches his father step into the water, he states,

> I looked at this old man, my old man with his old white feet in this cross-running stream, these moments the very last in his life, and I thought of him suddenly, and simply, as a boy, a child, a youth, with his whole life ahead of him, much as mine was ahead of me.... And these images—the now and then of my father—converged, and at that moment he turned into a weird creature, wild, concurrently young and old, dying and newborn. My father became a myth.[16]

Wallace's story is not only a collection of tall tales; it is a study of the process of myth-making as seen through a son's eyes. One episode of Edward Bloom's childhood tells of a time when the boy was bedridden for months and used his time to read "almost every book there was in Ashland," "A thousand books—some say ten thousand. History, Art, Philosophy, Horatio Alger.... Even the telephone book."[17] William notes, "They say that eventually he knew more than anybody, even Mr. Pinkwater, the librarian."[18] William's conclusion that "He was a big fish, even then" shows how stories are at the foundations of this one.[19]

With its roots in Wallace's novel, Burton's film performs as the cinematic tall tale that explores the competing versions of the story of Edward Bloom.

The viewer's introduction to Edward's stories is shaped by Will's reactions to them over the years. The story unfolds sequentially as the father tells the story to his son, his son's Boy Scout troop, his prom date (Morgan Grace Jarrett), and, finally, the guests at his son's wedding. As time passes in the sequence, we see that Will becomes disenchanted with the stories and tries to distance himself from them. Burton increases the distance between father and son in this sequence: the camera pans down the line of Boy Scouts to reveal a bored Will at the end; Will is down the hall with his mother (Jessica Lange) as his prom date is captivated by the tale (with high angle shots demonstrating Edward's control over her and the narrative); and, at his wedding, Will eventually walks out of the room and off the boat. When Edward confronts his son, Will reveals his frustration with his father and his stories. He tells him, "I don't love that story, not anymore, not after a thousand times. I know every punchline, Dad. I can tell them as well as you can."[20] After the wedding, Will becomes completely estranged from his father, not speaking to him for three years.

Edward becomes an absent presence in his son's life. A scene depicts Will and his mother talking on the phone when Will asks about his father. She tells Will that he is out, although we see Edward in the kitchen with her. The distance between the two is played out emotionally, physically, and symbolically. While the William of Wallace's novel is a college-aged young adult, Burton's Will is a married man living in Paris with his pregnant wife Josephine (Marion Cotillard) when he learns of his father's failing health. As this adult Will answers the phone at work, he identifies his occupation: he works for United Press International. This detail highlights the connection and disparity between father and son. When Will and his wife return to his childhood home, Will reminds his father that Josephine is a photographer who has been to the locations that Ed dreamily represents in his stories. Edward still insists on the veracity of his stories, saying to Josephine, "So you know...."[21] Speech continues to trump the reporter's writing, at least by Edward's account.

While Wallace's novel can be read, mostly, as a series of more conventional (though extraordinary) tall tales, Burton's representation of the tall tales on the big screen emphasizes the divide between the father's and son's versions as it navigates the space between them. Derrida states that speech is the original that writing attempts to re-present. Yet the idea of a logocentric order is itself a fiction, as speech exists relative to writing; it is through différance that meaning is made. Art Berman writes, "For Derrida, the 'structures' of reality purportedly discovered by philosophy are meant to account both for the generativity, change, and transmutation that characterize life and the world as it is known to humankind, and, as well, for the stable, unchanging ground of the structure itself."[22] In *Big Fish*, the son's desire to know the "truth" about his father is weighed against the father's insistence of the man he has always been. Will says that he only knows Edward through his speeches, including the one that leads to their estrangement: the wedding toast. After Will leaves the boat and Edward follows him, Will offers his interpretation of his father's story. He says, "I'm a footnote in that story, Dad, the context for your great adventure, which never happened, incidentally. You were selling novelty products in Wichita the day I was born."[23] Here, Will presents his position (as he sees it)—outside of his father's stories, themselves elaborate fantasies. Will doubts those speech acts and longs to find visible proof for the stories that his father has told him. After their reunion, Will continues his search for the "real story" before it is too late.[24] As a reporter, he says, he deals with facts.

Will destabilizes the father's authority from the very beginning of the film, casting doubt into the story as it is relayed. Burton begins the film with a voiceover by Will that says, "In telling the story of my father's life, it's impossible to separate fact from fiction, the man from the myth. The best I can do is to tell it the way he told me. It doesn't always make sense and most of it never happened."[25] Here, Will is identified as a storyteller, repeating what he had been told over the years. Through the voiceover, Will is afforded the role of storyteller and can be read as guaranteeing that, in and through speech, "we know what we mean, mean what we say, say what we mean, and know what we have said."[26] However, in these lines he indicates that he doubts the veracity of the stories. As Will renders his speech, he deconstructs its terms.

While the film establishes the tension between the two men—the ways that they see the world—Ed easily aligns them, telling Will that "We're the same. I tell the stories and you write them down."[27] For Edward, they are both storytellers; only their mediums differ. Will is initially resistant to this idea and continually attempts to distinguish the two. When Edward later tells Josephine the story of his courtship of Will's mother, Sandra Templeton (Alison Lohman), and its beginnings, Josephine tells Will that it doesn't matter if it is accurate, only that it is "romantic." Edward is surprised that Will never told her the story but then tells Josephine that "He would have told it wrong anyway. All of the facts, none of the flavor."[28] To punctuate this point, when Josephine asks Will about the story of how his father and mother met, Will simply responds, "They met at Auburn."[29] Style is imperative to the storyteller and, while Will and Edward are initially estranged over this very point, this is where Burton and Edward are inextricably connected. Burton realizes the vision of Edward's stories, translating it for the viewers. For example, when Edward tells the story of working at Amos Calloway's circus and seeing the "love of his life," Sandra Templeton, for the first time, he says, "They say when you meet the love of your life, time stops.... What they don't tell you is that once time starts again, it moves extra fast to catch up."[30] Burton exaggerates this effect by freezing all of the characters and objects surrounding Edward and Sandra. Edward moves toward her, pushing aside popcorn and stepping through a hula hoop. The scene is played in fast forward, with Sandra quickly leaving and the circus closing for the night. It is through Burton's cinematography that Edward's stories come to life, providing the "flavor" that Edward cites is imperative to stories.

The relationship between speech and writing, father's and son's stories, is redefined with Burton's cinematography. The father's stories do not exist only as speech acts. As the film takes us through the first "big fish" story, it becomes more than just a story. We see Edward struggle with the big fish. From the film's beginning, we are presented with a different perspective than Will's. It is complementary and yet contradictory to the story Will tells. While Will's doubts about the truth of his father's stories frame the film, the audience is immediately cast into Edward's story-world. What Will discounts as fantasy is realized for the audience onscreen. According to Peter Brunette and David Wills, "Like spoken language, conventional cinema, through the careful suturing of sound and image, offers an illusory wholeness."[31] The suturing of sound and image fills the space between speech and writing, father and son, allowing the viewer accessibility to the world(s) of the stories.[32]

Will's quest to find the truth about his father ironically brings him into Edward's story-world. Burton stages this development with the use of props. Will seeks out material facts, objects and documents that will verify his father's accounts or provide the "real story." When his mother asks him to go through his father's things, Will is immediately and literally dismissive. He starts throwing things away without reading them until he finds an official document and becomes a more thoughtful reader. This document is a notice of his father's death, part of the story that Edward tells about his disappearance during the war. Will's mother tells her son, "Not everything your father has told you is a complete lie."[33] Will (and the audience) glimpse the "Handi-Matic" device that is featured in Edward's stories of his time as a traveling salesman. Here, the material facts complement the stories. The most significant object that Will uncovers is a deed with the name Jennifer Hill written on it. Will again plays the role of the reporter, following the lead to find Jennifer Hill (Helena Bonham Carter) and Spectre. Edward's stories are brought to life.

As the film explores the space between speech and writing, Spectre, signifying liminality, is a productive site in *Big Fish*.[34] It provides a middle ground for both father and son. Describing Edward's return to Spectre, Jenny says, "Fate has a way of circling back on a man, and taking him by surprise."[35] Her comment offers a way of reading the film's circular narrative. Spectre, that absent presence, is a transformative site for both the storyteller and the listener. Everything comes together for Will. The story of his father's life becomes more than a speech act: it is materialized in and as the film. Jenny's retelling of Edward's story corroborates Edward's account and brings it to life. As the story—and Will's journey—circles back to Spectre, Burton shows how the allusive and elusive site has been transformed in Edward's absence. A storm drives Edward back to Spectre where he rediscovers the "girl in the river" and his key to Ashton. Edward realizes that he has been there before but, as Jenny puts it, "A man sees things differently at different times in his life."[36] Spectre's altered appearance takes Edward by surprise. After the road had come to Spectre, outsiders bankrupted the town; it is about to be auctioned off when Edward rediscovers it. Without Edward, the magical quality of the place disappears. He turns to his resources, those characters central to his stories, to procure the funds to buy the town. In essence, his stories breathe new life into Spectre. In the novel, Wallace refers to the circle that is completed within and by Spectre, as Edward tells one of Spectre's own, Al, "When I saw Spectre, I knew I had to have it.... I had to have it all. I suppose in part it has to do with circles, with entireties."[37]

In the film, Jenny has something to do with that circularity. Not only is she the last owner to turn over her house and land to Edward but she is also the character who first introduced him to its magic. She is Jenny Beaman, the mayor's daughter who had stolen Edward's shoes. She is the catalyst to his early departure as well, for her mother (Missi Pyle) tells Edward that "Jenny thinks [he's] quite the catch."[38] Remaining the biggest fish by virtue of never being caught, Edward must leave. Contrary to Will's supposition, the two do not have an affair. Wallace writes, "IN SPECTRE, HISTORY BECOMES what never happened. People mess things up, forget and remember all the wrong things. What's left is fiction ... the story keeps changing. All of the stories do."[39] There is no one "real story"; instead, "What's left is fiction." Although Jenny is enamored by Edward, she realizes that there are only two women in Edward's life: his wife and everyone else. After Edward leaves Spectre, her house, one that he had repaired to become a dreamhouse, falls to disrepair. The world of and beyond Spectre appear to be extensions of Edward; without Edward, Spectre ceases to exist. Jenny's life, as one of Edward's characters, is dependent upon the storyteller's construction. According to Jenny, "As for the girl, the common belief is that she became a witch, and crazy at that. She became somewhat of a legend herself. And the story ended where it began."[40]

Although Will initially tells Jenny that it is impossible that she is the witch, as the witch was old when Ed was young, she highlights the possibilities of this nonlinear narrative. Burton's casting supports the claim: Helena Bonham Carter plays both roles. Will tells Jenny, "My father talked about things he never did and I'm sure he did a lot of things he never talked about it. I'm just trying to reconcile the two."[41] Jenny's story helps Will to sort through the facts and fictions of his life, including the assertion of his father's fidelity to his mother.[42] All of the pieces of the story start to come together for Will. As Edward's wedding ring is made the focal point of the stories, it comes to emphasize the circularity of the film and its meaning. Initially, the ring is introduced in the story that Will resists and grows to resent. It is central to the "big fish" story that opens the film, as the catfish that Edward catches on the day of Will's birth takes it. The ring remains prominent as Edward narrates the story in the opening sequence, and, as Burton depicts the evolution of the "big fish" story over the years and the gradual estrangement between father and son, he constantly uses close-up shots of Edward's hands, focusing on the ring. As Edward's words are accompanied by gestures that help to create the story-world and translate meaning, the ring helps define the content and performance of the stories. The story of the "big fish" appropriately concludes at his son's wedding, where the ring is most symbolic. After the wedding, the two characters do not talk for three years, as Will is upset that his father always needs to be the center of attention, even on his wedding day.

The scene is indicative of Derrida's description of "decentering." Derrida writes, "The concept of structure" "must be thought of as a series of substitutions of center for center, as a linked chain of determinations at the center."[43] Following the rupture that Derrida identifies in structuralist thought, creating the path for deconstruction to follow, "it was necessary to begin thinking that there was no center" and, in that absence, "everything became discourse," extending "the domain and the play of signification infinitely."[44] Although Edward tries to tell Will that he is at the story's center, his son replies that he is only a footnote, pure context for the story of Edward Bloom. Burton extends the "domain and the play of signification infinitely" in the film through the presentation of the ring. It figures in the estrangement between father and son but is also the key to their reunion, as Will is about to become a father himself. When Will talks to Josephine one night, his ring becomes a focal point, catching the light in an otherwise dark scene. Ultimately, the ring plays a significant role in the story that concludes the film. The circle connects all of the points of Edward's life and gives shape, form, and meaning to the film.

A film focusing on a father's passing, *Big Fish* is self-conscious of its own attempts at closure and resolution. Recalling Johnson's characterization of the act of writing that attempts to signify presence despite loss, *Big Fish* depicts the struggles both father and son face in letting go. While the ending provides the key for understanding the transformations of Will, the character, and the story itself, the end is already suggested in the beginning. As Jenny says, "[T]he story ended where it began," with the legend of the witch.[45] As a boy, Edward (Perry Walston) is dared to steal the witch's eye that reveals the future. Although he initially questions if he should see his own death, Edward decides that you can survive everything else if you know what the ending will be. This knowledge guides the shape of the narrative. For instance, when Edward is almost swallowed by a tree, he says, "Wait, this isn't how I go," and the tree promptly drops him.[46] Taking its cue from the novel's chapter "How It Ends" and William's line "The ending is always a surprise. Even I was surprised by the ending," the metafictionality of the story is highlighted throughout the film when Edward tells Will—and the audience—"It's a surprise ending. I wouldn't want to ruin it for you."[47] Will himself substantiates the claim, "As unlikely as his stories got, the endings were always the most surprising of all."[48] Jenny's story suggests that Edward is the source of Spectre's transformation, if not creation; here, Edward's storytelling directs his actions, even sustaining his own life. The line separating reality from fiction, or distinguishing "real-world fact, fictional 'fact,' or fictional 'fiction,'" is displaced, perhaps entirely erased in Burton's retelling.[49]

The unexpected result of the story is that the man becomes the stories. At the end of Wallace's novel, William resists closure and loss by offering a final transformation of that story and the man at its center. William says, "And that's when I discovered that my father hadn't been dying after all. He was just changing, transforming himself into something new and different to carry his life forward in. All this time, my father was becoming a fish."[50] The last lines of the novel conjure his father as a myth, as Will says, "Already I've heard stories, of lives saved and wishes granted..." but, he concludes, "... no one believes them. No one believes a word."[51] At the novel's end, the stories continue to exist, despite disbelief.

Burton takes *Big Fish* in a slightly different direction so that the ending highlights the transformation in/of storytelling achieved by film. At the hospital, Will is the last to remain with his father. When Edward awakens and begins to speak with him, the two begin one last adventure after Edward makes a request: "Tell me how it happens."[52] When Will asks him "How what happens?" Edward replies, "How I go."[53] Trying to decipher his father's meaning, Will asks, "What you saw in the eye?" and then responds, "I don't know that story. You never told me that one."[54] When Edward remains silent, Will says, "I need your help. Tell me how it starts" and Edward provides the foundation: "Like this."[55]

In the sequence that follows, Will demonstrates his ability to render his father's story visually, in the space beyond the hospital room, between (or beyond) speech act and writing. The characters are in a dark hospital room, yet the room becomes illuminated, transformed, as Will begins. His father excitedly sits up, and, as Will notes, Edward is better, different. With Will shaping the narrative in the voiceover, an extradiegetic narration spoken in the hospital room that transforms the story-world, the scene becomes animated with the two characters' escape plot. Will, Edward, and the audience are transported from the hospital room, down the hallway as Sandra and Josephine divert the orderlies, to the car, and, finally, to the river, the site of the final story. Unlike Edward's more escapist narratives, however, Will's story is grounded by the reality of the hospital room. Burton focuses on Edward's face as he reacts to the story that Will tells, cutting between fantasy and reality. And yet Will's story is no less fantastic than Edward's; in fact, it is a compilation of all of Edward's stories.

Here perhaps is the middle ground afforded by magical realism, a transformation of reality with the introduction of the fantastic. Eugene L. Arva writes, "magical realism, a postmodern phenomenon *par excellence*, does not so much create new realities as re-create our own reality—often by pushing its limits, true, but even more often by enhancing its black holes, its inaccessible spaces."[56] In the story, Will and Edward can resist if not transcend death and closure to his story. The transformation of Edward's stories allows that possibility. The father and son travel in Edward's old Charger, now brand-new. En route to the river, elements of Edward's stories become part of the landscape: Will notes his father's thoughts about church traffic and, when they become stuck in it, Karl the Giant (Matthew McGrory) flips a car out of the way before waving to Edward. After they arrive at the river, Will carries his father through a huge crowd awaiting him. Josephine grabs Edward's slippers and throws them on the line, imitating Jenny's actions upon Edward's arrival in Spectre. All of the chapters of Edward's life are present and accounted for.

Will comments, "It's unbelievable," and Edward reflects that it is "The story of [his] life."[57] It is not a time of mourning; instead, loss is transformed into something beautiful and meaningful. The girl in the river, a manifestation of the big fish and projection of what the viewer wants it to be, becomes what it was always meant to be: Edward's wife. As Edward comments, "My girl in the river," he touches Sandra's chin in an intimate gesture the two share throughout the film.[58] Returning to the film's beginning, Edward produces his ring from his mouth and gives it to her. In the film's final sequence, Will lowers Edward's body into the water and, after Edward crosses his hands, staging himself for burial, Edward is transformed into a catfish. With the shot returning to the hospital room, Will offers the story's conclusion in his last words to his father: "You become what you always were—a very big fish.... And that's how it happens."[59] Edward responds with one last word, "Exactly," asserting the truth behind this version.[60]

The next scene offers another "take" on Edward's death and a final redefinition of the relationship between speech, writing, and film. As the camera presents a bird's eye view of a street leading to a church, a recurring scene, it suggests that the location is both Ashford and Spectre. The chapters of Edward's life converge at this site. Nondiegetic music is the only sound the audience hears. Without the characters' words, the images signify meaning. The funeral is viewed through Will's eyes, at times through point of view shots and, at others, reaction shots depicting his perspective on what he sees. Finally, Will is able to see what the audience has all along: the characters of Edward's stories come to life.

Yet this final sequence does not merely affirm the reality of the stories; instead, it highlights what Edward's storytelling had done: it had offered hyperboles. Karl is not a giant but incredibly tall. Ping and Jing are twins, although they are not conjoined. Burton shoots each character with a suspension of disbelief: we see the characters as extraordinary and then he reveals the "reality." Ping (Ada Tai) and Jing (Arlene Tai) appear to be conjoined in a two shot until Norther Winslow (Steve Buscemi) separates them by leading one away. We see Karl emerge from a car, seemingly larger than life, but we then see him in relation to the objects and people around him. After the funeral, the people in Edward's life gather in front of the church to retell Edward's stories, like Edward, wildly gesticulating with their hands. We cannot hear them, yet the scene, like the stories, bears meaning. Accompanied by the sweeping music and the characters' pantomime, Will's voiceover reframes the narrative, asking, "Have you ever heard a joke so many times…?"[61]

By the film's conclusion, a next generation—the future of the Bloom family, Will's son—continues the tradition of storytelling. As Will's son (Trevor Gagnon) excitedly tells his friends about Karl the Giant's size, he asks for corroboration to his story. Will neither fully asserts nor denies the existence of the fantastic, saying, it's "Something like that."[62] With Will's son's story, we only have access to the world of speech; we do not enter the world of the story but instead remain present, with the Bloom family in the backyard of the family home. Yet, as Will acquiesces, partly affirming and partly denying the story's veracity, Burton offers one last version of the story. The camera pans from a high angle shot overlooking the pool to take us back to the river, to the big fish, and Will's voiceover completes the circle. He says, "I guess that was my father's final joke.... A man tells his stories so many times that he becomes his stories. They live on after him, and in that way he becomes immortal."[63] The meaning of the father's stories is re-presented, signifying meaning, through cinematic effects.

Burton uses *Big Fish* as a metatext to examine not only his own mark left on the world of Hollywood cinema but also expands the frame to consider the medium. With Will's inauguration into Burton's world, *Big Fish* highlights the possibilities found in the exchange between creator, text, and audience in the space between speech, writing, and film. At the end of *Edward Scissorhands*, Kim (Winona Ryder) tells her granddaughter (Gina Gallagher) a story about the magical world that she inhabited when she was young. Snow begins to fall in their world, becoming an extension of the story-world. As Will's son tells the story to his friends, in the Blooms' swimming pool, a ripple is felt and a catfish emerges, pure cinematic magic. Following Derrida's argument that "The absence of the transcendental signified extends the domain and the play of signification infinitely," Edward's death does not translate to the end of his stories; they continue to signify meaning, covering the distance between speech and writing in Burton's adapted medium.[64]

Notes

1. Michelle LeBlanc and Colin Odell, *Tim Burton* (Harpenden: Pocket Essentials, 2001), Nook file, 9.
2. Ibid., 81.
3. Molly Hite, "Postmodern Fiction," in *The Columbia History of the American Novel*, ed. by Emory Elliott (New York: Columbia University Press, 1991), 701.
4. Ibid., 703.
5. Julie Levinson, "Adaptation, Metafiction, Self-Creation," *Genre* 40.1–2 (2007), 158–159.
6. *Big Fish* can be considered more broadly as reflecting developments in narrative and literary theory in the twentieth and twenty-first centuries. For example, Ken Hada explores how the self is depicted as a "product of storytelling" in *Big Fish*; he connects Walter Benjamin's account of storytelling to theories about social interaction in the work of Jean-Paul Sartre, George Herbert Mead, and Mitchell Aboulafia in his reading of the film. "Fishing for the [Mediating] Self: Identity and Storytelling in *Big Fish*," in *The Philosophy of Tim Burton*, ed. by Jennifer L. McMahon (Lexington: U of Kentucky P, 2014), 11. My focus is on the poststructuralist dimensions of the work represented in Will's insistence upon the "real" story and the construction of the divide between Edward's oral storytelling, Will's career as a reporter, and film. *Big Fish* reflects Art Berman's description of deconstruction as a critical practice that "disassembles a text to reveal that what perhaps has appeared to be a consistent and unified work is a structure of rhetorical strategies and maneuvers. The uncovering of that structure subverts the presumption of a coherent, non-contradictory, comprehensible (clearly interpretable) meaning." *From the New Criticism to Deconstruction: The Reception of Structuralism and Post-Structuralism* (Urbana: U of Illinois P, 1988), 211.

7. Ibid., 700.
8. Patricia Waugh, *Practising Postmodernism/Reading Modernism* (London: Arnold, 1992), 50.
9. Barbara Johnson, introduction to *Dissemination*, by Jacques Derrida (Chicago: The U of Chicago P, 1981), viii.
10. Ibid.
11. LeBlanc and Odell, 81.
12. Ibid., ix. Peter Brunette and David Wills state that the "act of writing" assumes "that writer and reader are involved in a *rendez-vous manqué*: they will not be present at the same time, now or in the future, or there would be no need for writing." *Screen/Play: Derrida and Film Theory* (Princeton: Princeton University Press, 1989), 61. Edward's imminent death is the crisis of the film—how his stories will be passed on.
13. Edwin Page, *The Gothic Fantasy of Tim Burton* (London: Marion Boyars Publishers Ltd, 2007), Nook edition, 166, 167.
14. Ibid., 166.
15. Daniel Wallace, *Big Fish: A Novel of Mythic Proportions* (New York: Penguin, 1998), 4.
16. Ibid., 2.
17. Ibid., 12.
18. Ibid., 12.
19. Ibid., 12.
20. *Big Fish*, writ. by John August and dir. by Tim Burton (Sony, 2004), DVD.
21. Ibid.
22. Berman, From the New Criticism to Deconstruction, 200.
23. Big Fish.
24. In her reading of Vladimir Nabokov's *Pale Fire*, Hite writes that the reader must evaluate what is "real" "in terms of the fictional universe of the novel" and what is "unreal," "fantasized, fictionalized, hallucinated, mistaken, and so on." "Postmodern Fiction," 707. Her description is applicable to the work that Will does with his father's stories, performing as *Pale Fire*'s reader in another metafictional loop.
25. Ibid.
26. Johnson, Introduction, viii.
27. Big Fish.
28. Ibid.
29. Ibid.
30. Ibid.
31. Brunette and Wills, *Screen/Play*, 63.
32. Eugene L. Arva discusses Jacques Ellul's argument about the relationship between images and one's sense of reality, writing, "Visual imagery turns out to be more than just a representation of reality: it ends up as its appropriation by complete identification with it. The image, just like reality, cannot be questioned: it is the ultimate evidence of its existence. The image *is* reality." "Writing the Vanishing Real: Hyperreality and Magical Realism," *Journal of Narrative Theory* 28.1 (2008), 63. He then turns to Jean Baudrillard's work to define hyperreality: "Caught in the web of a myriad of images, people no longer tell or listen to stories—the traditional carriers of meaning—nor seem to distinguish between reliable and unreliable media. Information conveyed through images is surrounded by an aura of plausibility that stories (particularly in written form) cannot match." Ibid., 64. Drawing on Arva's argument, the film screen presents images to the viewers where Will has access only to the words. The visual element of film lends an embodied form to the stories and, with it, weight and meaning. *Big Fish* represents this sense of a "vanishing real" that is the condition of postmodernism.

33. Big Fish.
34. Burton's Spectre is adapted from Wallace's novel, which itself borrows from many sources (from Greek mythology to Dante's *Divine Comedy*), but it also visually recalls the fantastic landscape in Victor Fleming's film *The Wizard of Oz* (1939). When Edward enters Spectre for the first time, he walks over expansive green grass (an Emerald City) and under a clothesline strung with shoes. One pair is at the center—red high-heeled shoes. In Spectre, Edward learns that the idea of home is relative and that his journey has just begun. Burton's return to Oz offers a lens for examining the director's ideas about film. 1939 was a remarkable year for film with the release of *Gone with the Wind* and *The Wizard of Oz*, which experiment with the introduction of color. Burton's worlds are richly colored and patterned, from costumes to the landscapes, seen in films like *Batman* (1989), *Edward Scissorhands*, *Alice in Wonderland*, and *Sweeney Todd: The Demon Barber of Fleet Street* (2007). Spectre, true to its name and nature, is uncanny—both familiar and strange. With Spectre, Burton illustrates how his film landscape is "haunted" by other stories, including his own. From his mise en scène to casting, Burton's films are intertextual and self-reflexive. While Helena Bonham Carter is a constant presence in Burton's films, other actors make reappearances: Danny DeVito is borrowed from *Batman Returns* (1992) to play Amos Calloway and his attorney is played by Deep Roy who is later cast in *Charlie and the Chocolate Factory* (2005). Page, *Gothic Fantasy*, 172.
35. Ibid.
36. Ibid.
37. Wallace, *Big Fish*, 150. The town is referred to as Specter in the novel but Spectre in the film.
38. Big Fish.
39. Wallace, *Big Fish*, 159.
40. Ibid.
41. Big Fish.
42. Burton's film highlights the fidelity of Edward Bloom and devotion to the love of his life. Wallace's novel is less romanticized; affairs are mentioned and Edward's life with Jenny is depicted. There is a magical transformation in that story as well—when Edward abandons her for a length of time, her house becomes surrounded by a swamp and the two never meet again.
43. Jacques Derrida, "Structure, Sign, and Play in the Discourse of the Human Sciences," in *Modern Criticism and Theory: A Reader*, 2nd ed., ed. by David Lodge (New York: Longman, 2000), 90.
44. Ibid., 91.
45. Big Fish.
46. Ibid.
47. Wallace, *Big Fish*, 164.
48. Ibid.
49. Hite, "Postmodern Fiction," 701.
50. Wallace, *Big Fish*, 180.
51. Ibid.
52. Big Fish.
53. Ibid.
54. Ibid.
55. Ibid.
56. Arva, "Writing the Vanishing Real," 69.
57. Ibid.
58. Ibid.

59. Ibid.
60. Ibid.
61. Ibid.
62. Ibid.
63. Ibid.
64. Derrida, "Structure, Sign, and Play," 91.

Bibliography

Arva, Eugene L. "Writing the Vanishing Real: Hyperreality and Magical Realism." *Journal of Narrative Theory* 28.1 (2008): 60–85. Accessed February 12, 2014. ProjectMuse.

Berman, Art. *From the New Criticism to Deconstruction: The Reception of Structuralism and Post-Structuralism*. Urbana: The University of Illinois Press, 1988.

Brunette, Peter, and David Wills. *Screen/Play: Derrida and Film Theory*. Princeton: Princeton University Press, 1989.

Derrida, Jacques. "Structure, Sign, and Play in the Discourse of the Human Sciences." In *Modern Criticism and Theory: A Reader*, 2nd edition, edited by David Lodge, 89–103. New York: Longman, 2000.

Hada, Ken. "Fishing for the [Mediating] Self: Identity and Storytelling in *Big Fish*." In *The Philosophy of Tim Burton*, edited by Jennifer L. McMahon, 9–29. Lexington: The University of Kentucky Press, 2014.

Hite, Molly. "Postmodern Fiction." In *The Columbia History of the American Novel*, edited by Emory Elliott, 697–725. New York: Columbia University Press, 1991.

Johnson, Barbara, translator. Translator's Introduction. In *Dissemination*, by Jacques Derrida, vii–xxxiii. Chicago: The University of Chicago Press, 1981.

LeBlanc, Michelle, and Colin Odell. *Tim Burton*. Harpenden: Pocket Essentials, 2001. Nook file.

Levinson, Julie. "Adaptation, Metafiction, Self-Creation." *Genre* 40.1–2 (2007): 157–180. Accessed February 12, 2014. MLA International Bibliography.

Page, Edwin. *The Gothic Fantasy of Tim Burton*. London: Marion Boyars Publishers Ltd, 2007. Nook file.

Wallace, Daniel. *Big Fish: A Novel of Mythic Proportions*. New York: Penguin, 1998.

Waugh, Patricia. *Practising Postmodernism/Reading Modernism*. London: Arnold, 1992.

Mixing Man and Monkey in *Planet of the Apes*

KIMIKO AKITA *and*
RICK KENNEY

The *Planet of the Apes* franchise, comprising eight movies released between 1968 and 2014, is based on the 1963 science-fiction novel *La Planète des Singes*, by Pierre Boulle, about three space explorers who crash-land onto a planet where apes are the dominant, civilized species and humans are savage slaves or pets. The original *Apes* film was released in February 1968 and starred Charlton Heston as George Taylor, an astronaut who time-travels to and from his home planet, Earth. Taylor discovers that in the future, apes rule the planet after mankind nearly self-destructs with nuclear weapons. In 2001, Burton "re-imagined"[1] *Planet of the Apes*, with Mark Wahlberg as U.S. Air Force Colonel Leo Davidson, an astronaut who, on a rogue mission, crash-lands on a strange planet ruled by apes who have enslaved and domesticated wild humans. The original ended with Heston's Taylor on horseback with his mate, Nova, discovering a shattered Statue of Liberty on the beach, evidence that he is on a post-apocalyptic Earth. Burton's remake ended with Wahlberg's Davidson returning to a future Earth that his nemesis, General Thade, has reached first and turned into an ape world where even the visage of Abraham Lincoln at the memorial on The Mall in Washington, D.C., has been remade in Thade's image.

Both the original 1968 *Planet of the Apes* movie and its 2001 remake by Tim Burton "transport" audiences from their respective current civilizations to a dismal and primitive future world but eventually leave us looking back at societies with uncertainty, confused over where (and when) we stand in relation to one another as races and as species. What seemed, early on in both films, to be an alien planet turns out to be an unfamiliar Earth or its parallel. These transitory moments created by the crossing of space and time can dislocate and disorient audiences in provocative ways. We are drawn to, confused by, and entertained by the apes' mimicry of humans as slaves in Stone Age clothing on a planet colonized and controlled by apes. That leads us to wonder who are the colonizers and who are the colonized; in what epoch the wild humans are living and where; who is alien and who belongs; who are the advanced and who are the primitive; and whether, in the end, we humans have advanced or regressed culturally and morally as a civilization.

As a blockbuster film, Burton's 2001 "reimagining" of *Planet of the Apes* received ample attention from movie critics, reviewers and bloggers. Whereas Taylor, in the original, had clearly traveled to a future Earth, the ending of Burton's remake was roundly criticized as ambiguous, implausible, or impossible[2]—even for science fiction.[3] Cultural critics have long interpreted the original *Apes*, its many sequels, and its TV adaptations, along with Burton's remake, as, *in toto*, an allegory for race relations and the struggle between the colonized and the colonizer for civil rights. Subsequently, some critiques of *Apes* have problematized Whiteness as the dominant hegemony, with humans representing Whites and apes, Blacks.[4]

Our critical essay applies postcolonial and postmodern notions of hybridity, mimesis,[5] and *simulacra*[6] in examining interspeciesism and representations of apes and humans in Burton's *Planet of the Apes*; and of audiences—in Althusserian[7] and Maynesian[8] terms—as *spectators*, ideological subjects of the Western discourse with new cultural orders in late capitalism.[9] Our discussion extends further to spectators' *imagined community*.[10] We argue that although Burton's *Apes* appears to be, and attempts to be, a postmodern and postcolonial project, it fails to achieve postcolonial and postmodern values.

Spectators in an Imagined "Post-Apes" World

Postcolonial thought argues that history is a product of colonizers, written by them and written for them to justify their economic and political enterprises. Colonizers were self-deceptive, manipulative, and oppressive. Unable to resist, the colonized imitated colonizers out of fantasy for the other. It is not just that one culture imposes power and dominance over another to colonize or homogenize it. Cultural production is collaborative work. "Domination even at its most violent can still be permeated with ambiguity, uncertainty, and peculiar mixtures of fantasy and reality; resistance can occur simultaneously with collusion."[11]

While trying to uncover the hidden voices from both the colonized and the colonizers, scholars such as Sider[12] and Bhabha[13] focused on collaborations of the colonized and their colonizers. Among postcolonial theoretical threads, Bhabha's[14] ideas of *hybridity, mimicry,* and *ambivalence* are crucial to an analysis of Burton's *Apes*. According to Bhabha, cultural differences confound tradition and modernity in a *hybridity* that can be achieved in borderline engagements: liminal (in-between) and contemporaneous space and temporal moments that may be displaced and decentered. Hybridity subverts the colonial power and the dominant discourse. In colonial discourse, *doubles* are created collaboratively by colonizers and the colonized. Colonizers need these doubles, who speak their language and understand their culture, whereas the colonized may attempt to *mimic* their colonizers to survive or succeed. Bhabha claimed:

> [C]olonial mimicry is the desire for a reformed, recognizable other, *as a subject of difference that is almost the same, but not quite*. Which is to say, that the discourse of mimicry is constructed around an *ambivalence*; in order to be effective, mimicry must continually produce its slippage, its excess, its difference.[15]

The more like the original, of course, the more effective the mimicry; but it must maintain some difference from the original. An unsolvable binary of sameness and difference—an ambivalence—must remain at the core of mimicry. Bhabha[16] asserted that mimicry was a sign of an articulation by the colonized, expressing a portion of the colonizer's self-identity; and, though it can be performed as mockery, delusion, or deception, if performed too well, it could alert the colonizer to a potential menace. Fanon rejected what he termed "a dangerous misunderstanding": that the colonized (in one specific example, the Malagasy people of Madagascar) must choose "between inferiority and dependency"; and yet, "if [the colonized] forgets his place, if he thinks himself the equal to the European, then the European becomes angry and rejects the upstart."[17] The colonized is seen as a threat. If too convincing, mimicry that is almost identical to the original (the colonizer) lacks slippage and ambivalence; then, it would no longer be effective mimicry.

The mimesis idea corresponds with Baudrillard's[18] idea of the *simulacrum*—neither original nor copy—which pervades late capitalist society. There must also be slippage between original and copy. The more blurred the distinction between originals and copies, the more realistic a film should appear to its spectators. When filmgoers compare versions—the original and the remake—and note or discuss changes, they are discussing in part, the idea of simulacra: how well (or not) the mimicry of the original is followed and performed. Postmodern audiences of Burton's *Apes* consume the original and the copy with equal vigor because their focus is the performance of the *simulacrum*: how well mimicry is performed. Burton uses *mimicry* abundantly in *Apes*.

The colonization of humans in *Apes*, all audiences understand, inverts the reality of actual domination, whether in zoos or in laboratories or in the wild, of apes by humans in history and in modernity. Burton's apes, though, play the colonizers, which at least achieves the feat of exposing the audience to formerly repressed voices and ideas. Furthermore, Burton's apes reject human civilization and live in their own political-economic system. Interspecies interaction occurs in human language in a dislocated space and antichronological time.

Since the release of the original *Planet of the Apes* in 1968, socioeconomic systems around the world have changed greatly, affecting the constituents of cultural production and ideology. Modernity shifted to postmodernity as societies experienced the advances of electronic (analog, then digital) media technology, beyond capitalism, and into late capitalism. We as consumers may now think we get to make choices, but we are actually the subjects of consumption by capitalism. Filmgoers, concomitantly, are powerfully affected by both media technology and capitalism.

Where and how we watch a film depends on the individual. We no longer need to go to a movie theater seeking only respite and fantasy. Whereas in modern society, people sought truth, realism, and materials, in postmodern society, consumers also seek certain non-material reality, such as *imaginary work*,[19] to make sense of our worldview and to identify ourselves with images and information from a film. Consuming mass media often provokes "resistance, irony, selectivity, and, in general, agency."[20] The collective experience of consuming mass media, such as watching a film, can seem to create solidarities and imagined worlds for spectators. Postmodernism will help us consider the relationship between Burton's *Apes* and its audience: spectators as cinematic consumers.

Postmodernism: Imagination as the Real[21]

Postmodernism challenges *modernism* and its values. Modernism aspired to advance technology and achieve central power, but postmodernism values displaced (or decentered) power and resources, time, and space. Unlike in modern society, in the postmodern power-decentered society, ordinary people deploy their imaginations in their everyday lives.[22] Imagination plays a central role in cultural production and is treated as real. The advance of media technology helped heighten the work of the imagination, which we rely on to live everyday life. For instance, someone self-identifies on the Internet by a cat avatar, and "the line between human and nonhuman increasingly blurs."[23]

This blurriness may be represented by mimesis, or *simulacra*, which is crucial for the cultural production of late capitalism.[24] The better the *simulacra*, the more stimulating the product (e.g., film). *Simulacra* stimulates consumers (including filmgoers) who seek ephemeral pleasure.[25]

Interpellation: Ideology and Illusion

Althusser (1992) spoke of *interpellation*: the constitutive process (various devices and components of the cinema function) in which individuals acknowledge and respond to ideologies, thereby recognizing themselves as subjects. Film scholars have long employed the concept of interpellation to suggest that institutional cinema acts as an ideological apparatus that manipulates the moviegoer to "misrecognize" oneself through illusion, identifying with fictional characters in the movie. Thus, film serves an ideological purpose not only through content, but also through the audience experience of watching a movie.

Building on Mayne's (1993) idea of *spectatorship*[26] and Anderson's (1983) concept of *imagined communities*, we contend that spectators are not passive subjects prone to the ideological, but rather that they belong to their imagined worlds, while constructing their *sociality*.[27] While watching a movie and seeking ephemeral pleasure, we as spectators collectively engage in imagining and flipping back and forth to our knowledge and memory, creating socially imagined worlds. Since imagination works like an ideology, provokes *agency*, and potentially fuels action, spectators may execute the ideology we acquired from a film.[28] Anti-postmodern representations, however, could prevent spectators from engaging in imaginary work and thus disconnect or destroy spectators' imagined worlds. A close reading of the film reveals that peril.

Imagined Nostalgia and Achieving Hybridity

Burton's *Apes* opens in a chronological time easy for audiences to imagine: 2029, a little into the future. U.S. astronauts are training chimps to fly spacecraft. The first character we see is the chimp Pericles, wearing an astronaut's helmet and flight suit, in a scene that startles because he appears to be piloting the spaceship *Oberon* independently, without any human help. Pericles is at best a semi-domesticated animal. There are more such chimps on board, kept in cages. In the opening scene, Captain Leo Davidson (Mark Wahlberg) and Pericles are already close friends, but Davidson continually patronizes Pericles in teasing, but paternalistic ways. Davidson is aware that chimps are less sophisticated than humans and that humans must protect chimps. Up to this point, it is a scene of modernism, in which humans control apes and teach apes an advanced technology. Pericles has gained the trust of humans who send him into space; his "thumbs up" mimics human behavior.

The extra chimps, though, like Pericles, are disposable. Pericles is dispatched in space pod, of which he loses control in an extraterrestrial electromagnetic storm. His inability is no surprise to the astronauts, to Davidson, or to the audience because all know a monkey cannot do a man's job. Interspecies colonial dominance exists. The spaceship's commander refuses to rescue him. Yet, Davidson defies orders and follows Pericles in a second pod, shouting, "Going to get my chimp! Never send a monkey do a man's job!" to the *Oberon*'s human crew while hurriedly ejecting in his pod. And thus, a man takes off on a suicide mission to save a monkey. This familiar theme of human as savior is in stark contrast to what occurs next. If it were a modernist film, Davidson would rescue Pericles by using humans' advanced technology and superior intellect. Because the film attempts to be a postmodern project, spectators are ushered to experience shifting time and space and to observe a provocative reverse colonialism.

Davidson pursues Pericles and crashes on Ashlar. It is the year 5021. Three thousand years have passed. The civilization Davidson finds is a primitive world (in stark contrast to the high-tech Oberon and even his tiny space pod) and features apes in antiquated military uniforms and clothing who control human captives in skimpy, stone-age clothing. The humans in this scene, except for Davidson, do not even speak. Davidson's disrupting entry into a primitive world is a metaphorical awakening in the film's narrative for the audience, which must adapt to a change in perspective, to understand and embrace the story. The audience must pay attention to Burton's invented history by immediately assuming an imagined nostalgia, a memory of a time that never existed.[29]

The audience explores Ashlar with Davidson, trying to identify where we are suddenly, what chronological time it is, what is going on, wondering whether we can return safely to the *Oberon*, but assuming that we can. Burton makes sure to educate Davidson and the audience about Ashlar's history, social system, culture, and interspecies relations so that Davidson and the audience will better appreciate the fact and timing Pericles' surprising arrival on Ashlar near the end of the movie. Pericles lands amid the mayhem as man battles monkey. The apes assume Pericles is their god, Semos, and immediately stop fighting. Davidson is happy to see his old friend. Still, this time, Davidson abandons Pericles, whom everyone on the ape-run planet is worshiping, and attempts to go back to 2029.

Though Pericles merely mimics the human as astronaut in the film's opening scene, by its end, he navigates his pod skillfully and lands safely and softly on Ashlar just in time to save Davidson and the human tribe from slaughter. This suggests that Pericles may after all be a superior astronaut to Davidson, who had crash-landed in a swamp. In colonial worlds, when the mimic surpasses the colonizer, it is perceived as a threat.[30] Pericles, however, is never a menace to the apes or to humans. He is a savior to humans as well as to the other apes in the story. Pericles is a real chimp who does not speak like humans. In Burton's film, these differences do not stifle the interactions between man and monkey. Burton has created liminal moments by displacing time and location and by reversing the status and situation of one another. Just enough ambivalence is maintained in the *simulacrum* between Pericles and Davidson.

In these borderline encounters, Pericles and Davidson's friendship blossoms, displacing tensions between humans and apes, offering an alternative vision of interspecies relations. In the opening scene, when Pericles had been tested and tricked by his human trainers (colonizers), he was a disposable commodity. The colonizers (the spacecraft's human crew) were self-deceptive, not knowing whether Pericles could safely carry out the mission, but sent him into space anyway. When Pericles returned and saved Davidson, the other humans, and the apes while using advanced space technologies—which the *Oberon*'s human crew, overthrown by the apes on board thousands of years earlier, no longer could—this odd combination demonstrated hybridity in a liminal spatial tempo. Davidson, the other humans, and the apes themselves all needed a savior like Pericles.

Stone, Chains and Other Artifacts

After he crash-lands on Ashlar, Davidson sees wild humans in Stone Age clothing being chased by gorilla soldiers in medieval military uniforms. Before he realizes it, Davidson is running with the humans and soon gets knocked down from behind. General Thade goes to him and stares at Davidson, then shouts, "This one looks at me!" Cringing and crawling backward, Davidson accidentally bumps into the leg of Attar, one of Thade's gorilla soldiers. Attar orders Davidson, "Take your stinky hands off me, you damn, dirty human!" and kicks him unconscious. Davidson and other captured humans are carted off in a crude, wooden cage pulled by humans in chains rather than by horses. Davidson is awed by the trappings of the apes' medieval society. He asks other humans where he is, but they shake their heads, stare at Davidson, or ignore him. At this point, the displacement of time and space disorients Davidson and the audience. It appears that apes and humans' social status has been reversed, but where are they? What has happened? Why do apes speak and not humans? Davidson's disorienting perspective is the audience's as well; we join his primitive journey on Ashlar.

Young gorillas hurl stones at Davidson as his cage-cart passes through town. Ari admonishes them: "Stop it! You're being cruel." She knocks away the stones they clutch, and the young gorillas run off. One turns, though, sticks out his tongue, and hurls an epithet at Ari: "Human lover!" Ari's sophisticated manner shows that she is not a beast. Ari, an ape anthropologist with womanly manners and behaviors, is a relief to Davidson. In postcolonialism, mimicry that is too convincing threatens the colonizer. Ari's mimicry of a human anthropologist with empathy for another species threatens Thade and other apes (colonizers), but it comforts Davidson.

Human slaves fight like animals against their jailers and appear more barbaric than the apes. During the capture of the humans, Davidson was the only one of them who glared in return at Thade's gaze, prompting him to say: "This one looks at me. He is feisty." As Attar observed the tense encounter between Davidson and Thade, Attar later commands the slave trader Limbo, "Keep an eye on this one!" and points at Davidson. Thade arrives with his daughter to check out the new prisoners. His daughter begs her father to allow her to take one little girl as a play-doll. Thade hisses her wish at Limbo, who immediately obeys, "I'll get that."

Burton's characters, man and monkey alike, mimic the other species' behaviors well. This corresponds to Baudrillard's[31] *simulacrum*, a representation of good mimicking. The better the quality of *simulacra*, the less distinction exists between reality and fiction. The more realistically an animal acts like an ensouled human, the more an audience might identify with it. For instance, Thade's daughter's treating a human girl as a doll, a commodity, allows moviegoers to buy into the premise that the apes in this foreign society possess self-consciousness and subjectivity. Primates, in reality, possess consciousness, which makes them different from the apes that Burton imagined, created, and represented through electronic media. Because Burton's apes and humans mimic well, however, the audience can easily believe these characters have a soul, an intersubjectivity, though what spectators are actually witnessing is the *simulacrum*—not beasts with a limited soul, a non-human soul or subjectivity. As Baudrillard wrote, "The object is without desire, it is that which escapes desire and belongs to the order of destiny."[32]

Consumers' focus is an object, a commodity. An image is a commodity, the destiny of "desire" for the consumers. Apes and humans in imagined nostalgia are commodities, which are similar to virtual pets for the spectators of late-capitalism to consume. The better *simulacrum* is, the more spectators can consume. The slippage, or ambivalence, is maintained because spectators are aware that Burton's history, imagined nostalgia, is a fiction. The audience, the consumers, are after all in control of the commodities; we know the narrative is fictive, even if we have willingly bought into the premise to be entertained. Ultimately, we know that apes could not colonize humans.

The film cuts to a political discussion at the elite apes' dinner party. Apes have clearly evolved. And humans have regressed, have devolved. The apes pray before dinner, yet are prone to violent, barbaric outbursts and treatment of their human slave servants. At the party, Thade criticizes Ari: "Your ideas threaten our prosperity. The human problem will not be solved by throwing money at it…." Ari counters that humans are capable of culture and displays the fine scarf they have woven for her, adding a layer of ambiguity about time. Thade observes, "Everything in 'human culture' takes place below the waist"—an allusion to the primitive lack of morality among them. Another ape adds, "Next, you'll be telling us that these beasts have a soul." Burton lets an ape speak as if he/she has a soul. In *simulacrum*, subjectivity does not exist, but it emerges within the layers of performances. The audiences know that Ashlar is a fictitious planet. Without reference to the real world (Earth) or the original world, spectators' imagination is stimulated. Imagination connects spectators and enhances the solidarity of their imagined worlds.

Davidson and Ari

Ari meets Davidson early in the film, shortly after he is captured and brought to the jail for the first time. She appears as a savior, suddenly swinging into the jail for runaway slaves, snatching a branding iron from Limbo just before he can mark a woman prisoner, and tossing it aside. Ari tells Limbo to stop and chides him and the other apes for their mistreatment of humans. Davidson and the audience are shocked, their curiosity piqued. When Limbo tells her that humans are dumb, Ari replies: "They are not dumb. They could be taught to live with us as equals." Davidson then picks up the branding iron and points it threateningly at Ari's neck. He quickly wraps an arm around her and tries to pull her toward his cage. Ari is obviously unsettled; humans are almost always submissive. Ari is startled again when he utters, "Please help me." Humans don't talk on Ashlar! Ari senses Davidson's intelligence right away. She implores Limbo to sell Davidson to her. When Limbo questions Ari's sanity and reminds her that both Davidson and Daena, a speechless woman, are wild, Ari responds, "Have them delivered at my house."

Davidson's gaze makes Ari uneasy and impels Ari immediately into buying him. Eventually, Ari accompanies Davidson when he escapes. During their flight, all are attacked by Limbo and his slave-hunters. Davidson fires a gun at a tree to scare Limbo. Ari defends Limbo, now, too; standing in front of Limbo, Ari says to Davidson, "If you kill him [Limbo], you will lower yourself to his level." And so, Davidson spares Limbo's life and takes him hostage. This is a striking postcolonial scene, in which a slave-trader ape is transformed into a slave to a human captor in the next moment. Ari, knowing that Davidson is more intelligent and rational than Limbo, asks Davidson not to lower himself to a colonizer's level by killing Limbo. Immediately after this, Krull, Ari's gorilla bodyguard, snatches the gun from Davidson and smashes it into pieces. Davidson says, "What's the hell are you doing?" Krull answers, "You could use it against us." Davidson says, "It could keep us alive." Ari says to Davidson that "we had better not carry a dangerous weapon like that with us." Daena challenges Ari, asking, "What do you mean by 'we'?" Ari asks Daena why she is so difficult, then Daena asks Ari why she does not act like a slave. Davidson shouts, "Shut up! … That goes for all species." In this scene, interspecies racial identity is negotiated. Burton challenges the audience with the fluidity of racial/species identity. Through Davidson's voice, Burton educates the characters and the audience that we are in a borderline time and space now in this ape society; species differences do not matter.

When the mixed group of humans and apes rides through the military encampment and tries to cross the adjacent river, Ari is momentarily left behind and about to be captured. Davidson leaps from his horse and grabs her hand. She is terrified because apes cannot swim. Davidson promises, "I won't let go of you." They leap into the river. Moments later, Davidson staggers out of the river, carrying Ari on his back. That night, Ari and Davidson sit and stare at the stars and talk quietly. Ari boldly states, "I'd like to see your world." Davidson responds, "No, you wouldn't. They'd prod you and poke you and throw you in a cage, too." Ari replies coquettishly, "You'd protect me." Her meaning is seductive, and Davidson responds with a slight smile. This is an astonishing scene in which the ape and human help one another across a river, which terrifies the apes. In liminality—borderline time and space—Ari and Davidson, both displaced from their social systems and identity, self-sacrifice for one another, protect each other, and achieve hybridity. Maintaining postmodern liminality in the film's end, Burton separates Ari and Davidson. Their experiences are ephemeral: temporal and fleeting.

In the final scene on Ashlar, when Ari asks whether Davidson is going to stay back with the other humans on the planet, Davidson retorts, "I never promised anyone anything." As he departs Ashlar, he tells Ari: "I have to leave now. I have to take a chance to get me back." Davidson kisses Ari, a mere peck on the lips. Moments later, he kisses Daena passionately. But ultimately, Davidson leaves them both behind. A man may pursue his selfish goal and desert his women; but they, who support and sacrifice for him, must endure after his departure. The too-familiar information about gender hierarchies and stereotypes are incongruent with postcolonialism and postmodernism. When information is too real, too well known to the audience, it fails to demonstrate *simulacrum* and thereby incapacitates our imagination.

Throughout the film, Davidson and Ari represent freedom fighters. Davidson wants only to flee Ashlar. Ari resists her father's power, Thade, and the expectations of ape society to uncover the myth of man-monkey history. Thus, Ari inadvertently, yet inexorably explores beyond the boundaries of her world, visiting the forbidden area. Though initially Ari is apparently romantically attracted to Davidson, she instead becomes his best friend and supporter.

Memorializing Thade in the "New" World

The most common complaint among the remade *Apes'* movie critics (e.g., Ebert 2001) relates to its denouement. If Burton's *Apes* had been a response to colonialism, the movie's ending would have given greatest voice to the former colonized or oppressed. Hybridity might have been achieved in the final scene at Thade's memorial in Washington, D.C., in place of Abraham Lincoln. However, in Burton's *Apes*, hybridity had already been achieved, upon Pericles' arrival and Davidson's takeoff for returning to earth. Had the movie ended there, postmodern audiences more likely would have been pleased with Pericles and Davidson's farewell scene. On the contrary, the film ends with the gaze of the statue memorializing Thade, a former colonizer of humans, as Lincolnesque—a well-played *simulacrum*—after Davidson has crash-landed on The Mall in Washington. Somehow, the audience must accept that Thade managed to escape his trap inside the wreckage of the Oberon, and flew to Earth far enough back in time to change American history. Davidson, meanwhile, has been quickly caught by ape police officers and recorded by journalists.

Thade triumphs, even over the image and meaning of Lincoln. This scene rejects Lincoln and U.S. history and denies Davidson's journey. Through Davidson's point of view, the audience can see and sense Thade's colonizing gaze. We wonder, as Davidson likely does, where we are; what was the point of the journey?

American—indeed, global—audiences know the original memorial all too well: who Lincoln was and what the iconic memorial should look like. Thus, Thade's sudden appearance, in mimicry of Lincoln, is jolting. Lincoln emancipated the slaves in 1863, but Thade was a colonizer of humans as slaves on Ashlar. Now we learn that, on Earth, Thade became a colonizer of our land. This scene, thus, is not the *simulacrum*, but becomes a new fact. But it requires too much work because it's too farfetched for any imagined nostalgia.

Burton's use of Lincoln's memorial unsettles the audience, who cannot help comparing Thade's visage with that of Lincoln's. Thade's statue, which appears to be a *simulacrum*, is no longer a *simulacrum*. Clearly, it turns out to be a newly created colonizer's visage, striking away any ambivalence. Thade is no longer mimicking a colonizer. He has become a colonizer himself. There is no slippage or ambivalence between a mimicker and the colonizer whom a mimicker was supposed to mimic.

Simulacrum stimulates spectators' imagination. When an image or an object becomes real, it is no longer congruent with the postcolonial or postmodern project. What was odd was that Thade became a human with an intersubjective, autonomous soul. The representation of Thade as very close to human is effective in intensifying the imagination. By displacing Lincoln, the colonizer Thade hinders spectators' imagination, their understanding of the represented world, and their connection with other filmgoers in their imagined worlds.

An Incongruent Journey

The simulacrum of apes and humans in Tim Burton's 2001 reimagining of *Planet of the Apes* amplifies the imaginary work of audiences while strengthening the connections among spectators in their imagined worlds. The advancements of media technology intensify the simulacrum production as well as its diffusion. To achieve successful simulacra successfully, ambivalence must be maintained between the original and the copy, and between colonizer and colonized.

In *Apes*, Burton navigates man (Davidson), monkey (Pericles, Ari &

Co.), and the audience and manages to usher us to Thade's statue. While Burton attempts to indoctrinate us into an imagined nostalgia throughout the film—in which Thade is a colonizer and both Davidson and Ari are freedom fighters—Thade's reappearance as a colonizer, with his gaze looking down upon Davidson and spectators, betrays us. It not only confirms Thade's colonialism but also reminds us that his colonialism is permanent and that we are his slaves forever. Disappointed, we struggle to justify our own journey in watching the film. The audience's experienced (lived) memory nullifies Burton's imagined nostalgia. In substituting Thade for Lincoln, Burton fails in an attempt to achieve *simulacrum*. Thade is nothing like Lincoln. Thade is a menace. The audience is left to feel that our land, our sacred memorial, has been overtaken by an alien colonizer. Burton's imaginary work all along has been to toy with us and, in so doing, to entrap and enslave our collective imagination.

Notes

1. Hughes, 46
2. Renowned movie critic Roger Ebert (2001) lamented that Burton's *Apes* "could have been a parable of men and animals, as daring as *Animal Farm*. It could have dealt in social commentary with a sting, and satire that hurt. It could have supported, or attacked, the animal rights movement. It could have dealt with the intriguing question of whether a man and a gorilla having sex is open-mindedness, or bestiality (and, if bestiality, in both directions?). It could have, but it doesn't."
3. Bradshaw 2001; French 2001.
4. Greene 1998; Foster 2003; Nama 2008.
5. Bhabha 1994.
6. Baudrillard 1994.
7. Althusser 1971/2001.
8. Mayne, 1993.
9. Fredric Jameson, *Postmodernism, or, the Cultural Logic of Late Capitalism*. (Durham: Duke University Press, 1991). As Fredric Jameson explained, first-stage market capitalism came about in the 1840s with the invention of photography and realism; second-stage monopoly capitalism, in the 1890s with cinema and modernism; then, multinational capitalism in the 1940s with electronic technology. second-stage monopoly capitalism, in the 1890s with cinema and modernism; then, multinational capitalism in the 1940s with electronic technology. By the 1970s, *late capitalism*, or informational capitalism, pervaded society and deeply impacted the way culture is formed and how we communicate via microelectronics, telecommunications, and computers.
10. Anderson 1983.
11. Sider 1987, 3.
12. Sider 1987.
13. Bhabha 1994.
14. ibid.
15. ibid., 86
16. ibid.
17. Fanon 1952, 74.

18. Baudrillard 1993, 1994
19. Appadurai 1996
20. ibid., 7.
21. *Postmodern* here refers to cultural conditions since the 1970s. *Postmodernism* points to a theoretical position. Theories of postmodernism emerged in France in the 1960s and were exported to the U.S. in the 1970s (Azuma 2001, 16).
22. Appadurai 1994.
23. Allison 2006, 178.
24. Baudrillard 1994.
25. Appadurai 1994.
26. Mayne (1993, 2) defined *spectatorship* as the "relationship that occurs between the viewer and the screen." Mayne described the "cinematic spectator" as intrinsic to the ideological institution of cinema.
27. Appadurai 1996.
28. Appadurai 1996, 7.
29. Appadurai 1993.
30. Fanon 1952, 74.
31. Baudrillard 1994.
32. Baudrillard 1988, 54.

Bibliography

Allison, Anne. *Millennial Monsters: Japanese Toys and The Global Imagination*. Berkeley, CA: University of California Press, 2006.
Althusser, Louis. "Ideology and Ideological State Apparatuses (Notes Toward an Investigation)." In *Lenin and Philosophy and Other Essays*, 85–126. Ben Brewster, trans. New York: Monthly Reviews Press (1971), 2001.
Anderson, Benedict. *Imagined Communities: Reflections on the Origins and Spread of Nationalism*. London: Verso, 1983.
Appadurai, Arjun. *Modernity at Large: Cultural Dimensions of Globalization*. Minneapolis: University of Minnesota Press, 1996.
Azuma, Hiroki. *Otaku: Japan's Database Animals*. Jonathan E. Abel and Shion Kono, trans. Minneapolis: University of Minnesota Press, 2001.
Baudrillard, Jean. *Selected Writing*. Mark Poster, ed. Stanford, CA: Stanford University Press, 1998.
Baudrillard, Jean. *Symbolic Exchange and Death*. London: Sage Publications, 1993.
_____. *Simulacra and Simulation, The Body, in Theory*. Ann Arbor: University of Michigan Press, 1994.
Bhabha, Homi. *The Location of Culture*. New York: Routledge, 1994.
Boulle, Pierre. *Planet of the Apes*. Paris: Livre de poche, 1963.
Bradshaw, Peter. "*Planet of the Apes*: Tim Burton's Reworking of the 1968 Classic Is a Dumbed-Down, Gibbering Festival of Nonsense." *The Guardian*, August 17, 2001. Accessed February 14, 2013. http://www.guardian.co.uk/film/2001/aug/17/1.
Fanon, Frantz. *Black Skin, White Masks*. Richard Philcox, trans. New York: Grove Press, 2008.
Foster, Gwendolyn Audrey. *Performing Whiteness: Postmodern Re/constructions in the Cinema*. Albany, NY: State University of New York Press, 2003.
French, Philip. "*Planet of the Apes*: The Make-up Is Faultless but Compared to the 1968 Epic, Tim Burton's Ape Tale Is Bland Fare." *The Observer*, August 19, 2001. Accessed February 14, 2013. http://www.guardian.co.uk/film/2001/aug/19/philipfrench.

Greene, Eric. *Planet of the Apes as American Myth: Race, Politics, and Popular Culture.* Middletown, CT: Wesleyan University Press, 1998.
Hughes, David. *Tales From Development Hell.* London: Titan Books, 2004.
Jameson, Fredric. 1991. *Postmodernism, or, the Cultural Logic of Late Capitalism.* Durham, NC: Duke University Press, 1991.
Keith, Michael. *Theories of Race and Racism: A Reader.* Les Back and John Solomon, eds. Florence, KY: Psychology Press, 2000.
Mayne, Judith. *Cinema and Spectatorship.* London: Routledge, 1993.
Nama, Adilifu. *Black Space: Imagining Race in Science Fiction Film.* Austin: University of Texas Press, 2008.
Sider, Gerald. "When Parrots Learn to Talk, and Why They Can't: Domination, Deception, and Self-Deception in Indian-White Relations." *Comparative Studies in Society and History* 29 (January 1987): 3–23.

"A Stranger in a Sea of Familiar Faces"[1]

Self-Referentiality, Bodily Hauntings and Materializing Identity in Dark Shadows

Lance Norman

> ELIZABETH: But she can't go on loving a dead man for the rest of her life.
> BARNABAS: It's been known to happen.[2]

Tim Burton's adaptation of Dan Curtis's 1960s gothic soap opera *Dark Shadows* (2012) opened to lukewarm critical reviews—to put it mildly. While many reviewers focused on the film's lack of narrative, perceived plotlessness, and campy gags to no purpose, *The New Republic's* David Thomson's vitriolic "How Johnny Depp and Tim Burton Became Shadows of Their Former Selves" is noteworthy for its personal attacks on Burton and the actors. Thomson finds Depp's turn as the vampire Barnabas Collins less than compelling: "Depp is a puppet made of blood, starch, and the actor's vanity that if he says dull lines with a putative languor it may seem as if Oscar Wilde had written them." Thomson goes on to confess to the suspicion "that at some time around 2000 Michelle Pfeiffer was body snatched," and Tim Burton has become a parody of himself.[3] Writing for *The Globe and Mail*, Stephen Cole suggests that "*Dark Shadows*' only meaningful relationship is between Depp and his audience. He's a persona now, no longer an actor."[4] Self-proclaimed *Dark Shadows* fan, and reviewer for *The Star Ledger*, Stephen Whitty bemoans the distance between the intent of the soap and the film:

> Yes, everything about the show was overdone—starting with that redundancy of the title. But it was never done out of mockery.
>
> Real melodrama—and that's what even the lowliest of daytime shows always aspired to—embraces heightened emotions. It's why there's an "opera" in "soap opera," acknowledging the genre's over-the-top plots and passions.[5]

While I appreciate the pleasure with which Thomson *et al.* eviscerate Burton's adaptation, I cannot help wondering what might be the appropriate means to pay homage to the series. Reviewer ire is particularly fixated on the arch performances of Burton's actors, and their refusal to fully commit to a realist style of representation. Such critiques are decidedly phenomenological in their import. Where the critics want to embrace the fantasy (or if you like structuralist) elements of a film's narrative, conflict, and characters, *Dark Shadows* keeps returning focus to the actors who are playing the roles. In so doing, the film may be Burton's most overt representation of the aesthetics of self-referentiality. Ironically, Thomson combats Burton's privileging of the reality of the material body by suggesting these acting bodies are not real enough: Depp is a puppet and a persona over an actor, and Pfeiffer was body snatched. Metaphorically transforming the authentic performing bodies into simulacrums of humanity allows Thomson to critique the revelation of the material performing body as a matter of artifice. Depp and Pfeiffer's bodies are artificial things to the degree they refuse to encourage the audience to view the characters and narrative with a "willing suspension of disbelief."[6]

For Thomson, authenticity is decidedly mimetic in origin as the film is compared unfavorably to the dominant acting style of realism and genre conventions. The critic evokes both Depp's failure to live up to the legacy of Marlon Brando, the Godfather of Hollywood realist acting, and *Dark Shadows'* lack of inheritance from its aesthetically rich generic ancestor *Nosferatu* (1922). Brando is largely credited with bringing the Method to Hollywood film in which the actor disappears into a role by imaginatively becoming the character. Based on the acting theories of Konstantin Stanislavski, a Method Actor's role becomes their reality.[7]

Not to overstate the obvious, but such an effort betrays the legacy of *Dark Shadows*. Embracing the melodrama of the narrative and having the performers disappear into their roles, turns *Dark Shadows* into a vampire narrative (and a not particularly well thought out one) that pales in comparison to *Nosferatu* and maybe even to *The Vampire Diaries* (2009). One of the defining features of the original iteration of *Dark Shadows* is its inherent campiness. The acting body never disappeared into the role. The actors seemed to take their roles seriously, but through their inability to fully actualize the melodrama, they laid bare the process of representation. The bargain basement production values of *Dark Shadows* repeatedly helped to reveal that more than a signifier in service of a realist narrative, the body can exhibit a comedic presence every bit as potent as narrative representation. Burton's playful retelling may strip *Dark Shadows* of its attempted seriousness, but in so doing it highlights and institutionalizes the theoretical and subversive camp of the soap opera.

Dark Shadows is a performative process as well as a narrative trajectory. The film's celebration of the process of bodies perpetually transcending representation embraces the earnest if less than proficient legacy of its antecedent. Rather than dominating the acting body and using it simply as a tool to reveal the *mise en scène*—rather than simply using the acting body to tell a narrative—Burton's adaptation tells the narrative of the acting body's material presence. In Burton's hands, Dark Shadows becomes a meta-commentary on performance and identity construction. The film considers whether a performing body can empower and define itself in the present, or whether the pull of an historical field inevitably strips the performing body of agency and refigures the body as a transparent site for representation. Somewhere between melodrama and comedy, Burton's Dark Shadows explores the confluence of a narrative past and a performative present in creating meaning. In trying to embrace the critical resonance of Burton's movie, I begin by close-reading a scene from the 1960s soap opera in which the identity of a character is determined by the conflict between historical representation and bodily presence. After I treat this melodramatic narrative with enough seriousness to appease Burton's toughest critics, I focus on the material bodies who performed the soap opera and how the amateurish acting and camerawork are as much a part of the series' legacy as its supernatural narrative. In privileging the performance it becomes clear that any radicalness the series finds in its performing bodies is integrally connected to its inability to represent melodrama other than as a comedic process. Finally turning to Burton's film, I suggest that its power lies in its choice to reject melodrama. Burton's Dark Shadows is consumed with adaptation of performance at least as much as adaptation of narrative.

"I Am Maggie Evans"[8]*: Representation Is a Matter of Black and White*

Following the introduction of the vampire Barnabas Collins via release from the Collins family tomb, the 1960s gothic soap opera Dark Shadows is consumed with the power of a dark and material past to reshape the always tenuous present identity. The supernatural becomes the process by which the past deforms, overwhelms, and redefines the present. Barnabas's love of everything family related and historical leads to his convincing family matriarch Elizabeth Collins Stoddard to let him renovate the ruins of the family's seemingly uninhabitable old-house. Barnabas's obsession with history is materially marked on the Old House. His miraculous restoration, and rejection of newfangled modern fads such as electricity, leave him proudly proclaiming that the house looks exactly like it did when the Collins ancestors inhabited it in the Eighteenth-century. The crown jewel of Barnabas's restoration project is the upstairs bedroom that formerly belonged to Josette Collins. The finished restoration includes: a portrait of Josette, Jasmine—her favorite perfume—and the music box which was a gift from Barnabas. Where the rest of Barnabas' work is celebrated as an uncanny return that is a temporal and spatial repetition—where the past has become the present—Josette's room is both the most overt rupture in the temporality of the present, and a spatial symbol of the inability of things to connote individual subjectivity. The room may allow the Eighteenth-century to emerge, but it also must serve as a haunted memorial to Josette's essential absence.

Perhaps unsurprisingly, in light of the overt anxiety surrounding any resistance to non-conservative gender roles and sexuality which is a defining facet of the vampire narrative,[9] Barnabas decides he will kidnap local waitress Maggie Evans and literally transform the modern woman into her traditional counterpart. This domination becomes a gendered conflict. Barnabas is determined to remake Maggie Evans so that her body becomes an historical receptacle—foreign to herself—for Barnabas to remake Josette, and recapture his past desire. Barnabas's plan is largely successful. Maggie is not the only one who begins to think she is Josette. David Collins sees Maggie walking through the Old House in a wedding dress and veil, and thinks he has seen the ghost of Josette. Herein lies the tragedy of Barnabas' project. Barnabas wants to transcend the meaning of the physical body and shift its signification. The body of Maggie shall become Josette not through any physical change, but more so in terms of how it can be read by any potential viewer. However, for David to think he is seeing Josette's ghost is different from thinking he is seeing Josette. A ghost is both absent and present, and is a reminder of a representational shortcoming. The ghost is a figure that can impact the present, but can never be fully part of the present, and whose presence is a reminder of a materiality and a temporality which no longer exists.[10]

Barnabas wants to look past the body and shape how it means, but it is through understanding that her body is essential to any meaning it creates that Maggie is able to banish Josette's ghost and reestablish her essential presence. Episode 249 opens with the viewer seeing Maggie sitting at Josette's makeup table reaching out to touch the mirror—one of the most common ways to reflect on signification. As she touches it, the point of view shifts and Maggie's reflected representation replaces the view of her body. We see a cut from Maggie touching the object of representation to a shot of Maggie confronting the essence of her own body as the viewer sees a reflection of her touching her face. Maggie Evans's self-awareness is reasserted (albeit momentarily) as through voice-over Maggie establishes her essential bodily coherence which any representation must account for.[11]

> Maggie. Yes Maggie. That's your name. Maggie Evans. I've got to remember that […] Never forget. Say it again, and again, and again. Maggie Evans. Maggie Evans. Maggie Evans.[12]

In a clumsy and overt way, Maggie inverts the Lacanian mirror stage as seeing herself touch her face, forces the disruption of the other. Maggie's interior monologue shifts from referring to herself in the third to the first person. To see her reflection allows Maggie to return home to her body, and to find this material site through language.

It is a short return. Barnabas has been encouraging Maggie to identify and define herself through Josette's music box rather than through any sense of bodily integrity. As the scene continues, music becomes a literal possession (in the *Exorcist* (1973) sense). The sound from the past usurps the physical essence of the present:

> (Maggie knocks music box open, and it begins to play. She moves away from mirror.)
> My name. My name. I must remember my name. Josette.
> (Goes to painting of Josette)
> Josette. Is that my name? Josette Collins. Yes.
> Turns away from painting.
> My name is Josette. No. No. That's not my name.
> Returns to mirror.[13]

Maggie's war with herself (or is that a war with Josette? A war with Barnabas? A war between material presence and musical affect?) over whether her body is the signifier of self-representation, or whether Maggie / Josette's corporal presence is simply the signified defined by outside forces, takes a decidedly traditional and temporal dynamic. Maggie tries to define herself as something self-contained and essential, and something with bodily integrity that can be understood and protected from the music box and its power to define the body in relation to the past. However, Maggie must learn that true empowerment involves a present divorced from the past. When Maggie first starts defining herself in front of the mirror, the naming is a representational act—she is describing what she sees. By saying her name over and over again, she will remember what she is seeing: the body known as Maggie Evans. Understanding self in terms of memory (you know the present self by remembering the past self), leaves Maggie with little agency in the process. It is simply the matter of finding the right word—be it Maggie or Josette—to accurately define what she sees before her. Subjectivity becomes an act of remembering instead of being. Essentially, Maggie is fighting for her right to define herself via the rules established by the music box. The past will define the present, and not allow the body to speak for itself. It is no wonder Maggie is losing herself to Josette as she seems unable to let her body announce its unique presence.

In the final moments of the scene, Maggie seems to take the first steps away from self-representation and toward self-construction:

> I must remember my name.
> (Closes music box forcibly)
> Maggie. Maggie Evans. Maggie Evans. Remember that. No matter what. Maggie Evans. Maggie. I am Maggie Evans.[14]

Maggie's assertion of "I am Maggie Evans" uses language performatively rather than representationally. In *How to Do Things with Words*, J.L. Austin describes how language can transform its representational function and perform an essential doing. Austin's famous example of performative language is a wedding ceremony. The only way to get married is to say "I do." These words do not just represent something, they commit an act through language.[15] Similarly, when Maggie says, "I am Maggie Evans," she is doing more than constructing a present through a remembered past. She is defining a present self that is liberated from the rhetoric of the music box and its demands that the present can only be understood in relation to the past. She is Maggie Evans not because she used to be Maggie Evans; such a rationale is as false as thinking of herself as Josette Collins. She is Maggie Evans because her present self announces and demands that her body be understood as Maggie Evans.[16]

"Stiff, Proper, and Old-Fashioned"[17]*: Camp and the Haunting of the Acting Body*

As I reflect on my comments on the 1960s television series above, it all comes across as somewhat ridiculous. Using the hyper-blown academic discourses of psychoanalysis, semiotics, and performativity to analyze a gothic soap opera best known for the way actors perpetually struggle with their lines, how shots are occasionally framed offering views of the boom mike (or at least its shadow), and in my favorite example: Kathryn Leigh Scott—the actor who played Maggie Evans—whispers the cue to Sharon Smyth—the actor playing Sarah Collins—who seems to have forgotten her line. Privileging

Dark Shadows' narrative over its performative resonance creates an essential absence akin to the restoration of Josette's room. However, recognizing I am missing something does not dissuade me from the notion that I am correct in analyzing Maggie Evans struggles through the tropes of academic discourse. Much like Jonathan Frid's portrayal of Barnabas Collins, I have become someone who tries to achieve their desire through language, but the material presence of the object of desire serves as a reminder something is missing, representation does not equate to meaning.[18] My efforts to banish the resonance of material presence exposes my own material presence in a comedic light uncomfortably close to the aesthetics of Camp, and uncomfortably close to Johnny Depp's over-the-top comedic portrayal of Barnabas Collins in Tim Burton's remake of *Dark Shadows* which led to him being savaged by critics of the film.

In her foundational "Notes on 'Camp,'" Susan Sontag emphasizes the seemingly contradictory statements that "To perceive Camp in objects and persons is to understand Being-as-Playing-a-Role. It is the farthest extension, in sensibility, of the metaphor of life as theater," and "In naïve, or pure, Camp, the essential element is seriousness, seriousness that fails."[19] This vision of Camp attempts to show the seriousness of theatricality—of playing a role—of being consumed by representation, but through its attempts to do so seriously, comically reveals the limits of representation despite the seriousness of the performer. In this sense, the narrative content of Maggie Evans in front of the mirror struggling to escape representation and the exterior efforts to dominate and define her offers a campy and melodramatic repetition of the act of performance. Maggie Evans's desire to become Maggie is paralleled by Kathryn Leigh Scott delightfully quixotic effort to portray Maggie Evans seriously.[20] Like Maggie, Scott finds the power of bodily excess even if in her over-seriousness she does not know it.

Many critiques can be leveled at Tim Burton's adaptation of *Dark Shadows*. However, despite the frequency with which the word campy appears in the reviews of the film it is certainly not that, if we take Camp in the Sontag sense of naïve seriousness. Burton's *Dark Shadows* carries its self-consciousness on its sleeve. Some prominent examples include the playful critique of capitalism that runs through the film (Barnabas equates McDonald's golden arches with a symbol of Mephistopheles and is certainly not the first Marxist or eco critic to evoke such a parallel), and Barnabas's characterization of *Scooby Doo* as "a very silly play" (which could very well be understood as a meta-pronouncement on Burton's film).[21] More a representation of Camp than Camp itself, Burton's *Dark Shadows* tries to eliminate all ambiguity surrounding the naivety of the camp gesture and representation. Barnabas may be naïve, but Depp (and the other performers) know enough to exempt himself from unknowingness. Where the 1960s precursor to Burton's film always took itself representationally serious thereby opening itself materially to the aesthetics of Camp, the remake suggests representation is no serious matter. Frid's Barnabas was narratively tragic in that he was a Jay Gatsby figure who tried impossibly to recapture his past. Depp's Barnabas is a figure to be laughed at both by the audience and the other characters for his inept efforts to fit into the present.[22]

When reviewers critique the film's plotlessness, it might be more accurate to suggest that there is a plethora of narrative trajectories that are introduced and disappear before reaching resolution in the film's conclusion. Or, in other words, the film mimics the plotting of a soap opera. Rather than a narrative shortcoming (or at least more than just a narrative shortcoming), I wish to suggest that the film's plotting undercuts the domination of narrative representation. Many of the narrative trajectories from Burton's film are greatly influenced by long-running plots in the original series. By short-circuiting the various narrative trajectories of the film, Burton's *Dark Shadows* offers its mission statement for adaptation. Like Maggie Evans who finds her freedom as she allows her body to speak for itself and thereby resists being foreclosed by Baranabas's representational tyranny, the *Dark Shadows* acting body in Burton's film is the most memorable and delightful when the distance between the body and the role it ostensibly performs becomes most transparent. More than your everyday vampire / witch / human love triangle with werewolves, Burton's film demands the body of the actor be understood in its historical context outside of the narrative of the film. In so doing, Burton's film embraces the transgressive nature of Camp, the comedic excess of which seems to preclude to possibility of fully absorbing bodily essence in narrative representation even if self-consciously staging such bodily awareness leads to the loss of naïve seriousness.

"I Love That Chick, Man"[23]: Romantic Fantasy and the Historical Body

> Tim constantly has me killing his wife in his movies. I don't know what that means.
> —Johnny Depp[24]

Where Maggie Evans individually resists being absorbed into history, Tim Burton's *Dark Shadows* exhibits a much more sustained historical encroachment. Early in Burton's film, newly hired governess Victoria Winters joins the Collins family for dinner. Even for a *Dark Shadows* novice, and even before the unearthing of Johnny Depp's Barnabas Collins, a viewer with a rudimentary familiarity with Tim Burton's filmography or vampire narratives may very well recognize that they are seeing something they have seen before. In addition to perpetual Burton performers Depp and Helena Bonham Carter, the film sees Michelle Pfeiffer's return to the world of Tim Burton.[25] Completing the Collins's around the table are Chloë Grace Moretz—an actor whose previous film credits include playing the role of the vampire Abby in *Let Me In* (2010), itself an adaptation of the Swedish film *Låt den rätte komma in* (2008)—and Jonny Lee Miller who would soon play the vampire Ruthven[26] in Neil Jordan's *Byzantium* (2012), and who Burton playfully suggests,[27] was cast as Roger Collins due to his strong physical resemblance to Louis Edmonds—the actor who originated the role.[28]

Victoria Winters is the character who materially as well as narratively is the most unfamiliar to the audience as well as to the Collinses. Playing Victoria, Bella Heathcote is certainly the least familiar face seated at the Collins dinner table, and probably the only one whose film career does not encourage a viewer to read her in terms of a genre specific film history. It is hard not to read Heathcote as less than the characters who share the *mise en scene* with her. In a sense, due to the relative lack of familiarity of Heathcote as an actor, she is the character who is the most fully immersed in the narrative. She is Victoria Winters. Portraying an orphan, Heathcote finds her orphanness doubled. Not only is Victoria an orphan character, but Heathcote portrays a character who is surrounded by actors whose very bodies encourage a genre specific perception of personhood which transcends the *Dark Shadows* character they play.

Adding to this perception of Victoria Winters as a character surrounded by actors, she is revealed to be a semiotic construct. While Vicky may not be campy in either the Sontag or the popular culture sense, in fact she may be the most self-aware (and realist) character in the film, she echoes Sontag's conception of being as playing a role. Victoria is initially introduced on a train, rehearsing introducing herself. Victoria's train arrival is a canonical image in the history of *Dark Shadows*. Vicky's introduction restages the series opening of both the original 1960s soap opera, and the short lived 1990s revival.[29] However, where previous Victoria Winterses proclaim a desire to discover their history, this Victoria appears to desire distance from her personal history and the history of *Dark Shadows*. Rather than introduce the audience to the world of *Dark Shadows* through Victoria Winters, Burton only allows such an introduction to occur after he has introduced the origin story of Barnabas Collins. Vicky believes history is unimportant, but by beginning his adaptation with the act of vampire creation, Burton's narrative suggests Victoria is mistaken. Deferring Victoria's introduction through Barnabas's origin disrupts the narrative if not the historical trajectory of the source material. Where previous manifestations have begun with Victoria Winters assured introduction to the audience via voice over, Burton's Victoria Winters is robbed of such internal revelation, and is instead introduced to the audience as she is practicing introducing herself. This Victoria Winters is constructing herself to seemingly escape the very idea of a past. Victoria is not just introducing herself to an audience, she is introducing herself to herself:

"Hello. My Name is Maggie Ev—"
"Hello. My Name is Victoria Winters. Please Call Me Vicky."[30]

The erstwhile Maggie Evans sees an advertisement for winter skiing in Victoria BC and thereby the persona of Victoria Winters is created. More than a wink to fans of the original series, it is tempting to read the newly christened Victoria as akin to Maggie Evans resistance to becoming Josette. Unlike the original series Maggie Evans finding herself through letting her body speak, Victoria is named through embracing an exterior linguistic construct that seems to have little to do with the person uttering it.

The difficulty of such a rebranding effort, and its possible lack of resonance is confirmed shortly after Victoria's naming as she hitches a ride to Collinwood with a van full of hippies. One of the women in the van refers to Victoria as Veronica. When, in an effort to reaffirm her new identity, Victoria corrects her, the hippy rewards Victoria with the mocking rejoinder: "*And its Victoria.* I love this chick, man." The hippy drives this point home by offering a goodbye greeting to Veronica after they drop her off in front of the Collinwood estate.[31] So, when Victoria joins the Collins around the table she makes an instructive contrast. Vicky's self-conscious performance of self reveals her to be an empty cypher constructed completely through language. In terms of identity it does not seem to matter whether she is Maggie, Victoria, or Veronica. Victoria (as I will continue to call her for convenience sake) adapts the name as a means of control. The film shows her introduction to every other cast member and her friendly rejoinder to "Please call me Vicky." However, Vicky in particular, and the language of naming in general, does not seem to mean anything other than a reminder of a woman's inability to construct herself through language. Where Vicky's name does not resonate and identify deeply enough, she is surrounded and contrasted by actors who through their very bodily presence announce their film histories.

Burton's film suggests that bodies matter and despite fantasies to the contrary—in terms of identity—language is superfluous.³² In *The Haunted Stage* (2003), Marvin Carlson defines ghosting as the way audiences become familiar with actors and develop expectations surrounding the appearance of the actor. Audiences are incapable of viewing a performance apart from previous roles and the actor's public persona. Ghosting is a two way process impacting the way actors approach roles as well as how audiences perceive an actor's performance:

> Before many appearances most actors, consciously or not, develop associations with particular ways of portraying even the most codified *emplois*³³ and so appear in new roles with a double ghosting, the cultural expectations of the *emploi* itself overlaid with those of the actor's own previous appearances.³⁴

Carlson's equation of the matrix forged by the memories of both the performer and audience with ghosting is particularly resonant in *Dark Shadows*. Just as the materiality of the well-known acting bodies encourage the view of Victoria Winters as a figure defined linguistically who cannot be understood as clearly as the bodies which surround her, and just as the film encourages itself to be understood in terms of past associations more than its own narrative representation, Carlson's insights emphasize the material body as the film's narrative as well as its visual resonance.

Shortly after Victoria Winters and her linguistically forged new identity is shown to be insufficient in comparison with the Collins acting bodies with which she is surrounded, she looks in the doorway, and sees a ghost. This is quickly revealed to be a comedic moment, as the apparent ghost reveals itself as David Collins—the child Victoria has been hired to educate—simply wearing a sheet. Victoria and David quickly bond over their shared belief in ghosts. It is only natural for David to be revealed as non-ghost because as the sheet is pulled off of him, he is revealed to be like Victoria. The body of the actor playing David Collins does not resonate beyond the narrative construct of the film. David fails as a ghost because there is nothing to be memorialized under the sheet. The bodies performing Vicky and David will not be historically appropriated like Depp, Carter, and Moretz. As Heathcote sees David Collins revealed to be a non-ghost, this serves as an indication that while she may be a narrative ghost in that she is playing a character that has been played by actors before, her relatively unknown acting body will not be absorbed into the historical matrix that is Burton's film. The comedy of David removing the sheet and demonstrating he is not a ghost announces what the film has already dramatized. Believing in ghosts is not the same as being a ghost. Heathcote has not entered the popular consciousness enough to be a character with a history like Maggie so she must create Victoria.

"Please Call Me Vicky.... My Name Is Josette"

Victoria Winters's desire for self-construction dramatizes *Dark Shadows'* struggle between the material body and narrative, between the present and past, and whether the body dictates how the self represents and is understood, or whether larger exterior linguistic and narrative forces absorb the individual. Victoria Winters believes in ghosts, and the existence of such ghosts serve as a reminder that a performing and narrativized body is haunted by the past despite whatever hopes a linguistic utterance may provide. In this light, perhaps it is not surprising that Maggie Evans is the name that Victoria Winters effaces. Immediately after the dinner scene where David is revealed to be a non-ghost, the film cuts to Victoria alone in her bedroom unpacking when she again sees someone wearing a sheet in her doorway. Vicky thinks it is David, but upon removing the sheet it is revealed to be the ghost of Josette Collins, and Josette is also played by Heathcote.[35]

Heathcote's self-confrontation serves as a primer on the workings of bodily ghosting. What haunts Victoria is the inability of the body to be self-contained. Seeing Josette's ghost, and recognizing that the exterior ghost is the self, is an almost uncanny moment in which Victoria may rename herself but the past cannot be left behind. The past is always a part of the present. Whether you call this present essence Vicky or Josette does not provide liberation from the material resonance of confronting an unchanging ahistorical body. Vicky's effort to change names from Maggie to Vicky is an effort to control who she is and to recreate herself. However, where the 1960s version of Maggie Evans found a present self through her body, in Burton's film Vicky finds what the actors playing the Collinses (and indeed all actors) already know. No one owns and controls their body. Vicky's efforts at liberation must deflate at seeing the ghost of Josette. Josette died before Vicky (or for that matter Maggie) was born but it is still her. The now cannot be divorced from the historical repetition of the ghost.

Upon confronting her living self, the ghost offers her only utterance in the film: "He is coming"—he being Barnabas Collins, he being Johnny Depp. Josette warns Victoria (or phenomenologically speaking: Heathcote warns Heathcote) that Barnabas's vampire and Depp's fame are about to escape from the analepsis which begins the film and enter the present of the narrative. Depp is a visual representation of what Vicky resists. As a past figure who remains continuous in the present, Barnabas / Depp serves as a constant reminder of someone whose self exceeds their own ability of contextualization. Barnabas/Depp is the ultimate outsider because his body and his utterance consistently reveals himself to be a thing from the past. Barnabas's critique of television, search for a sleeping space, and his desire to believe he knows Collinwood better than the present inhabitants announce a character (and an actor) who can never become present enough. Barnabas's desire to fit in and (for the most part) his obliviousness to his failures use the past to represent camp aesthetic. According to the diegesis of the film, Barnabas cannot fit in because he is too campy. Barnabas will never seem to be a normal person to Roger or Carolyn Collins despite his efforts, just like Johnny Depp's acting body has too long of a history to be embraced as Barnabas Collins, no matter how good or poor his performance. It is these comedic self-betrayals of a body in which the performer naively believes they can construct themselves seriously only to have their meta-audience reveal themselves as the ultimate arbitrators of meaning where Burton's *Dark Shadows* offers its clearest homage to the camp materiality of the struggling bodies of the original.

While it may be surprising and even clumsy narratively speaking for Barnabas / Depp to replace Vicky / Heathcote as the film's protagonist, it is also narratively essential. Vicky's desire to construct herself in the present is halted in seeing a past version of herself. In the logic of adaptation no matter how fresh faced of an actor you find they must be absorbed by the ghosts of the past in the same way Heathcote confronts herself. Vicky / Heathcote cannot carve out a new place for herself amid all the literal and performing ghosts of *Dark Shadows*, and therefore must be replaced by Barnabas / Depp and the vampire body where present comedically refracts the past. As Vicky / Heathcote's mission of a present self-constructed linguistic identity is proven to be a failure she to a large degree disappears from the narrative shifting from protagonist to love interest.

When Vicky re-enters the narrative—in a *The Sixth Sense* (1999)—like reveal—the film offers her backstory and refigures the Victoria Winters persona. Victoria Winters is not an effort to escape the historical persona that is Maggie Evans. Victoria Winters is a transitional moment, and an effort to find a sense of belonging in the past. The persona of Maggie Evans does not allow her to go back far enough. Lifting the sheet off of Josette when she was unpacking was not the first time she had seen the ghost. Josette has been leading Victoria to Collinwood from the beginning. The ghost led to her being institutionalized as a child, the ghost helped her escape from the asylum, and the ghost showed her the Collins's advertisement for a governess.[36] This knowledge transfigures Josette's announcement that "He is coming," from an uncanny vision of an exterior self to a promise of integration. Victoria is not trying to escape the ghost she is trying to become it, and thereby transcend her present-ness and her otherness. Victoria wants to be a ghost in the same way the acting personas of the other Collinses make them ghosts. She wants to transcend the transparent appearance of the ghost, embrace her historical legacy, and transform it into a material and bodily reality. This transition is the difference between Vicky and Barnabas, and in a metonymic kind of logic, Victoria's backstory paves the way for her wanting to become a vampire. Where the 1960s Maggie Evans wants to be in control of her body and thereby resist becoming Barnabas's object of desire, Burton's Maggie / Victoria embraces such a fate. In the world of *Dark Shadows* there does not seem to be any other option.

Vicky must submit to Barnabas's control because like Josette she has become a stranger in her own body. The film dramatizes this essential foreignness as Vicky literally loses control over herself. Vicky is forced to jump off of Widow's Hill by the witch Angelique. Barnabas leaps after her, and bites her on the way down. As Barnabas mourns the apparent death of Vicky, she transforms into a vampire and announces her name is Josette. This Josette is something new. Josette announcing her own personhood (or is that vampirehood?) is different from Maggie in front of the mirror. Rather than creating a self she announces a self that was created from the outside. As the film concludes with a Barnabas voice-over, Barnabas becomes Pygmalion to Victoria's Galatea. The romantic ending is only achieved through Josette's loss of power. Despite the way Burton's film flirts with representing a radical and campy body, the film only reaches narrative culmination once Vicky stops trying to control how her body is being represented and submits to the structures of meaning which surround her. Bella Heathcote's fluid transitions from Maggie to Victoria to Veronica and back to Victoria before finally coming to rest as Josette codifies Tim Burton's frequent collaboration with Johnny Depp. Despite the character he plays, Depp offers the representational stability to escape the campy rupture between body and meaning. Such stability promised by the Depp of future past may be denied to the body of Bella Heathcote but as her screen performances continue to accumulate, one day her body may be as haunted as Depp's or she may find the integration of Josette, thus she has learned the lessons of the famous haunted body.

Notes

1. *Dark Shadows*, created by Dan Curtis.
2. Ibid.
3. Thomson, "How Johnny Depp."
4. Cole, "Dark Shadows: Stock, Stale, and Best Kept in Shadows."
5. Whitty, "Screwy Gothic."
6. Coleridge, *Biographia Literaria*, Chapter 14.
7. The Method lives on in actors such as Daniel Day Lewis, who reportedly insisted on being referred to as Mr. President on the set of *Lincoln* (2012).

8. *Dark Shadows*.
9. The conservative depiction of gender in the vampire narrative can be seen in a continuum from the horrific desire exhibited by Lucy Westenra's after she becomes a demon in Bram Stoker's *Dracula* to Bella Swan exulting in being a kept woman in Stephenie Meyer's *Twilight*. For a dissenting view which acknowledges the conservative perception of vampires see Nina Auerbach's *Our Vampires, Ourselves*: "Vampires were supposed to menace women, but to me at least, they promised protection against a destiny of girdles, spike heels, and approval." Auerbach, *Our Vampires, Ourselves*, 4.
10. Unlike this typical description of a ghost, *Dark Shadows* is never able to completely separate the ghost from material presence. Maggie finally escapes Barnabas with the help of Barnabas's sister's ghost, Sarah Collins. Perhaps it is the unconventional notion of a ghost as something that has a material legacy as well as an historical/representational one which causes Maggie's father Sam Evans to initially dismiss the possibility of Sarah being a ghost because he can touch her.
11. The tenuous nature of Maggie's empowerment is underscored by the voice-over by which such power is asserted. In *The Acoustic Mirror*, Kaja Silverman asserts: "Hollywood dictates that the closer a voice is to the 'inside' of the narrative, the more remote it is from the 'outside,' i.e., from that space fictionally inscribed by the disembodied voice-over, but which is in fact synonymous with the cinematic apparatus. In other words, it equates diegetic interiority with discursive impotence and lack of control, thereby rendering that situation culturally unacceptable for the 'normal' male subject" (53–4). In this context it is worth noting that it is Victoria Winters and other female narrators who are given the control intrinsic with the exterior voice-over, but in Burton's remake he reinscribes the power as a representationally masculine one, giving the power of the exterior voice-over to Barnabas. Silverman, *The Acoustic Mirror*.
12. *Dark Shadows*.
13. Ibid.
14. Ibid.
15. Austin, *How to Do Things With Words*.
16. The horror of the past trying to force a woman's body into signifying an essential historical foreignness was a repeating trope in the series. After Maggie escapes, Barnabas turns his sights onto David's governess Victoria Winters as the candidate to become the next Josette Collins. Barnabas gives the music box to Victoria, and often sneaks into her bedroom to turn it on so she will listen to the tune all night. Victoria's fiancé Burke Devlin is just one of many characters who think Victoria should live in the present, and it is unhealthy for her to be so consumed by the past. I will address Burton's combining of Maggie and Victoria with particular attention on his problematic ending below.
17. *Dark Shadows*, directed by Tim Burton.
18. Auerbach notes: "Barnabas's backward quest is, by definition, a lost cause" (138).
19. Sontag, *Against Interpretation*, 280, 283.
20. The viewer of this conception of Camp revels in their superior knowledge—the viewer understands the performative shortcoming. However do they really? Can I ever be really sure Sharon Smyth has forgotten her line or might this be a performance of failure for the viewer's benefit? In the trusting of appearance and surface, the source of naivety can never be foreclosed.
21. *Dark Shadows*, Burton.
22. Where the 1960s characters who inhabit Collinwood find Barnabas (for the most part) charming, Carolyn Stoddard leads the charge of characters in the Burton film who emphasize his oddness.
23. *Dark Shadows*, Burton.
24. Depp is referring to his character's murder of Dr. Julia Hoffman played by Burton's

real world wife Helena Bonham Carter in the film. See the special features of the *Dark Shadows* DVD release. Depp's Sweeney Todd also murdered Carter's Mrs. Lovett in Burton's film adaptation of the musical *Sweeney Todd* (2007).

25. Pfeiffer played Selina Kyla/Catwoman in Burton's *Batman Returns* (1992).

26. In another metatextual reference, the name Ruthven is a clear homage to the foundational early 19th-century vampire narrative *The Vampyre* (1819) by John William Polidori.

27. See the DVD extras.

28. The film's insistence on using the performing body to contextualize the adaptation within the larger career trajectory of the performers perpetuates beyond the Collins family. Vampire (and horror) movie legend Christopher Lee has a small role, and in playing the role of the witch Angelique, Eva Green is essentially repeating the same genre type from her portrayal of Morgan on the Starz series *Camelot* (2011). And, of course, there is also the gratuitous and seemingly obligatory cameo of actors from the original series which is a staple of the Hollywood remake.

29. The television remake was much less invested in calling attention to the performing body. While there are some delightfully over-the-top performances—most notably Jim Fyfe as Willie Loomis and Lysette Anthony as Angelique—the 1990s version is much more adept at performing its melodramatic narrative than either the original or Burton's film. *Dark Shadows: The Revival*, created by Dan Curtis.

30. *Dark Shadows*, Burton.

31. Ibid.

32. Barnabas takes a dissenting view upon meeting Victoria. He is dismayed at the thought of her being known by a nickname: "Surely you do not let them call you Vicky. A name like Victoria is so beautiful that I couldn't bear to part with a single syllable of it." Ironically, Depp's Barnabas here provides the film's most nuanced call back to the original series as Frid's Barnabas almost says exactly the same thing upon meeting Victoria. Despite Victoria's experience to the contrary, Barnabas's pronouncement both emphasizes the aesthetic delight in speaking names and uses names to establish the historical legacy between Burton's film and the antecedent soap. This gestures toward Barnabas as a character being more naïve than Victoria and his desire to be in control of the language she wants to use to define herself.

33. Line of business.

34. Carlson, *The Haunted Stage*, 59.

35. The film's introduction prepares the viewer for the reality of Heathcote being a ghost of narrative even if our understanding of her does not transcend the film's limits. The introduction sees Heathcote as Josette forced to commit suicide by jumping off Widow's Hill while under the control of the witch Angelique.

36. The innocent orphan's actual or metaphorical institutionalization by a society that mistreats and does not understand them is a long trope of the Burton oeuvre from *Beetlejuice* (1988) to *Dark Shadows*. *Dark Shadows* may take this critique of institutionalization to new heights. The montage which reveals Victoria's past is scored to Alice Cooper's ode to insanity: "The Ballad of Dwight Fry." Cooper plays himself in the film.

Bibliography

Auerbach, Nina. *Our Vampires, Ourselves*. Chicago: University of Chicago Press, 1995.
Austin, J.L. *How to Do Things with Words*. Cambridge: Harvard University Press, 2001.
Carlson, Marvin. *The Haunted Stage: The Theatre as Memory Machine*. Ann Arbor: The University of Michigan Press, 2003.
Cole, Stephen. "Dark Shadows: Stock, Stale, and Best Kept in Shadows." *The Globe and*

Mail, May 11, 2012. http://www.theglobeandmail.com/arts/film/dark-shadows-stock-stale-and-best-kept-in-shadows/article4107371/.

Coleridge, Samuel Taylor. *Biographia Literaria*. 1817. Project Gutenberg, 2013. http://www.gutenberg.org/files/6081/6081-h/6081-h.htm.

Silverman, Kaja. *The Acoustic Mirror: The Female Voice in Psychanalysis and Cinema*. Bloomington: Indiana University Press, 1988.

Sontag, Susan. *Against Interpretation and Other Essays*. New York: Delta Book, 1966.

Thomson, David. "David Thomson on Films: How Johnny Depp and Tim Burton Became Shadows of Their Former Selves." *The New Republic*, May 15, 2012. http://www.newrepublic.com/article/film/103321/dark-shadows-tim-burton-johnny-depp-soap-opera-remake.

Whitty, Stephen. "Screwy Gothic: 'Dark Shadows' Abandons Melodrama for Camp." *The Star Ledger*, May 11, 2012. http://www.nj.com/entertainment/movies/index.ssf/2012/05/dark_shadows_review_johnny_depp.html.

"Attend the Tale"
Burton's Transformation of Sweeney Todd *from Stage Epic to Screen Intimacy*

Brian D. Holcomb

Stephen Sondheim and Hugh Wheeler's 1979 stage musical *Sweeney Todd, the Demon Barber of Fleet Street* opens with a chorus of unnamed London residents imploring the audience to "attend the tale of Sweeney Todd."[1] In doing so, they create a relationship between themselves and the audience: the chorus is the authority (both in the sense of knowledge and in the sense of justice), and the tale of Sweeney Todd is *their* story, one that they are desperate to share. As Joanne Gordon points out, the chorus "informs the audience that what they are about to see is a tale, a legend, a parable that will teach of corruption, oppression, and revenge" and that "it will have universal implications."[2] It is a story of community, and of communal guilt: whatever horrors Sweeney Todd commits, he does so because he is a part of a society that creates monsters. This musical shows that the potential for madness lurks within every Victorian subject.[3] It also reflects the class anxieties of the Industrial Revolution, which saw the rise of industry, but also the social devastation that accompanied it. Society feared what it created, and what further dangers might be ahead. Sweeney Todd is one of these by-products, a bit of the social experiment gone terribly wrong.

By contrast, Tim Burton's 2009 film of the musical focuses on Sweeney Todd as an individual. This is *his* story; the audience (and the citizens of London) are bystanders to his murderous rage, but are neither involved in nor responsible for it. While the stage musical has a Cold War mindset, fearing enemies from within, Burton's is a post–9/11 tale, one in which the enemy is clearly *other*, and who terrorizes victims who are not responsible for the violence visited upon them. Burton has replaced the collective experience with the singular. Todd becomes a kind of steampunk terrorist: he is a madman acting out his impulses upon London, but he is not truly *of* London. Steve Winn said in his review of the film that "*Sweeney* seems more interested in distancing than captivating an audience," reflecting Burton's interest in outsiders rather than inclusivity.[4] Burton investigates individuality rather than community in multiple ways: by trimming the script to remove most material that does not directly focus on Todd; by framing shots and deploying color palettes in such a way as to call attention to Todd's singularity; and by increasing the importance of Judge Turpin as a second madman who mirrors Sweeney Todd.

Some critics claim that this focus blunts the critique implicit in the stage musical. Patrick Riley addresses the difficulties of adapting a work so beloved in its stage productions into a film. His mostly negative assessment of Burton's film contains elements typical of much commentary surrounding the adaptation, much of which disparages the film simply because it is not the stage musical. He criticizes Burton for eliminating the chorus, explaining "Burton does include brief shots of customers enjoying the pies, but without their vociferous participation and persistent demands for 'more,' the focus remains primarily on Lovett and Todd. The scene is less communal, less celebratory, and hence less unsettling; as a result, the scene does less to suggest the complicity of Lovett's customers—and by extension, of ordinary consumers, including those in the audience."[5] Riley claims that Burton focuses on individuals, not on communities, and in doing so, he does not ask viewers to consider their connection to Todd. While he claims to be confused by this, he actually reveals that he understands Burton's vision; he simply does not agree with it.

A.O. Scott said of the film: *Sweeney Todd* "is as dark and terrifying as any motion picture in recent memory.... Indeed, *Sweeney* is as much a horror film as a musical."[6] In a similar, but less laudatory turn, Carrie Rickey labels the film a "splatter operetta."[7] The nature of the horror film is to produce an affect in the viewer: to create fear. The heightened 'slasher' elements of the film, particularly the blood-drenched violence, are a direct appeal to the audience. This shows a kind of mixed intent in the film: the narrative has been trimmed to be intimate and personal, focused on characters more than on society. The visuals of the film, though, create direct connection with the audience *as a crowd*: when Todd slashes a throat and blood spurts several feet across a room, there is nothing personal or intimate at work: the audience is unified as a generalized humanity, particularly in its horror. Thus, while Burton's impulses lead us toward the close and individual in this film, his techniques scare and horrify the audience at a communal level.

On stage, Todd is a character bent on revenge, in restoring social justice.

He is a monster, but is part of a social order: he presents the boundaries of social norms, but is, therefore, part of that system. His actions begin as a rational, if immoral plot to take revenge upon the specific person who wronged him; when that plan fails, Todd embarks on an unfocused murderous rampage, seeking retribution from an entire social order. In Burton's film, these collective goals are eliminated, because there is no collective, no social order to be responsible to. Revenge, however misguided, is a logical construct, where an action elicits a response. Burton's Todd is not interested in revenge, but only in rage. By transforming the character from a social evil to an individual one, Burton also removes the possibility for collective redemption. Todd acts as an individual because there is no society to which he (or anyone) owes responsibility. His is the world of terrorism, of random, undeserved violence. Burton's film reflects its moment as much as Sondheim's play did its own.

This emphasis on maniacal, out-of-control rage, rather than on murder with a focused purpose is shown in the way that Burton depicts Todd's acts of violence. The original Broadway production of *Sweeney Todd* was noted for its gruesome onstage murders, but the film turns murder into wildly perverse spectacle, a reflection of Todd's insanity. For Burton, there can be no justification for Todd's acts, for they are irrational, born of madness rather than revenge. They are not the limits of social norms, but entirely outside of them. This proves true with the very first murder Todd commits. It is a murder of "necessity," as Signor Pirelli has revealed that he knows Todd's true identity and plans to blackmail him.

In the stage musical, this murder is an act of desperation, not of rage. Burton transforms this into a scene where Todd is utterly out of control: even if he has a reason for the murder, the form it takes is barbaric, and Todd delights in the killing. As a barber, Todd's razor is the most obvious weapon with which to kill Pirelli, and this is what happens in the stage production. On film, the razor is only an afterthought. Johnny Depp, who plays Sweeney Todd, initially grabs a steaming kettle of water and uses it to violently beat Pirelli. It is a murder of hideous, uncontrolled, unfocused rage. Todd does not merely murder Pirelli, but does so in a shockingly violent manner. He metaphorically boils over, much as the kettle he grabs as his weapon. Burton frames the shot from Pirelli's point of view, with Todd bent over him, swinging the still-steaming kettle. Blood flies as Todd swings his weapon. The razor comes in only to finish the task, but then, even more blood splatters the scene, eventually ending with a shot from above. Pirelli's blood drips from a skylight that Burton has positioned between the viewer and the murder: we observe the act, but are removed from it in its final moment. We remain outside the action, much as we remain outside Todd's mind.[8] The horror of the moment is intensified, transformed from a violent crime of opportunity into the rage of a madman. This is accomplished through the filmcraft itself, allowing Burton to use his medium to make new observations about his text. On stage, this murder is sloppy because it is unplanned, in the film, it is sloppy (and gruesome) because it is an enactment of preexisting rage that has finally been released.

Much of Burton's focus is accomplished by trimming the text: eliminating the chorus and reducing the romantic sub-plot to its necessary minimum. As exemplified in Pirelli's murder, a great deal has also been accomplished with choices of images, framing of shots, and the manipulation of the visual in particularly filmic ways to reinforce the emphasis of this *Sweeney Todd*. Christopher Rawson describes the look of the film as a whole: "Burton's extraordinary visual palette—relentlessly dark, occasionally brightening into sepia, with copious amounts of brilliantly red blood, poured, sprayed and gushing with viscous insistence ... except for a few excursions into warm hues (mainly in flashbacks)."[9] Terry Teachout discusses "the film's grim palette, in which the only bright color is the spurting red blood of the victims whose throats the revenge-crazed Sweeney slashes with his razor."[10] The color of the film is specifically linked to the emphasis on Todd's madness: it is black and white, the classic "othering" binary, and smeared with red. The opening credits show an animated sequence of London being pelted with huge, oversized raindrops.[11] The individual raindrops signal Burton's focus on isolated individuals within a context usually assumed to be collective. Some drops are even further individualized, colored a menacing red. Against the sterile color scheme of the opening, each of the red drops screams from the screen, demanding attention. Again, the emphasis here is on the individual, the unique, not the universal. There are precious few of these ruby drops, though. Almost as soon as the audience becomes aware of their existence, the title sequence shifts to a different set of images: meat being ground into the ingredients for Mrs. Lovett's meat pies.

The sequence continues as the blood from the meat forms into streams, which eventually run into the sewers of London, transforming the sanitation system into an abattoir. This contradicts the impulse of the opening scene, for here the individual victims are merged: first by their bodies becoming indiscriminately transformed into food, then as their blood mingles with each other's, and eventually with all of London, leading to the Thames.[12] In this context, though, the transformation of individuals into a collective is important, because Todd is not one of these individuals. All other people, with their own stories, lives, dreams, and hopes, have been subsumed by

Todd's rage. They are merely the materials of his story, not stories of their own. Even as their blood rushes through the sewers, and directly toward the audience, they are nameless people (in fact, we don't yet even know for certain that they are people) lending their bodies and blood to whatever story we are to hear. That story begins properly on the Thames itself, this river of blood created by Todd's madness, as the good ship Bountiful brings him home after years of criminal exile in Australia.

We first meet Anthony, a teenaged sailor who rescued Todd from a sinking raft in the Pacific Ocean and has brought him to London. It has apparently not occurred to Anthony that a lone man on a raft off the coast of Australia might be an escaped convict. That naïveté establishes Anthony as a willing dupe in Todd's plans, and he becomes a significant tool in the later developments of the story. The 1982 television broadcast of the original Broadway staging shows this scene as part of the busy life of the London docks. Merchants, fishmongers, beggars, and dockworkers crowd the stage. Todd and Anthony's entrance is mechanical: a dockworker pulls a rope that draws their dinghy center stage by means of a huge pulley.[13] The machinery of the docks reflects the social machine that is London. Todd and Anthony are part of a busy crowd, part of a community of dockworkers and sailors onstage together. By contrast, Burton's mise-en-scène for this moment is a heavy London fog. Slowly, the prow of the Bountiful emerges from this fog, thrusting to the left of the screen.[14] This establishes that the ship is separate from the fog; it is somehow other within its setting, much as Todd is figured in the film.

The first words in the film are Anthony's, who sings of his joy to have returned to London. The lyrics are unchanged from the stage version, but Burton asserts his vision onto the text. On stage, Anthony sings:

> ANTHONY: But there's no place like London!
> I feel home again.
> I could hear the city bells
> Ring whatever I would do.
> No, there's no pl-
>
> TODD: (*Sings grimly*) No, there's no place like London.[15]

Todd interrupts Anthony, replacing the young man's happiness with his own world-weariness. On stage, the pair are relatively equal: they stand on a relatively bare stage, on the same level, and Anthony, although a young character, is usually played by an adult, making his physical presence similar to Todd's.[16] Burton, however, has cast a teenager (Jamie Campbell Bower) as Anthony. He is a particularly young-looking, feminine youth with large eyes, full lips, and long hair. He is in no way a physical equal to the mature Todd, played by Johnny Depp, with an ashen face, dark-rimmed eyes, and a wild mane of black hair with a skunk stripe of white across his brow. Additionally, Burton has framed the shot so that initially we see only Anthony, dreamily looking toward London as he sings. Todd then jarringly enters the frame in the extreme foreground, replacing Anthony as the focus of the shot, and all but obscuring him.[17] Burton visually asserts that this is Todd's tale. Everyone in the film serves Burton's exploration of Todd's character; other characters exist only to the extent that they help us focus on Todd.

Todd tells Anthony (and thus the audience) the story of a foolish barber who was sentenced to Australia for crimes he did not commit. Again, it is a sign of Anthony's naïveté that he does not realize that the story he hears is Todd's own, but believes it to be a generalized tale of injustice. On stage, this is a moment of exposition, but also a moment of bonding between characters. Their friendship is displayed through Anthony's rapt attention to Todd's tale, even while not knowing its significance, and through Todd's insistent delivery: he wants Anthony to hear his story. In the film, though, Depp does not reciprocate: he is communicating *to* Anthony, but is not engaged *with* Anthony. Even at this early moment, Burton places Todd firmly within his own mind, acting within the world, but not connected to it. It is not the world of a wronged father and husband, but of a sociopath.

Through the use of a flashback sequence, Burton transforms this moment into one focused entirely on his title character, rather than on his interaction with Anthony. We see a young Todd and his beautiful wife with their infant daughter in a London flower market, and a lustful Judge Turpin so instantly infatuated with the woman that he instructs his Beadle to arrest her husband on the spot in order to have her for himself. This scene is painted in vibrant, saturated colors, and is shot in soft focus.[18] It is both a hazy memory of Todd's past, as well as incredibly present for the audience, and stands in shocking contrast to the muted palette of the rest of the film.

In the stage musical there is no flashback; this scene focuses on the interaction between Todd and Anthony. Burton visually calls our attention away from this relationship and places Sweeney, not only as the center of the story, but also as its only substantive element. In addition to the shocking color, we are shown Johnny Depp as a younger Todd (at the time, named Benjamin Barker), thus making sure that the audience is not allowed to make the same mistake that Anthony does. We cannot assume this to be a general story of events that happened to *someone*, because we can see the particular person to whom they happened. We also see the legacy of those events on Depp's face, as he transforms from a young, pink-skinned lover into a ghostly pale, masklike shell of a person. This shows the past, but as a fantasy, not a reality. The film reveals facts that are ostensibly true within the diagesis of the film, but in a visual manner that alerts the viewer that there is something distinctly un-real about what s/he sees. The *facts* may be accurate, but Todd's telling of those facts shows his disconnect from them.[19] Much as the sequence is visually distinct from the rest of the film, Todd is separated from the world in which he finds himself. His inability to connect with Anthony emphasizes this; Sweeney Todd is a lone actor in a crowded world, and Burton demonstrates this from the moment we first see him interact with another human.

After the full-color flashback, Todd and Anthony enter the metropolis. Burton's London is a bleak, desolate, unpopulated city. Somehow, they have docked at the busiest harbor in the Empire, in the largest city in the world, but are alone. The fog has disappeared; we clearly see block after block of empty London streets. Todd is the only person on the wharf, or in streets he claims are now foreign to him. He is a solitary person, not part of a crowd.[20] There may be other people somewhere, but Todd does not see them, and neither do we. As David Edelstein claims, "Burton has scaled *Sweeney Todd* to his favorite leading man. [...] Sweeney sings to himself, not the audience."[21] Peter Marks claims that "highlighting the sorrow within the sordidness of Sondheim's wit-strewn score, Burton invites us into a more intimate communion."[22] Burton's Todd is isolated: he is not a product of this society, because he is not even a part of it.

The moment of Todd's re-entry to London also presents a visual cue about Burton's trajectory. As Todd and Anthony leave the ship, they step into a gas lamp-lit London street. For the remainder of this scene, both characters have a warm skin tone: they each look human. As the scene ends and Todd races through London, his skin tone changes to a chalky pale color. He literally becomes less human as he gets closer to his destination.[23] If there was even a shred of humanity left in Todd as the film opened, Burton has drained him of it almost immediately. Burton uses still animation of London through which Todd travels incredibly, inhumanly quickly, to bring us to Mrs. Lovett's pie shop (and the location of his previous home and barber shop). This technique both gives the audience a taste of Victorian London, as well as shows Todd's lack of interest in it. As the camera races through streets and alleys, it occasionally pauses. At one point, we peek into a window at a group of women. The camera, and Todd, then race on, with no interest in the human lives on display.[24] The lightning-quick pace and the brief investigations of people seem almost animal-like, as if a dog is sniffing out his prey. Burton's Todd rushes towards Mrs. Lovett and his gruesome plans, anxious to begin the slaughter.

The centerpiece of *Sweeney Todd* is the song "Epiphany," which in the stage production is the moment when Todd turns his internal rage outward, committing himself to mass murder after his attempt to kill the Judge has been thwarted. It is a transition from a desire to murder one specific person into a desire to exact vengeance upon the entire world. Burton has somewhat blunted this moment by making Todd a violent madman from the outset; the transition here is less significant than onstage. What he does in exchange, though, is to have Todd interact with Londoners, something that he does almost nowhere else in the film. He rushes into the street, confronting person after person with his razor, asking if they want a shave, and begging to kill them. The Londoners, though, do not notice Todd; he is invisible to them. They walk by without noticing the crazed man singing at them and swinging a razor, or they freeze in place while Todd moves around them. Here, Burton shows the fundamental disconnect between Todd and society. He cannot form human connections, because he cannot even make other people see him. As frozen figures, they are projections of his mind: they are not real people, but only things he wants to kill. He is not just a killer, but a sociopath. Burton's staging of this sequence changes it from a transitional moment into an escalation of an already-established motif.

Burton narrows the source material's epic scope by focusing on the character of Sweeney Todd, to the (almost) exclusion of all others. On stage, the cast comprises dozens of actors, most of whom play multiple roles. The effect is of a crowded, busy city, and places Todd within a social context. Burton has trimmed all of the chorus numbers from the script; while the majority of the songs remain in the film, they are performed only by the principal actors. The film's effect is more personal, almost an intimate chamber opera. Similarly, the bulk of the romantic subplot between Johanna (Todd's daughter) and Anthony is removed. Some of it is preserved for plot reasons (rescuing Johanna from Judge Turpin is initially part of Todd's motivation), but its existence as a romantic plot is irrelevant to Todd's own madness. He needs Anthony to help him lure the Judge to his death, but he does not need (or care about) Anthony as a son-in-law. To the extent that their romance is essential to Todd's plans, it is preserved for the film. As a story of youthful love or hope for the future, it has been eliminated in Burton's vision. This emphasizes Burton's reimagining of Todd's motivation, and the extent to which Todd is a character propelled by rage and madness, not one interested in restoring his family or correcting social injustice.

While Burton removes large sections of the story and streamlines characters, he adds one substantial element to his *Sweeney Todd*: a series of scenes involving Judge Turpin. On stage, he is a secondary character at best, more of a mechanism that advances the plot than a three-dimensional character. He is motivated primarily by lust, and has few barriers to his power. As such, he is almost cartoonishly evil, but is not especially interesting. While he shares duets with Beadle Banford ("Ladies in Their Sensitivities") and Todd ("Pretty Women"), he has no song to himself. In some ways, this shallowness of character actually helps the focus of the stage musical, because Judge Turpin becomes part of a nameless and unaccountable system that has both produced and condemned Todd without cause. His actions are unchecked, which makes them part of the chaotic social machine of Victorian London, like the oversized pulley that initially dragged Todd onstage.[25] In Burton's *Sweeney Todd*, the Judge still has no solo song, but a number of scenes centering on him have been added, and other scenes have been framed in ways that focus on him. Considering that Burton has cut so much material in order to focus the film on Todd, his elevation of a smaller character is unexpected. In doing so, though, he has made Judge Turpin into a madman, like Todd. He is not a social evil, but a personal, individual evil. This emphasizes Todd's own madness, as the story becomes a competition among madmen, rather than one madman against the world.[26]

One of the first times we see this focus on the Judge is a scene inserted into the first iteration of the song "Johanna," a romantic soliloquy sung by Anthony when he first sees Todd's lovely daughter in an upper window of Judge Turpin's house. After the first verse, the Judge opens his door, welcomes Anthony inside, pours him a drink, and invites Anthony to view his extensive collection of pornography. When Anthony claims "I think there has been a mistake" and rises to leave, the Judge attacks him, verbally and physically.[27] This attack is filmed from Anthony's point of view, much like Pirelli's murder is filmed from the victim's perspective, thus visually linking Todd and Turpin in their madness and rage. Both moments also feature windows as framing devices: Anthony is seen from the house through a window, ultimately luring him to his beating, and Pirelli's murder is shot partially from outside a window, positioning the audience again as spectators. This scene fleshes out a moment missing in the stage version, and establishes the Judge's rage. After having done nothing more than look at Johanna's window, Anthony is savagely beaten and threatened, which reveals the degree of the Judge's madness, similar to that of Todd's own.

The score of *Sweeney Todd* presents Burton with some challenges. Although he cut the chorus numbers, there was one song that he could not cut without significant outcry from fans (who were already upset with several of his cuts). "Green Finch and Linnet Bird" is one of the best-loved melodies of the musical, but is problematic to Burton's vision. It reveals and deepens the character of Johanna, but does nothing to emphasize Todd. While part of the romantic storyline, it is not actually important to the plot (unlike

Anthony's song "Johanna," which could not be cut without significantly changing the plot in ways important to Todd). To adapt it to the film's focus, Burton introduces the Judge as a voyeur, and also uses the song as a way of establishing the intimate focus he brings to the material in general. On stage, Johanna is alone, singing of her desire to be free, but feeling caged like the birds she sings of and to.[28] On screen, Johanna is decentered, with much of the scene shifting between Anthony watching Johanna through the window, and the Judge watching Johanna through a peephole cut into the wall.[29] This reiterates the Judge's obsession with her that verges on madness, and also turns Johanna into a product or commodity for consumption, much like the victims that Todd uses as materials for Mrs. Lovett's meat pies.

After one intervening scene, we return to Judge Turpin's house, where Anthony is visiting for a second time. Much of this scene is shot through the peephole. The camera becomes the eye that watches Johanna. It is hand-held, so the image moves and bobs within the frame, making us aware of the physical movement of the voyeur, as well as evoking his turbulent mental state. The shot then cuts away to show the Judge with his eye against the peephole, revealing him as the surreptitious observer. At this point the camera is fixed and steady, positioning the audience outside of the Judge's mind, which the earlier camera movement has shown to be an unsteady and chaotic place. This also mirrors the exterior position of the end of Pirelli's murder, where we watch Todd's madness, but have no access to his mind. On stage, the Judge's desire to marry his young ward is unusual and problematic, but his desire remains abstract. In the film, the movement of the camera indicates the Judge's masturbation while he watches Johanna, making the nature of his desire specific, graphic, and deeply upsetting. When the scene focuses on Johanna and Anthony, the camera alternately cuts between an interior shot looking out onto the street through the window, and a shot from the street, showing Johanna in her window above. The foreshortening of this scene, particularly from the street level, compresses the image, flattening it. This again shows that this is a story of individuals, not of a society. There is no long shot of the street filled with Londoners, but only two people, who are brought together visually. This scene emphasizes the focus on the individual that Burton has chosen for the film.

Other moments, specifically involving Todd, highlight Burton's use of film technique in his crafting of *Sweeney Todd*. The first time that the Judge visits Todd for a shave, the camera travels around the pair in a steady motion. It alternately moves closer and further away, as well as circling, creating a seductive sense of bonding between the pair. They sing the duet "Pretty Women," an ode to women in general, and to young Johanna in particular.

As Scott F. Stoddart points out, "it functions as a sort of homosocial lovesong—in which two men draw treacherously close to one another through their mutual sexual regard for women who figure as the apex to their erotic triangle."[30] It is no coincidence that the only time these characters bond in any way is when they encounter a fellow madman. The ability of the camera to enter the space they share highlights the various types of intimacy in the scene, both between Todd and Turpin, and between the audience and the characters they see on screen. Burton has made the viewer into a third party in this relationship, lovingly moving in and around the men as they sing of their love for the women they share (even if the Judge does not know this). The sound of the Judge's whiskers being scraped from his face is a sensuous nod to the closeness of these men, and for what is happening between them (a shave), which stands in place of what could be happening (a murder, a shared love). The screen is filled with a communion of sociopaths, sharing this moment with each other and with the audience.

Burton's emphasis on creating a sense of intimacy by streamlining the story causes him to substantially alter the finale. This scene maintains the essential plot of the stage play, but significantly shifts the focus and tone. In the script, after Todd commits his final murder, Tobias enters the scene to pass judgment on the barber. It is a collective judgment, reinforcing the values of an organized society. After noticing the body of the Old Beggar Woman, Tobias states: "It's the old woman. Ya harmed her too, have ya? Ya shouldn't, ya know. Ya shouldn't harm nobody."[31] He then slits Todd's throat with his own razor. Following this, the stage directions indicate: "TODD dies across the body of LUCY as the factory whistle blows. ANTHONY, JOHANNA, and OFFICERS OF THE GUARD come running on. Seeing the carnage, they all stop."[32] While the play proper ends here, there is a final Epilogue, in which the entire cast returns to stage to sing of Todd's evil deeds, ending in a condemnation of the audience itself:

> COMPANY: There he is, it's Sweeney!
> Sweeney! Sweeney!
> (Pointing around the theater)
> There! There! There! There! There!
> There! There! There![33]

The finale of the stage musical emphasizes that Todd is a product of his society, and also shows society's guilt about and horror of what they have created (and may create again). Tobias murders not out of revenge, or madness, but as a means of recuperating Todd into a societal norm. After Tobias executes (literally) society's sentence upon Todd, the rest of the cast returns to stage as witnesses. First are the young lovers, Johanna and Anthony, who represent the hope for the future. With them are the officers of the law, the most obvious evocation of social order. The play then ends with the cast pointing at the audience, claiming that Sweeney is "There!" everywhere they look.[34] Sweeney is everywhere, because we are all Sweeney.

Burton has altered the finale in significant ways. As he has done throughout the film, the chorus is eliminated entirely. There is no return of the masses to sing of Sweeney's evil deeds or to pass judgment on him, or to render Sweeney as an example of societal madness. Instead, Burton ends the film on a smaller, more intimate note. As Todd realizes that the Old Beggar Woman he has just murdered is in fact his own wife Lucy, they are framed embracing in a stone archway: a smooth, rounded shape amidst the general harshness of the film.[35] The tableau as Todd holds her body is a loving evocation of personal loss. This is not a moment of society gone wrong, but a very personal tragedy. Likewise, when Tobias enters the scene, he is exacting a personal revenge, not a social one. After Todd's throat is slit, a fountain of blood flows from the wound. In the film's other murders, blood spurts violently from victims' throats; in this case, it is a gentle, although substantial, torrent that spills from Todd onto Lucy's dead face, uniting the two in death. There, the film ends: there is no chorus, no police, no social judgment, and no lovers other than the dead pair themselves. Sweeney Todd is a madman with an individual story, a personal madness, and his story comes to a private ending rather than a social manifesto.

Burton's vision for *Sweeney Todd* is as bleak as the palette he uses in the film. The source material enacted Cold War–era anxieties through a reconstruction of Victorian Gothic horror. The *Sweeney Todd* that Sondheim and Wheeler wrote, and that Hal Prince staged, was of a character who sprang from within a society. Almost mirroring a Soviet defector, he left London for a remote location, then returned, changed, but still able to operate surreptitiously. By doing so, he revealed the worst elements of his own society, but offered no viable alternative. Burton has transported this character into an era more concerned with terrorists than defectors. The enemy still lurks among us, but he is not *of* us. We did not create him: he is an outsider who hides among us until he can attack. While this attitude removes society's responsibility for Todd's actions, it also renders his victim as helpless. There is no uprising of society to return the social order. Todd is not stopped by any sense of authority or order, but by another madman: young Tobias, who has been driven to insanity by Todd's influence. Society, in this vision, is not guilty, but also has no agency. London remains as Todd sees it in "Epiphany": it is full of bodies for him to kill, but these bodies are not actual people. The only moment of human connection that he experiences is with the dead body of his wife, whom he has just murdered. Burton paints this moment softly and tenderly, offering his Todd a bit of absolution, or at least a momentary return to humanity before he meets his own end. On stage, this moment is one of horrific realization, a return to the humanity that Todd had, but has lost. Burton has never allowed his Todd that kind of humanity in the first place. Sweeney Todd is a dangerous figure for the Burton oeuvre. This director has always had an interest in the ghoulishly delightful, in finding the dark side of even the most tender of stories. In this case, he has removed what little tenderness there was in Todd. In doing so, he creates a monumental cinematic figure, but one that is relentlessly evil. The way Burton fashions Todd's end is disturbingly redemptive. It rings perhaps a bit false, because the audience is invited to almost feel pity for a character who has been so far removed from humanity throughout the film. The humanizing element comes too late, and results in shock rather than compassion. But then, that feeling of shock and a lack of compassion are exactly the terrain of terrorism, which perhaps makes it the most fitting ending the film could have. Society is not held responsible for creating Todd, but they can neither rejoice nor take comfort in his demise, for they are not aware of it. He dies, unseen, in a cellar beneath a pie shop. The community may bear no responsibility for Todd's actions, but neither can it do anything about them, nor claim victory over him. Burton's *Sweeney Todd* is a world of victims without any communal sense of hope, except in the most disturbing and unexpected of moments.

Notes

1. Stephen Sondheim, and Hugh Wheeler, *Sweeney Todd, the Demon Barber of Fleet Street* (New York: Dodd, Mead & Co., 1979), 1.

2. Joanne Gordon, *Art Isn't Easy: The Theater of Stephen Sondheim* (New York: da Capo Press, 1992), 213.

3. The 19th century fascination with socially created monsters has a substantial pedigree. Mary Shelley's *Frankenstein* was published in 1818, and takes on this subject explicitly and influentially. In historical events, the century ended with the Whitechapel Murders of 1888, committed by a still-unknown person nicknamed Jack the Ripper, who is often seen as a natural outgrowth of Victorian strictures. While an entirely fictional character, Sweeney Todd does certainly have resonances to Jack the Ripper, albeit complicated and retroactively formulated. Sweeney first appeared as a character in a serialized form in 1846, several generations prior to the Whitechapel Murders. The original stage production of Sondheim and Wheeler's *Sweeney Todd* is set in 1846, according to the 1982 television broadcast of that production (the published script indicates no specific date). One of the first shots of Burton's film of *Sweeney Todd* shows a ship coming to dock in London, after passing beneath the Tower Bridge. That bridge was not constructed until 1894, almost fifty years after the setting of the play. An early poster for the film showed the clock tower at the Houses of Parliament (which houses the famous bell Big Ben) in the cityscape behind Todd. The tower, however, was not constructed until 1859. (The poster was redesigned after fans made note of the impossibility of the

famous tower in Sweeney Todd's London.) Nothing else about the film indicates that it takes place as late as the dates of the clock tower or Tower Bridge; the costumes and design of the film indicate an earlier decade of the 19th century, closer to the 1840s of the play. Burton is relying upon contemporary audiences' expectations of London, and the fact that they will not have specific information about the dates associated with these landmarks. Instead, he created a generalized fantasy version of London that is understandable to viewers, if not entirely accurate. For Burton's film, though, it also calls to mind the very timeframe of the Whitechapel Murders, which were still being investigated (and according to popular news sources of the day, still being committed) in the 1890s.

4. Steven Winn, "Review: Depp in 'Sweeney Todd' nails revenge, but he can't sing," *San Francisco Chronicle*, Dec. 21, 2007. http://www.sfchronicle.com/movies/article/Review-Depp-in-Sweeney-Todd-nails-revenge-but-3299330.php.

5. Brian Patrick Riley, "'It's Man Devouring Man, My Dear': Adapting *Sweeney Todd* for the Screen," *Literature/Film Quarterly* 38:3, 2010: 211.

6. A. O. Scott, "Murder Most Musical," *New York Times*, Dec. 21, 2007. http://www.nytimes.com/2007/12/21/movies/21swee.html?_r=0.

7. Carrie Rickey, "Burton, Depp cut to the quick with 'Sweeney,'" *Philadelphia Inquirer*, Dec. 21, 2007. http://www.philly.com/philly/entertainment/movies/20071221_Burton__Depp_cut_to_the_quick_with_Sweeney.html

8. *Sweeney Todd: the Demon Barber of Fleet Street*, directed by Tim Burton (2007; Universal City, California: Dreamworks SKG, 2007), DVD.

9. Christopher Rawson, "'Sweeney Todd': Bloody musical awash with Burton's flair for the ghoulish," *Pittsburgh Post-Gazette*, Dec. 21, 2007. http://www.post-gazette.com/ae/2007/12/21/Sweeney-Todd/stories/200712210158.

10. Terry Teachout, "The Hollywood Musical Done Right." *Commentary* 125:2, Feb. 2008, 51.

11. Burton, *Sweeney Todd*.

12. Burton, *Sweeney Todd*.

13. *Sweeney Todd: the Demon Barber of Fleet Street*, directed by Terry Hughes (1982; Burbank, CA: Warner Home Video, 2004), DVD.

14. Burton, Sweeney Todd.

15. Sondheim and Wheeler, *Sweeney Todd*, 5.

16. Hughes, *Sweeney Todd*.

17. Burton, *Sweeney Todd*.

18. Burton, *Sweeney Todd*.

19. Another important sequence that uses concrete visuals to establish fantasy is Mrs. Lovett's dreamy wish for her future with Todd in the song "By the Sea." This sequence is tonally different than the rest of the film, as it takes place in a bright, colorful, sun-dappled world. Not only does the color palette expand considerably here, but the fashion and makeup choices take a turn toward the whimsical and costume-like. Mrs. Lovett at one point wears tiny round sunglasses that are more a 21st century steampunk look than authentically Victorian. Todd's striped bathing suit and other outlandish clothing, as well as his stiff appearance and physical awkwardness, evoke Michael Keaton in Burton's own *Beetlejuice*. The visual distinction of the scene marks it as wildly unrealistic, which Burton uses to cue his impression of Mrs. Lovett's dreams themselves. While on stage this is a comic number between Lovett and a physically uncomfortable Todd, in the film it becomes a visually-realized exploration of the breadth of the disconnect between them. This is accomplished through specifically filmic techniques: cutaway and montage are utilized to create artificiality, thus projecting the fact that Mrs. Lovett's hopes are themselves unrealistic, and will be frustrated. Burton magnifies

this by the outlandishness of the visuals: this scene is clearly from the point of view of Mrs. Lovett, and its visual disconnect with the rest of the film shows her own misunderstanding of her relationship to Todd, and of the world in which they live. As David Edelstein remarked, "even in her pipe dreams, Sweeney stares out of dead eyes, dreaming of throats to be cut." Burton assures that, even in Mrs. Lovett's fantasy, there is a realization that she and Todd do not connect, which portends the dangerous (and evil) choice she later makes.

20. Burton, *Sweeney Todd*.
21. David Edelstein, "It's a Gusher! Oil, blood, Iran and the CIA: Four year-end films worth the trip outdoors," *New York Magazine*, Dec. 24, 2007. http://nymag.com/movies/reviews/42087/.
22. Peter Marks, "'Sweeney Todd': A Savory Pie, Any Way You Slice It," *Washington Post*, Dec. 21, 2007. http://www.washingtonpost.com/wp-dyn/content/article/2007/12/20/AR2007122002473.html.
23. Burton, *Sweeney Todd*.
24. Burton, *Sweeney Todd*.
25. Hughes, *Sweeney Todd*.
26. By contrast, Burton minimizes the role of the Old Beggar Woman, Sweeney's wife Lucy, whom he believes to be dead. She is not eliminated from the script, because she serves several important plot functions, but her screen time is limited, and she is rarely highlighted within the frame. She is a problematic figure in Burton's vision of the story, because she is the one character who is recognized as mad by the general public. Her madness is socially produced, as it is a reaction to Judge Turpin's cruelty to her and her husband. In this way, she personifies the kind of madness that Burton tries to minimize in Sweeney. While the Judge's role is magnified in order to show his similarity to Todd, Lucy's is diminished in order to achieve the reverse.
27. Burton, *Sweeney Todd*.
28. Hughes, *Sweeney Todd*.
29. Burton, *Sweeney Todd*.
30. Paul M. Puccio and Scott F. Stoddart, "'It Takes Two': A Duet on Duets in *Follies* and *Sweeney Todd*," in *Reading Stephen Sondheim: A Collection of Critical Essays*, ed. Sandra Goodhart (New York: Garland, 2000), 123.
31. Sondheim and Wheeler, *Sweeney Todd*, 187.
32. Sondheim and Wheeler, *Sweeney Todd*, 187.
33. Sondheim and Wheeler, *Sweeney Todd*, 191.
34. Sondheim and Wheeler, *Sweeney Todd*, 191.
35. Burton, *Sweeney Todd*.

Bibliography

Edelstein, David, "It's a Gusher! Oil, blood, Iran and the CIA: Four year-end films worth the trip outdoors." *New York Magazine*, Dec. 24, 2007. http://nymag.com/movies/reviews/42087/.

Gordon, Joanne. *Art Isn't Easy: The Theater of Stephen Sondheim*. New York: Da Capo Press, 1992.

Marks, Peter. "'Sweeney Todd': A Savory Pie, Any Way You Slice It." *Washington Post*, Dec. 21, 2007. http://www.washingtonpost.com/wp-dyn/content/article/2007/12/20/AR2007122002473.html.

Puccio, Paul M., and Scott F. Stoddart. "'It Takes Two': A Duet on Duets in Follies and Sweeney Todd." In *Reading Stephen Sondheim: A Collection of Critical Essays*, edited by Sandra Goodhart, 121–129. New York: Garland, 2000.

Rawson, Christopher. "Sweeney Todd': Bloody musical awash with Burton's flair for the ghoulish." *Pittsburgh Post-Gazette*, Dec. 21, 2007. http://www.post-gazette.com/ae/2007/12/21/Sweeney-Todd/stories/200712210158.

Rickey, Carrie. "Burton, Depp cut to the quick with 'Sweeney.'" *Philadelphia Inquirer*, Dec. 21, 2007. http://www.philly.com/philly/entertainment/movies/20071221_Burton__Depp_cut_to_the_quick_with_Sweeney.html

Riley, Brian Patrick. "'It's Man Devouring Man, My Dear': Adapting *Sweeney Todd* for the Screen." *Literature/Film Quarterly* 38:3, 2010: 211.

Scott, A. O. "Murder Most Musical." *New York Times*, Dec. 21, 2007. http://www.nytimes.com/2007/12/21/movies/21swee.html?_r=0.

Sondheim, Stephen, and Hugh Wheeler. *Sweeney Todd, the Demon Barber of Fleet Street*. New York: Dodd, Mead, 1979.

Teachout, Terry. "The Hollywood Musical Done Right." *Commentary* 125:2, Feb. 2008, 51.

Winn, Steven. "Review: Depp in 'Sweeney Todd' nails revenge, but he can't sing." *San Francisco Chronicle*, Dec. 21, 2007. http://www.sfchronicle.com/movies/article/Review-Depp-in-Sweeney-Todd-nails-revenge-but-3299330.php.

Zadan, Craig. *Sondheim & Company*. New York: Da Capo Press, 1994.

Navigating the Risks of Re-Adaptation
Burton's Charlie and the Chocolate Factory *After Dahl and Stuart*

Pamela Krayenbuhl

Adapting a popular novel to the silver screen is nearly always a risky venture.[1] Inevitably, a horde of naysayers will insist that the film version is an inadequate bastardization of the beloved original text. To remake a film is to face similar dangers[2]; the new set of actors will, for some viewers, "never measure up" to the original cast, and these viewers' nostalgia for their pleasurable experience of the first film will usually cloud their opinion of an updated version. To adapt a book that has already been adapted, then, is to remake the initial adaptation and engage in *re*-adaptation.[3] Thus, when Tim Burton agreed to direct a new version of Roald Dahl's 1964 children's novel *Charlie and the Chocolate Factory*, which Mel Stuart had already adapted into the musical film *Willy Wonka & the Chocolate Factory* in 1971, he risked upsetting both fans of the novel and lovers of the original film.

The story of *Charlie* originates in Britain with Roald Dahl, whose dark themes and unforgiving caricatures brought a great deal of criticism from parents, teachers, and literary critics.[4] Despite *Charlie and the Chocolate Factory*'s frequent appearance on banned book lists since its publication in 1964, Mel Stuart's daughter convinced him in 1969 to make a film version. Warner Brothers negotiated for a second version as early as 1991 (the year after Dahl's death), when the rights to the property returned to the Dahl estate.[5] A great deal of time elapsed before an agreement was finally reached, and public knowledge of the family's dissatisfaction with the 1971 final product made this project especially risky.[6] However, Tim Burton was well equipped for this challenge. Already a renowned Hollywood auteur by the time he received the Charlie project in 2003, his corpus up to that point exhibited a clear "Burtonesque" style—often characterized as "dark," much like Dahl's—and comprised a celebrated array of films. Bearing in mind that he had already completed several other adaptations and remakes, it came as no surprise to both viewers and critics when he took on a re-adaptation of Dahl's novel that bore the distinct "mark of Burton." Unlike Mel Stuart's original adaptation, whose whimsical if eccentric Wonka (Gene Wilder) guides his guests through a candied wonderland, Burton's film emphasizes the mysterious and "creepy" side of Wonka (Johnny Depp).[7] While both qualities are evident in Dahl's original Wonka, Burton's affinity for dark or garish colors, strange characters, and unsettling dialogue shine through in his adaptation.

But the differences and changes viewers might notice in this latest *Charlie and the Chocolate Factory* cannot be attributed to Burton's virtuosity alone; the film is as indicative of its historical moment as its director's vision. Indeed, each iteration of what I call "the *Charlie* story" has necessarily been imagined and realized in (and thus to some extent, produced by) a specific cultural milieu. While this is true of any story, the several versions of the *Charlie* narrative offer us an unusual opportunity to track its changes over time. In this essay, I will do just that: while addressing Tim Burton's re-adaptation of *Charlie and the Chocolate Factory*, I consider not only what Burton's auteurist style and voice bring to the film, but also how his version fits into his historical moment (while also keeping in mind the previous versions and their historical moment). As I will indicate, what may on the surface appear to be simply a refashioning of the *Charlie* story to fit Burton's personal aesthetic is actually an intersection of the story, his perspective, *and* the early 21st century American zeitgeist. That is, Burton's signature dark and, at times, discomfiting style in *Charlie and the Chocolate Factory* serves as an effective vehicle through which to address contemporary cultural anxieties and "new norms" regarding family, amusement, race, colonialism, and neoliberal subjectivity.

Tim Burton seems to acknowledge the necessity of being respectful to his source text, but as an experienced filmmaker and adapter, he also gestures toward the necessity of personal interpretation, particularly in the case of *Charlie*:

> I had to feel comfortable with what I feel is Dahl's sensibility, but I feel it's close to my own. We added new elements that aren't in the book, but I always felt comfortable that everything was in the spirit of his work. Also, it's an interpretation, and there's an anarchic spirit there, so you kind of take it a few different ways.[8]

Although Burton was unable to dialogue with Dahl about his new version because Dahl had passed away by the time Burton received the project (unlike

Stuart,* who was able to work from a screenplay Dahl himself wrote), Burton did visit the Dahl estate to get a sense of the project's "roots." Dahl's widow, Liccy, showed Burton the original handwritten manuscripts, in which Burton identified strongly with the "slightly out-of-touch" Wonka character, as well as the "in the background" Charlie.[9] Here, then, are the "Burtonesque" entry points Dahl's work provides for the Hollywood star auteur: a vaguely dark, cynical but playful sensibility, and characters who are quirky and/or isolated.

Critics' anticipation of Burton's *Charlie* remake was marked specifically by their knowledge of his stylistic signature. As Mick LaSalle of the *San Francisco Chronicle* writes, "director Tim Burton does his best work in years. The story provides endless opportunities for him to let loose his visual imagination, and his caustic humor finds outlet in the baroque mishaps that befall various deserving characters and in the personality of Willy Wonka."[10] And, according to A.O. Scott at the *New York Times*, "Mr. Burton's world, for all its weirdness, is by now a familiar place ... in this case the source material seems to have reawakened the director's imagination, as he has found both Dahl and his most famous creation to be kindred spirits."[11] Thus, whether critics praised or castigated *Charlie and the Chocolate Factory* for its relationship to the source material, they invariably acknowledged evidence of the "mark of Burton." However, in the following sections, I expand on these critics' observations to show that *Charlie* is not simply the result of Burton's auteurist signature, but emerges from key social concerns of the new millennium. I thereby suggest that re-adaptations like *Charlie and the Chocolate Factory* do more than express the relationship between author and text; they also track and give voice to the relationship between auteurist style and contemporaneous cultural anxieties.

Morality Tales

As many critics have noticed, one of Burton's biggest changes to *Charlie and the Chocolate Factory* is his addition of Wonka's "daddy issues."[12] These are evidenced by his inability to verbalize the word "parents" at multiple points during the film and highlighted by several glassy-eyed flashbacks to his youth, which feature a towering dentist father (Christopher Lee) wearing medical gloves. In interviews, Burton has explained this change with reference to his personal past (similar paternal relationship issues exist in both *Batman* and *Big Fish*).[13] As a child, he explains, he was forced to wear elaborate orthodontic headgear, which he found to be "such a painful, isolating experience ... when you have this ugly-looking thing on your head and you already feel like an outsider, you don't have lots of friends and can't really communicate."[14] Burton has also spoken about missing the opportunity to reconcile with his own parents, and gestured toward his awareness of "the fear now, in becoming a parent: What trauma are you going to unwittingly inflict upon [your children]?"[15] Indeed, in the decades since 1971, during which large numbers of middle and upper class Americans have been regularly seeing a therapist, popular media have developed a hyper-awareness of such dysfunctional and/or traumatic familial relationships. Moreover, during these decades, the nuclear family has become increasingly fragmented; this, coupled with the perception that Americans have come to lead more mediated lives, has no doubt further contributed to a national desire for stronger family bonding.

On a certain level, then, Burton's own awareness of the family issues circulating in the popular consciousness at the time (as well as his own) leads him to guide his film toward a voicing of these anxieties. Young Charlie (Freddie Highmore) is willing to give up the factory he has just inherited for the sole reason that he refuses to leave his family.[16] Although Charlie's decision is explicit in the plot and dialogue, Burton relies on visual cues to further emphasize the importance of such a decision—of particular note is the cold, bluish lighting in the Bucket house when Wonka's elevator crashes in and he makes his offer to Charlie, which is in distinct contrast to the warm, comforting light at both the very beginning and very end of the film. Indeed, the lighting warms up again as Charlie facilitates Wonka's reconciliation with his father. In so doing, our hero proves himself and encourages the viewer to regain confidence in the nuclear family. Indeed, the end of the film suggests a "moral" to the *Charlie* story, something like "Remember, kids, you always have your *family,* even when you have nothing and no one else." But this family is not always as idyllic as Charlie's; as we will see later, 1970s and 2000s stereotypes about naughty children also figure centrally here.

The historical specificity of Burton's adaptation becomes clear when we contrast his film with Stuart's version. The American public of Stuart's time was less focused on family matters than the questions of trustworthiness and loyalty. This was the era of the Vietnam War and Watergate, in which powerful government officials were found to be lacking both of these virtues, and as such, one in which themes of corruption and betrayal were common in top box office hits—see, for example, *Serpico* (1973) and *The Godfather Part II* (1974). In this environment it made sense to choose a different moral for *Willy Wonka*. Thus, Stuart played up Dahl's Slugworth character, a sneaky, evil candy man in competition with Wonka, only mentioned once in the novel. As each winning child is celebrated for finding a golden ticket, the film cuts to a close-up of a suddenly present Slugworth (Gunter Meisner), whispering in the child's ear. When it is finally Charlie's turn, we learn that Slugworth intends to poach Wonka's everlasting gobstopper recipe, offering a bribe to whomever will steal a gobstopper for him. This setup lends a palpable sense of uneasiness to the scene in which Wonka distributes an everlasting gobstopper to each child, made more emphatic by Veruca Salt (Julie Dawn Cole)'s crossed fingers when Wonka asks them all to promise they will not let anyone else have their gobstopper.

The fear of betrayal reaches its pinnacle near the end of the film, as Grandpa Joe (Jack Albertson) in his vengeful anger makes plans to approach Slugworth with Charlie's gobstopper. It is precisely at this juncture that Charlie (Peter Ostrum) proves himself by returning it—slowly, his face plastered with consternation and regret—and trudging away while Wonka's back remains turned. Charlie thus keeps his promise. Just as Burton's Charlie relieves our familial anxieties, Stuart's Charlie relieves our ethical anxieties. We are again presented with a moral, but in this case, one more to the tune of "Remember, kids, be true to your word and loyal to everyone, even those who don't believe in you." And, as a means of highlighting his pedagogy, Stuart's Wonka reveals at the last moment that the "Slugworth" who offered bribes to the children is actually a Wonka employee, planted to tempt and test the prospective heirs. Thus, whether they face quandaries real or imagined, both Charlies serve as a beacon of hope for the audience. Unlike the variously spoiled and greedy other children, both Charlies are *good*; their reassuring functions vary based on the cultural root of the concern they work through. What makes Burton's version important is the commingling of this historical anxiety with his *auterist* additions—in this case, the insertion of *his own* anxieties and a visual dialectic between dark and light.

Changing Amusements

In reflecting back on the historical moment in which he made *Willy Wonka and the Chocolate Factory*, Mel Stuart refers to the Vietnam/Watergate era dissatisfaction I mentioned above: "There was a great deal of cynicism in the land because of the conflict over our involvement in Vietnam and the pressure of the civil rights movement."[17] In 1971, the year *Willy* came out, the "big hits" were *Dirty Harry, Sunday Bloody Sunday, A Clockwork Orange, Klute,* and *The French Connection*—notably, there are no family films in this bunch. Stuart surmises that these heavy-hitting films make clear the reason for *Willy*'s lack of success at the box office: "Where did *Willy Wonka* fit into that group of commercial and critical hits at a time like that? It didn't."[18] While this is certainly a reasonable analysis, it does not capture the whole picture; *Willy* does address 70s era fears in its own way, offering reassurances rather than bloody nihilism. Because the film versions of the *Charlie* story are first and foremost family entertainment, they each invoke culturally normalized forms of family amusement in their respective eras.

Coincident with Vietnam-Watergate era political strife and anxiety was the formation of an aggressive counterculture. Now fairly cliché in American cultural history, the late 60s and early 70s were the era of flower children, free love, and recreational drugs. The pleasures of psychedelia rapidly expanded beyond the bounds of counterculture and into the mainstream, thus coming to dominate mainstream aesthetics—including family movies. Indeed, Stuart's means of depicting the experience of the chocolate river boat ride through Wonka's factory betrays precisely this fascination, and could easily be described as an "acid trip" scene. In it, a series of colored strobe lights illuminates the boat in the midst of total darkness, creating a spinning sensation sometimes punctuated by "creepy" images (of bugs, Slugworth, etc.) and accompanied by disquieting and discordant music. Violet Beauregarde (Denise Nickerson) asks, appropriately, "Is this some kind of freakout?" Seventies audiences would have identified with the nervous and frightened guests, but simultaneously taken pleasure, as Wonka seems to, in the unpredictable "trip."[19]

But, beginning in the late 70s and becoming particularly marked in the new millennium, there has been a shift in what constitutes ideal family amusement. During this period, theme parks have seen exponential growth and continual upgrades to more traditional amusement park roller coasters; the new rides build elaborate "other worlds" whose roller coasters serve as the exhilarating means of navigating visitors through their enclosures. This is part of a larger shift toward immersive entertainment in general—the trend includes big screen TVs, surround sound, IMAX and 3D films, motion-controlled video game consoles, etc.[20] Burton's version of Wonka's boat ride inherits a great deal from this amusement park aesthetic. Not coincidentally, Burton has had an intermittently close relationship with Disney—the reigning king of the theme park—throughout his career.[21] Indeed, *Charlie*'s sometimes calm, sometimes turbulent boat ride through expansive spaces, including its emphasis on the jostling of the boat's passengers, is reminiscent of several of the popular immersive world-building roller coaster rides at Disneyland: "Indiana Jones Adventure," "Pirates of the Caribbean," "Space Mountain," and "Splash Mountain" ("Pirates" and "Splash Mountain" are both boat rides themselves). Thus, if we place Burton's millennial immersive experience in juxtaposition with Stuart's early 70s psychedelic experience, we might sum up the differentiation between the cultural amusements as that between a "crazy trip" and a "wild ride"—countercultural versus corporatized fun.[22] But who exactly participates in these journeys? From the 70s to the 00s, parents are overpowered by an increasingly discomfiting confectioner and increasingly powerful, threatening children.

Evolving Stereotypes

Whether consisting of a trip or a ride, each film's boat scene was piloted by a particular kind of captain. Wonka as portrayed by Gene Wilder is something of a harebrained scientist in the tradition of *The Absent-Minded Professor* (1961), with wild hair reminiscent of Einstein and the socially awkward commentary of a genius cooped up with his inventions. The Johnny Depp Wonka, on the other hand, has been compared to Michael Jackson and read as a maladjusted outcast figure, one who has become successful precisely at the expense of familial or social relationships. Indeed, nearly all reviewers insist on the similarity between Burton's Wonka and Michael Jackson: "The preternaturally smooth features and high-pitched voice—as well as the fantasy kingdom into which selected children are invited—may suggest Michael Jackson"[23]; "Willy appears, in his Prince Valiant haircut and green gloves, looking almost as pale and acting almost as strangely as Michael Jackson"[24]; and "Johnny Depp may deny that he had Michael Jackson in mind when he created the look and feel of Willy Wonka, but moviegoers trust their eyes, and when they see Willy opening the doors of the factory to welcome the five little winners, they will be relieved that the kids brought along adult guardians … in a creepy way we're not sure of his motives."[25]

Despite all of this, however, Burton has explained his thought process for Wonka in a different way. Though critics seem to be somewhat uneasy about Depp-Wonka, Burton feels this way about the entirety of Stuart's version: "It's a strange movie; it has the oddest tone. I found it to be quite disturbing. With that weird acid flashback, when they're on the boat. And Willy Wonka turns nice at the end, out of the blue."[26] His approach was instead inspired by characters from his own childhood, such as Captain Kangaroo and Chucko the Clown, to which he added the assumption that "people who are considered geniuses or leaders of their field, they're usually kind of crazy.… We always thought that Wonka as the Citizen Kane of candy became mythic then kind of went underground and became a recluse. He's hidden, he's out of touch."[27] Thus, while Burton's thought process harkens back to the "crazy genius" type that Wilder-Wonka thoroughly evinced in 1971, his final

2005 Depp-Wonka subtextually performs timely anxieties about child molestation and repression.

As far as gendered stereotypes of naughty children are concerned, the comparison between society's worst 1960s and '70s children and its worst 2000s children is an interesting one to undertake. Some of these types have not changed; childhood obesity is even more problematic in recent years, and the same might be said for the spoiled-rotten princess type. The changes to the Mike Teavee character, on the other hand, are obvious and also emphatically technological. What in the 60s and 70s was a familiar child—obsessively watching old Westerns (or gangster films, in Dahl's text) and awaiting his first real gun—would be less legible to a 2000s audience, as young boys no longer have direct access to these older genre films. Thus, Burton wisely replaced Stuart's cowboy Mike (Paris Themmen) with a gamer, whose apparent addiction to video gameplay (importantly, still of the shoot-'em-up variety) would ring as a familiar contemporary social issue to audiences in the 2000s. Both versions indicate a nascent masculinity, as demonstrated via an obsession with the violence that flashes across both eras of TV screen but with minimal demonstrations of actual violence. However, the Mike Teavee of the new millennium (Jordan Fry) is not simply hooked on violence—this characteristic has become such a presumed truism that love of violence in itself is no longer the mark of an *unusually* obnoxious child. The new Mike is coded as obnoxious because he is also a hacker, a know-it-all, and an overactive proponent of technological innovation. Once again, as with Charlie's refusal to leave his family, Burton's distinctly "dark" visual selections supplement what his plot and dialogue intend to convey: whereas the boxy white TV room in Stuart's version is accented by and tinted orange (perhaps to denote the warmth of the Wild West), Burton's is tinted blue, and populated by the cold, rounded and smooth, almost ominous contours of futuristic technology. As for plot progression, what leads Burton's Mike to be shrunk by the Wonkavision is not the prospect of being on TV, as it was for the Mike of the 70s, but rather the notion of being teleported. Thus, Burton's Mike Teavee character marks the shift toward an immersive aesthetic mentioned above, but is also indicative of a technological savvy that has helped breed a sense, for adults, that our children are artificially independent and therefore even more uncontrollable in the new millennium.

Equally indicative of changes in the forces shaping youth behavior is the evolution of the Violet Beauregarde character. Whereas Stuart's Violet is more of a garden-variety catty child with bad manners (her gum chewing is coded as part of this vaguely scummy character, which is then emphasized by her sleazy car salesman father), Burton's Violet (AnnaSophia Robb) is a specific millennial stereotype: the hyper-competitive brat who has been conditioned by an equally competitive mother to achieve at any cost. A well-groomed "winner," she is a model budding neoliberal subject, perhaps the most obviously neoliberal subject in the film (a topic I discuss in more detail to conclude this essay).

Race and Colonialism

The weightiest criticism Dahl received from the NAACP for his portrayal of the Oompa Loompas as little black pygmies from Africa, "rescued" by Willy Wonka and subsequently enslaved in his factory. Historically, the first release of *Charlie* fell precisely in the middle of the Black Power movement in the United States, when racial tensions were high and criticism from the NAACP was perhaps more damning than it might be today. Dahl responded positively to these complaints: "It didn't occur to me that my depiction of the Oompa-Loompas was racist, but it did occur to the NAACP and others.... After listening to the criticisms, I found myself sympathizing with them, which is why I revised the book."[28] Thus, as Dahl states, a revision was released, though it did not appear until 1973—two years after Mel Stuart's *Willy Wonka and the Chocolate Factory* was released. The revision replaced the African pygmies with little white dwarfs from "Loompaland," ostensibly removing the colonialist undertones objected to by the NAACP.

No doubt due to the visible controversy over Dahl's original version of the novel, Stuart was also acutely aware of potential racial pitfalls in his film version. He has explained that he changed the title of the movie to *Willy Wonka and the Chocolate Factory* (rather than *Charlie*) because of the racialized connotation of the name—specifically, its connoted meaning of "white boss standing over black workers."[29] With equal caution, Stuart designed his Oompa Loompas as little orange people with green hair, thus carefully avoiding any and all accusations of racism. However, it is important to recognize that neither case of removing or changing color makes the story any less affected by colonialist ideology and discourse. Because race was at the forefront of American consciousness in the 60s and 70s, there was little push to trouble notions of the West's postcolonial power relations to Africa and India, but these are the deeper issues that underlie the racial concerns brought to the fore originally.

What is perhaps more disturbing than the persistence of these power relations in the previous versions of the *Charlie* tale is Burton's continued incorporation of them into his 2005 film. It could even be argued that, in many ways, the postcolonial ideological subtext exhibited in the film is worse because it is evident, yet remains largely uncommented upon.[30] This omission draws attention to a core problem: while the U.S. in the new millennium presents itself as a melting pot in which, in this case, Indian Americans are a successful "model minority" who stereotypically exhibit much-coveted technological savvy (which is itself problematic), the many facsimiles of Deep Roy are nonchalantly presented as a limitless supply of imported indentured labor in Burton's film. Indeed, the presence of these undifferentiated, non-individualized, exotic workers—as opposed to the similar but not identical Oompa Loompas in Stuart's version—is legitimized with Wonka's safari tale, which is eerily reminiscent of European states' justification of their colonization of Africa and India. The viewer is not encouraged to think critically about the power-laden economic and social relations between Wonka, his labor force, and the production apparatus. Instead, the narrative of the Oompa Loompas' heroic rescue by the enterprising and generous Wonka (this is merely mentioned in Stuart's version, but receives an extensive visual cameo in Burton's) is naturalized in Wonka's storytelling: "So I told the chief, 'Come live in my factory. You can have all the cocoa beans you want! I will even pay your wages in cocoa beans if you wish!' They are such wonderful workers." In this way, Burton's film—knowingly or not—reflects the embedded postcolonial attitudes of American society, which presume that subjugation can no longer be an issue in a "post-racial" and "equal" society.

Neoliberalism

As I implied above, one cannot separate postcolonial discourses from market discourses. Indeed, the race and labor relations in *Charlie* are guided by neoliberal logic. By way of definition, "Neoliberalism is in the first instance a theory of political economic practices that proposes that human well-being can best be advanced by liberating individual entrepreneurial freedoms and skills within an institutional framework characterized by strong private property rights, free markets and free trade."[31] However, its reach extends beyond economics and into nearly all aspects of cultural life:

> While [neoliberalism] entails submitting every action and policy to considerations of profitability, equally important is the production of all human and institutional action as rational entrepreneurial action, conducted according to a calculus of utility, benefit, or satisfaction against a microeconomic grid of scarcity, supply and demand, and moral value-neutrality. Neoliberalism does

not simply assume that all aspects of social, cultural, and political life can be reduced to such a calculus; rather, it develops institutional practices and rewards for enacting this vision.[32]

All of this may at first seem irrelevant to the whimsical world of Wonka, but many argue that neoliberal philosophy has been hegemonically pervasive (that is, it has come to dominate all spheres of society through often invisible institutional power structures) since the early 1970s, and the *Charlie* story is no exception. All versions of the story operate according to neoliberal logic, but whereas Stuart explicitly addresses society's market-driven nature, Burton's version assumes it as natural. Consider what defines Wonka as a figure of success: his personal ingenuity, control over his own means of production, and ability to enter and reach the top of a competitive candy marketplace. Under his control, the Oompa-loompas conform to the classical industrial model of efficient factory production. Indeed, their docile bodies become not only regulated but also *identical* in the Burton's version—they are as utterly interchangeable as cogs in a machine.

But Wonka is not the only neoliberal actor in the story. In one sense or another, most of the main characters in all iterations of the *Charlie* story are neoliberal subjects; at the very least, they are implicitly measured against specifically neoliberal ethics. What has changed with Burton's most recent iteration (and which reflects a shift in American culture more generally) is the concealment and normalization of these underlying ideological logics. In Stuart's version, for example, Charlie and his schoolmates are overtly encouraged to participate in the market, both by their teacher's modeling (he abruptly ends class to purchase candy in pursuit of the final golden ticket) and his assumption during their percentages lesson that all have purchased hundreds of chocolate bars themselves. Charlie's inability to afford more than two bars marks him as aberrant, which implies to the viewer that good children have mastered market navigation before the basic arithmetic they are being taught in school. Charlie is only redeemed as a successful neoliberal subject at the end, when he embraces his factory-owning future.

In Burton's film, Charlie's father (who is deceased in Stuart's version) at first seems to serve as a casualty of the ideal neoliberal system; in an effort to increase production efficiency, the toothpaste factory where Mr. Bucket (Noah Taylor) works replaces many of their human workers with automated machines. However, the Buckets' resultant employment problem is soon resolved by Bucket's entrepreneurial streak, as he is rehired as the mechanic who fixes the machines. Conveniently, no mention is made of the many other laid-off workers who were not so skilled or fortunate. On a broader scale, Wonka's entire plan for bequeathing of his factory to the winning child is a (hegemonic) neoliberal project. His distribution of the golden tickets into the marketplace encourages not only a great deal of consumption of his products, but also a necessary act of entrepreneurship in order to obtain one. Charlie himself may have simply been lucky, but the rest of the children exhibit competitive characteristics. As obnoxious as they all may be, they understand the concept of scarcity in the market and make their various greedy interventions (which Charlie's wizened, impoverished grandparents see as wrong from their traditionalist perspective) in order to obtain tickets. Burton's iterations of Mike Teavee and Violet Beauregarde, as opposed to Stuart's versions per my discussion above, are particularly cutthroat, the former being an unapologetic hacker and the latter an almost robotic "winner."

The Risks of Re-adaptation

Bearing in mind the interpretive license Burton knowingly takes in his work, it would seem that the "risks" of re-adaptation to which I referred in the title of this essay are not simply limited to the possibility of alienating audiences with changes in plot or direction. Rather, and perhaps more importantly, they also include inheriting and thereby updating or reinforcing (increasingly hegemonic) ideological elements from previous versions of a story. Of course, there is always more to a historical moment than its ideology, which is why I have highlighted how re-adaptations such as Burton's *Charlie and the Chocolate Factory* also reflect (and sometimes work through) additional elements of their cultural zeitgeist. As such, the analysis of re-adaptations as juxtaposed with their predecessor film(s) and book(s) need not focus simply on fidelity to the story itself—differences in media and directorial style will always stand in the way—but rather, can be a fruitful means of tracing the dynamics of evolving cultural norms across time periods. Thus, when re-molded by the hands of Tim Burton, the *Charlie* story seems to offer the viewer more than just a dark and weird but well-known morality tale— the auteur's signature style both shapes and is shaped by its historical moment of creation at the dawning of the new millennium.

Notes

1. Scholars and theorists of film adaptation have been wrestling with issues of translation, fidelity, and transformation (usually in relation to literature) for decades. For some of the first arguments in this ongoing discussion, see: André Bazin, "Adaptation, or the Cinema as Digest," Alain Piette and Bert Cardullo, trans., in James Naremore, ed., *Film Adaptation* (New Brunswick: Rutgers University Press, 2000); François Truffaut, "L'adaptation littéraire au cinéma," *Le plaisir des yeux* (Paris: Flammarion, 1990);

George Bluestone, *Novels into Film* (Baltimore: Johns Hopkins Press, 1957). More recently, film scholar Robert Stam has claimed that the very question of fidelity is inappropriate for several reasons, including the differing conditions of production between novels and films as well as the flawed assumption that there exists an "essence" to literary texts that can and should somehow be preserved in the adaptation process. In "Beyond Fidelity: The Dialogics of Adaptation," Stam argues, "Each medium has its own specificity deriving from its respective materials of expression. The novel has a single material of expression, the written word, whereas the film has at least five tracks: moving photographic image, phonetic sound, music, noises, and written materials" (65). The solution to the quandary for many—one with which the present author agrees—is the notion of intertextuality.

2. Even once we have dispensed with the question of book to film "fidelity," what remains is the question of the remake, which I consider here as a subcategory of adaptation. We might imagine that remakes are born of a slightly different intent—rather than aiming to translate a written story to the screen, the remake constitutes the drive to transform an *already visual* memory audiences ostensibly hold. Scholars have struggled to categorize types of remakes; descriptive terms have included update, homage, readaptation and others. For a discussion of these terms, see: Thomas M. Leitch, "Twice-Told Tales: The Rhetoric of the Remake," *Literature/Film Quarterly* 18, no. 3 (1990), 138–149.

3. I have borrowed "re-adaptation" (but added a hyphen to emphasize the "re") from Thomas Leitch, for whom "[t]he goal of the readaptation is fidelity (however defined) to the original text, which it undertakes to translate as scrupulously as possible (presumably more scrupulously than earlier versions) into the film medium." "Twice-Told Tales," 142.

4. Dahl has been a widely read and beloved author since his first children's book, *The Gremlins* (1943), though he also wrote popular short stories for adults—several of them were adapted for the popular television show *Alfred Hitchcock Presents* in the 1950s and 1960s. Many of his children's novels have been adapted as well, including *Matilda, The Witches, The BFG,* and *Fantastic Mr. Fox*. In fact, Dahl's *James and the Giant Peach* (1961) was adapted for Disney in 1996 by Henry Selick, who brought in Tim Burton and Denise Di Novi as producers. The three had also worked together on *The Nightmare Before Christmas* (1993), and their combined visual style is similar in both films.

5. Mel Stuart, and Josh Young, *Pure Imagination: The Making of Willy Wonka and the Chocolate Factory* (New York: St. Martin's Press, 2002), 1; Benedict Carver, "WB to taste 'Chocolate,'" *Variety*, February 4, 1999.

6. Michael Fleming, "Warners takes whack at 'Wonka,'" *Daily Variety*, May 22, 2003.

7. This "creepiness" has been discussed in terms of Mikhail Bakhtin's "carnivalesque," a conjunction between humor and the grotesque. See: Schuy R. Weishaar, "Tim Burton's Two Worlds," *Masters of the Grotesque: The Cinema of Tim Burton, Terry Gilliam, the Coen Brothers and David Lynch* (Jefferson: McFarland & Co., 2012).

8. Tim Burton, and Mark Salisbury, *Burton on Burton* (London: Faber & Faber, 2006), 226.

9. Burton and Salisbury, *Burton on Burton*, 227.

10. Mick LaSalle, "Depp brings a nutty center to Willy Wonka adventure," *San Francisco Chronicle* (San Francisco, CA), July 15, 2005.

11. A.O. Scott, "Looking for the Candy, Finding a Back Story."

12. For the most part, critics admonished Burton for his addition of the father subplot. Ann Hornaday writes for *The Washington Post*, "Burton has labored so hard to make Wonka his own—giving him a tedious back story, replete with daddy issues—that he's lost all the subtle humor and understatement that made Roald Dahl's original story,

and Mel Stuart's 1971 adaptation ... so charming in the first place." In *The New York Times* A.O. Scott writes, "I'll grant that it was clever to make Wonka's dad a mad, sugar-hating dentist ... but to force a redemptive story of father-son reconciliation onto this story is worse than lazy; it is a betrayal."

13. In this case, as in many others, Burton brings more than simply his *style* to bear on the source text; by uncovering parallels between the story and his own life and expounding upon them with plot additions that reflect his personal experience, Burton clearly asserts his own *voice* as well.

14. Burton and Salisbury, *Burton on Burton*, 228–229.

15. Burton and Salisbury, *Burton on Burton*, 243; 228.

16. Notably, in the Stuart version, family is not an explicit issue; Stewart-as-Wonka immediately invites the whole family to join Charlie in the chocolate factory, assuming the close-knit family unit as a given rather than a site of conflict.

17. Stuart and Young, *Pure Imagination*, 104.

18. Stuart and Young, *Pure Imagination*, 105.

19. It is worth mentioning that, despite its initial lack of popularity, *Willy Wonka* saw a revival in the 1980s and 90s, when it was frequently aired on television and released on VHS. This is likely also due in part to nostalgia for the amusements of the prior decades, when suburban adults with young children reminisced about counterculture youthfulness (whether experienced directly or indirectly). It is in this context that *Willy Wonka* has become something of a cult classic—which is precisely why Burton's re-adaptation confronted the risks I mentioned at the beginning of the chapter.

20. I do not mean to imply that the notion of immersive entertainment is new; film and television have both been conceived and/or advertised in terms of their potentially immersive qualities since their very invention. What has changed in the new millennium is the ubiquity of forms these ideas have taken.

21. Burton was recruited by Walt Disney Productions soon after graduating from the California Institute of the Arts in 1979. He did concept art, storyboard art, and animation until he and Disney "parted ways" due to Burton's too-scary *Frankenweenie* (1984), though he worked with them again for *The Nightmare Before Christmas* (1993), *James and the Giant Peach* (1996), *Alice in Wonderland* (2010), and the reboot of *Frankenweenie* (2012). Burton describes his early Disney experiences in the second and third chapters of *Burton on Burton*.

22. For further reading on the impact of Disney on family fun, particularly in the context of globalization and cultural imperialism, see: Janet Wasko, Mark Phillips, and Eileen R. Meehan, eds., *Dazzled by Disney? The Global Disney Audiences Project* (London: Leicester University Press, 2001). Regarding Disney's affect on American children specifically, see: Nicholas Sammond, *Babes in Tomorrowland: Walt Disney and the Making of the American Child, 1930–1960* (Durham, NC: Duke University Press, 2005).

23. A.O. Scott, "Looking for the Candy, Finding a Back Story."

24. Mick LaSalle, "Depp brings a nutty center to Willy Wonka adventure."

25. Roger Ebert, "Charlie and the Chocolate Factory," *Chicago Sun-Times* (Chicago, IL), Jul. 15, 2005.

26. Burton and Salisbury, *Burton on Burton*, 223–224.

27. Burton and Salisbury, *Burton on Burton*, 233.

28. Mark I. West, *Trust Your Children: Voices against Censorship in Children's Literature* (New York: Neal Schuman Publishers, 1988), 72.

29. Stuart and Young, *Pure Imagination*, 18–19.

30. In her book *Tim Burton: The Monster and the Crowd: A Post-Jungian Perspective*, Helena Bassil-Morozow briefly begins to address race and colonialist discourse in relation to industrial capitalism: "The Oompa Loompas' identical appearance, apart from

the classic 'those natives all look alike' attitude, alludes to the replaceability of the workforce within the impersonal production apparatus" (136). Yet her attention to the "natives" issue is bracketed off as if either blatantly obvious or irrelevant and uninteresting to her point about industry and production.

31. David Harvey, *A Brief History of Neoliberalism* (Oxford: Oxford University Press, 2005), 2.

32. Wendy Brown, "Neo-liberalism and the End of Liberal Democracy," *Theory & Event* 7, no. 1 (2003), n.p.

Bibliography

Bassil-Morozow, Helena. *Tim Burton: The Monster and the Crowd: A Post-Jungian Perspective*. London: Routledge, 2010.

Bazin, André. "Adaptation, or the Cinema as Digest." Alain Piette and Bert Cardullo, trans. *Film Adaptation*. James Naremore, ed., 19–26. New Brunswick: Rutgers University Press, 2000.

Bluestone, George. *Novels into Film*. Baltimore: Johns Hopkins Press, 1957.

Brown, Wendy. "Neo-liberalism and the End of Liberal Democracy." *Theory & Event* 7, no. 1 (2003): n.p.

Burton, Tim, and Mark Salisbury. *Burton on Burton*. London: Faber & Faber, 2006.

Carver, Benedict. "WB to Taste 'Chocolate.'" *Variety*, February 4, 1999.

Dahl, Roald. *Charlie and the Chocolate Factory*. Revised ed. New York: Alfred A. Knopf, 2001.

Ebert, Roger. "Charlie and the Chocolate Factory." *Chicago Sun-Times* (Chicago, IL), Jul. 15, 2005.

Harvey, David. *A Brief History of Neoliberalism*. Oxford: Oxford University Press, 2005.

Hornaday, Ann. "Sorry, Charlie." *The Washington Post* (Washington, DC), Jul. 15, 2005.

LaSalle, Mick. "Depp brings a nutty center to Willy Wonka adventure." *San Francisco Chronicle* (San Francisco, CA), Jul 15, 2005.

Leitch, Thomas M. "Twice-Told Tales: The Rhetoric of the Remake." *Literature/Film Quarterly* 18, no. 3 (1990): 138–149.

Sammond, Nicholas. *Babes in Tomorrowland: Walt Disney and the Making of the American Child, 1930–1960*. Durham: Duke University Press, 2005.

Scott, A.O. "Looking for the Candy, Finding a Back Story." *The New York Times* (New York, NY), Jul. 15, 2005.

Stam, Robert. "Beyond Fidelity: The Dialogics of Adaptation." *Film Adaptation*. James Naremore, ed., 54–76. New Brunswick: Rutgers University Press, 2000.

_____. *François Truffaut and Friends: Modernism, Sexuality, and Film Adaptation*. New Brunswick: Rutgers University Press, 2006.

Stuart, Mel, and Josh Young. *Pure Imagination: The Making of Willy Wonka and the Chocolate Factory*. New York: St. Martin's Press, 2002.

Truffaut, François. "L'adaptation littéraire au cinema." *Le Plaisir des yeux*. Paris: Flammarion, 1990.

Wasko, Janet, Mark Phillips, and Eileen R. Meehan, eds. *Dazzled by Disney?: The Global Disney Audiences Project*. London: Leicester University Press, 2001.

Weishaar, Schuy R. *Masters of the Grotesque: The Cinema of Tim Burton, Terry Gilliam, the Coen Brothers and David Lynch*. Jefferson, NC: McFarland, 2012.

West, Mark I. *Trust Your Children: Voices against Censorship in Children's Literature*. New York: Neal Schuman Publishers, 1988.

The Kids Aren't All Right
Childhood Liminality and the Monstrous-Cute in Burton's Roald Dahl Adaptations

SARAH DOWNES

James Henry Trotter, an orphan cared for by his two cruel Aunts, has been given some magic creatures that cause a giant peach to grow on the old, dead peach tree in his garden. One evening James finds an entrance in the yielding pink flesh and clambers inside the fruit. As he approaches the stone, silhouettes dance before him upon a membranous wall. The shadows cast by creatures with many hands, hooked jaws and claw-like fingers bob and twirl as they speak in oddly human voices. The loud yet strangely melodic voices assault James' ears as he watches, bewildered and afraid. Falling through the membrane—an act that symbolizes the crossing of boundaries and implies the structural weakness of those boundaries—James is surrounded as the creatures loom above him, crowd him and swathe him in shadows. They ponder his appearance, question who he might be (fearing initially that he is Aunt Sponge or Aunt Spiker) as James cowers and covers his face with his arm.

A voice with a strange but familiar intonation dominates the soundscape and announces the arrival as neither Sponge nor Spiker, but James as the owner of the voice, a spider of some four feet across descends from the roof of the peach stone. Bathed in shadow and cowering before an unnatural collection of beasts, James fears for his life. Until Glow-worm turns up the lights and the monsters become familiar: ladybugs, centipedes, worms, spiders and grasshoppers. With their large eyes, bright colors, familiar clothing and recognizable accents the insects invoke the Japanese culture of *kawaii*—the brand of cuteness that structures the aesthetic of Hello Kitty—that draws upon creatures and characters that adopt humanized neonatal features in a way that influences the consumer's instinctual emotional reaction to them. Upon revealing their faces and the signifiers of their humanlike ordinariness in the growing light the insects are revealed to be of no threat. Not monsters after all but really rather familiar, friendly and *kawaii*. Like James' ambiguous insect friends, introduced by the protagonist's literal and symbolic descent into "the other" realm of monsters and animation, however, *kawaii* is never simply cute but is infused with the monstrous *anti*cute as well. In a "not only, but also" dialectic the two concepts of monstrous and cute feed from each other, unite, transmute and becomes something altogether more.

This essay will explore the use of the notions of monstrous and cute in relation to the figure of the child within Tim Burton's work. Drawing upon the polarity and mutuality of Maja Brzozowska-Brywczyńska's notion of the fusion of the monstrous-cute, and Julia Kristeva's theory of the abject, this essay will propose that Tim Burton's aesthetic constructs childhood as a state of liminality, of belong to no single category while inhabiting many simultaneously. Most eloquently expressed in the convergence of Burton's distinctive aesthetic with the darkly humorous tales of Roald Dahl—*James and The Giant Peach* (1996, directed by Henry Selick, produced by Tim Burton) and *Charlie and The Chocolate Factory* (2005, directed by Tim Burton)—I contend that Burton's artistry utilizes the connotations of monstrosity and cuteness to question whom the films are intending to communicate with and what the child and the monstrous-cute represents. Moreover, I propose that the synthesis of the monstrous-cute with the figure of the child poses an unanswered challenge to the adult culture that creates the symbolic juvenile: is this really what children are, or are these anxieties symptomatic of an adult generation more uncomfortable with itself than with its offspring?

Monstrous Cute Oppositions

Following in the wake of the rich 19th century literary tradition, the "flexible, multiuse concept" of monstrosity encompasses a range of physical and psychological criteria ranging from deformity to deviation from textual norms.[1] Yet, if a monster is considered to be a deviation, then the norm from which it evolved must be implicit in its particular brand of monstrosity. As Jasia Reichardt discusses: "The essential condition for a monster is that the human characteristics it possesses must not be changed too far. [...] Transforming a person into a monster is achieved by the exaggeration of one or two features."[2]

This intimate connection between the ordinary and its monstrous deviations has contributed to the evolution of the label *monster*: where once in visual culture, and cinema in particular, the monster was physically extraordinary in more recent times the monster has been recast as increasingly *kawaii*.[3] These "adorable" monsters, it may be said, "are our children."[4]

Although speaking figuratively about the cultural dialectic in which the monstrous body is seen as "a construct and a projection" of the parent generation's anxieties, Jeffrey Jerome Cohen's choice of metaphor is surprisingly revealing.[5] Produced and reproduced by the ambiguities of the dominant culture, monsters are liminal and evolving symbols of anxiety that reflect society. Monsters are, as Asma claims, omens; or literally *The Omen* (1976), as the child—the paradigmatic symbol of all things cute—is made monstrous by its association with amorality and evil.[6] Children are, of course, the representation, both practically and metaphorically, of the future of humanity: the bespoke cultural image of purity, innocence and *kawaii*. Ethnographic studies have demonstrated that "more infantile facial profiles and more infantile body builds were judged to be cuter, more cuddly, and more defence provoking than mature stimuli." Indeed, the most recognizable traits of human infants—large eyes, large foreheads, narrow noses, narrow chins and wide ear sets—can be extended to other species of animal and anthropomorphized creatures as measures of cuteness.[7]

Yet these monsters are not simply our children but ostensibly *for* our children, for their entertainment and education. If, as Lois Drawmer notes, "what we understand to be children's culture (films, media, games, television for example) are created, produced and disseminated by adults on behalf of children, with a specific concept of children and childhood underpinning them" we must move to question the representation of the child being propagated.[8] Moreover, if we are reproducing combinations of *kawaii* and abhorrent monsters then what is the significance of their "cuteness" or "monstrosity"?

Maja Brzozowska-Brywczyńska's notion of the monstrous-cute may help us to reconcile the conflicting connotations of the monstrous child: "Monstrous-cute is ... cute read through its thesaurus (endearing, loveable, delightful, darling, pretty) and then re-read through the notion of strangeness and marvel (something that is not as it seems, something that suffers from innate contradictions); to read cute as monstrous is—in brief—to read it as an other."[9] Monstrous-cute is a subversion of terms, a refusal of both through the reciprocal affect they have upon one another. The viewer is manipulated by the monstrous-cute aesthetic into what Julia Kristeva calls "a vortex of summons and repulsion" that at once attracts through its familiarity and disgusts through its difference.[10]

In Tim Burton's *James and the Giant Peach*, childhood is portrayed as a time of innocence and of becoming that is embodied by James Henry Trotter

(Paul Terry) and the differences drawn between him, the adults and the monstrous insects. In Roald Dahl's original text James' innocence is signified by the use of short simple sentences to introduce and describe him: "Until he was four years old, James Henry Trotter had a happy life. He lived peacefully with his mother and father in a beautiful house beside the sea." The consistent use of James' full name not only promotes identification with him but also emphasizes the familiar quality of his character. In contrast, when James' Aunts are first introduced, Dahl's sentences become longer and more complex as monstrosity begins to materialize in his description: "They were selfish and lazy and cruel, and right from the beginning they started beating poor James for almost no reason at all."[11] The winding nature of the sentences produces a labyrinthine-like narrative as the vocabulary transitions from words of happiness to those of cruelty. In both the form of the sentences and the specific words adopted the negative connotations of the vocabulary are emphasized.

Burton's incarnation of the two women visualizes in physical distortion the difference crafted by Dahl's linguistic choices. Aunt Sponge (Miriam Margolyes) is a short, rotund woman and the physical opposite of Aunt Spiker (Joanna Lumley) who's long and pointed body towers above her sister.[12] The contrast between the bloated Sponge and pointed Spiker emphasizes the extremity of their physical monstrosity while their obsessive self indulgence and enslavement of James indicate that their physical forms are manifestations of their moral difference.[13] The Aunts' influence upon James' depiction of childhood is represented through the rendering of color in Burton's film. In a scene leading up to the appearance of the giant peach, James is shown symbolically attempting to escape the overbearing adults. Shot with a muted palette that approaches a monochromatic scheme, the grey sky above James combines with the darkness of the bare soil and dead trees as he ventures down the steeply inclined garden of his Aunts' house. As he travels down, symbolically descending away from adult influence, James remains small within the frame and the peculiar grey hue given to his skin by the color wash results in him alternately merging with similarly greyed elements of the scene or standing out against the harsh black of the larger trunks and branches that frame it. Both visible and invisible, James has no consistent power of his own.

Set apart from these monstrous adults, James retains an air of childlike innocence even as he undergoes a physical and symbolic metamorphosis. Standing to the side of the peach one evening, the frame is typically dark with most colors being muted almost to monochrome. In a foreshadowing of the liberating nature of the peach, however, it remains a vivid pinkish-orange hue as James takes and eats some of the flesh.[14] Under the influence of magic, James changes from being represented by an actor to becoming an animated character as he enters the giant peach. As he does so his limbs take on some of the elongation evident in Burton's signature *The Nightmare Before Christmas* (1993) style: his head becomes slightly enlarged, his eyes increase in size and his face takes on an inverted triangular shape as James becomes visually more *kawaii*. This conformation to a neonate version of cute serves to further separate James from his Aunts: in his animated state there can be no ambiguity, James is the innocent party and the designated hero of the film. Despite the subtle distortion James remains in the realms of the familiar: his large head and prominent eyes reinforce his status as both human and child. Moreover, the transition from live action to animation during this scene restores the depressed and muted palate of earlier scenes and the increased color at first suggests a positive change. James' status as the innocent child is, however, complicated and influenced by the monsters in the film.

As he enters the peach stone the color scheme again changes from the warm orange of the peach flesh to a foreboding green hue akin to the night-vision effect seen in Jonathan Demme's *The Silence of the Lambs* (1991). The subsequent connotation of blindness and the high contrast between light and shade within the scene disempower James and render him, along with the viewer, at the mercy of whatever he may meet.

Once inside the peach stone he is indeed met by creatures much better suited to the darkness than he: an ensemble of giant insects, including a centipede and a spider. When one considers the reality of a six-foot long centipede or a four-foot wide spider, the monstrosity of the creatures becomes apparent. One need only compare the entertainment of *James'* human-sized creatures to the disturbing quality of Gregor Samsa's transformation in Franz Kafka's novella *The Metamorphosis* (1915) to appreciate the true horror that such creatures would evoke. *James'* creatures differ to Kafka's insect protagonist, however, in their adoption of specific and well-defined human cultural stereotypes. The spider, for example, despite being resident in the United Kingdom is portrayed as Eastern European through the adoption of an accent that bears a striking similarity to Béla Lugosi's 1931 performance of *Dracula*. In making such a connection the spider becomes at once threatening, a foreign other in the nature of the eponymous vampire that plays upon the fear of being bitten, but also familiar as contemporary audiences are accustomed to the accent and related persona being parodied by the likes of *Sesame Street*'s Count Von Count. The fear associated with the personification of the giant spider as a threat is tamed and made cute by the intertextual knowledge of the viewer. In addition to this intertextual referencing, the ominous green color scheme is quickly rectified by the glow-worm "turning up the lights" and restoring a full color palette. Indeed, while James is at first afraid of the anthropomorphized insects he is quickly able to reinforce his authority over them as he solves their dilemmas.

As Paul Wells discusses, a key function of the juxtaposition of human and animal within a narrative is to create a dialogue of opposition, of sameness and difference. The two apparently oppositional characters are set against one another, the animal representing irreconcilable difference, wildness and nature to the human connotations of civilization, culture and refinement.[15] This traditional animal/human binary bears resemblances to the binary often drawn between child and adult—the instinctual child set against the rational adult, for example—and yet the binary is not as oppositional as it might seem. In *James*, the animals are anthropomorphized to the extent that they assimilate human qualities; they have crossed the metaphorical boundary between the two states and stand with one foot in each category. Indeed, James literally fell through the boundary membrane between the ordinary and its monstrous counterpoint when he entered the extraordinary realm of the peach. It is within this slippage of meaning that Burton's aesthetic reaches towards the abject, towards a fundamental oscillation between same/other, me/not me that draws upon multiple aspects of the spectrum lying between those oppositional terms. Julia Kristeva's abject is a primal feeling of ambiguity that lies at the very boundaries of perception. In perceiving the abject,

> A massive and sudden emergence of uncanniness [is felt], which, familiar as it might have been in an opaque and forgotten life, now harries me as radically separate, loathsome. Not me. Not that. But not nothing either. A "something" that I do not recognise as a thing.[16]

The abject is a complex dynamic of boundary subversion that at once accepts and denies the binary terms. It draws upon the connotations of one term that enable the other to be—the strict cultural rules of human that enable animal to be differentiated—such that both terms oscillate between the poles of meaning as what was denoted by one becomes increasingly consumed by the other. The dynamic signification of the animal depends not upon its definition as either same or other but on the fluidity of its representation. The true uncanny meaning of "animal" plays out in the space between the terms that seem to be in opposition—a space that needs both terms in order to exist. The two terms involved in this kind of abjection-reaction exist in a mutual relationship with one another. What we understand as "human" is partly constituted by what we understand as "animal": each term is both a parent and child of the other. In *James*, then, the adult/child opposition becomes correlated with human/animal, monstrous/cute. The fact that James must take on aspects of his "opposites" in order to succeed—he must adopt the responsibility of an adult, the ingenuity of an animal and the suggested "maturity" of the monstrous in order to find his way to his destination—goes some way toward questioning the constitutive role of adults in the formation and the representation of children. A represented child is never simply a child but also a repository for the memories and experiences of the adults who constructed it. James is, literally and figuratively, a man-child.

Thus, the figure of the man-child becomes a model of the monstrous-cute as the innocent, asexual boy assimilates into the role of the experienced, connotatively libidinal, male parent. The man-child, like the monstrous-cute insects, stands on the border of two apparently discrete states of existence and questions the construction of childhood as a process whereby the blank slate of the child is inaugurated into, and prepared for, the adult spectrum of development. The implication being that in order to make the journey from child to adult, some fundamental aspects of childhood (imagination, irresponsibility, the fantastical) need to be overwritten by other fundamental aspects of adulthood (rationality, responsibility, accountability). Parental influence and responsibility for the maturation of children is subtly questioned, however, as neither Sponge nor Spiker appears to have any lasting or detrimental influence over James' development.[17]

Monstrous-Cute Mutuality

While *James* emphasizes the polarity of the monstrous-cute through the juxtaposition and implicit mixing of categories in order to question the representation of the child, *Charlie and the Chocolate Factory* (2005) explicates the mutuality of the two concepts more forcefully.[18] In *Charlie and The Chocolate Factory* the monstrous-cute emerges through the subtleties of Burton's casting, wardrobe, color and lighting choices. While the animation found in *James* allowed the insects to physically embody elements of monstrosity that set them apart from James' version of cute, the lack of animation in *Charlie* necessarily restricts how monstrosity can be portrayed. As a result, monstrosity is often enmeshed with cute in a more complex way that foregrounds the need for both terms in the spectrum in order retain the dynamism of its signification. Johnny Depp's casting as the morally ambiguous Willy Wonka, for example, represents a manipulation of viewer expectations on multiple levels. Depp's international status as a classical Hollywood actor and his physical appearance, which has been conventionalized into a Hollywood norm of its own throughout his successful career, bring with it a highly specific set of connotations that are gradually broken down. The formal, somewhat old-fashioned costume contrasts with Depp's youthful look; the dark, harshly-styled haircut sits uncomfortably against his pale white skin and the high, almost childishly inflected voice stand in contrast to the viewers' expectations. Burton's blasé dialogue combines with Depp's delivery to create the most striking moments of monstrosity within the film, including Wonka's reaction to Veruca Salt disappearing down the bad-nut chute. When Veruca's father worriedly enquires where the chute goes Wonka nonchalantly responds "to the incinerator. But don't worry, we only light in on Tuesdays." "Today is Tuesday" Mike Teavee replies; Wonka's expression changes slightly as he shrugs before stating calmly, "Well, there's always the chance they decided not to light it today" and continuing with the tour, leaving Veruca's father understandably dumbfounded in the nut sorting room.[19]

Without the benefit of Burton's traditional animation style or heavy prostheses, the character of Willy Wonka becomes infused with the viewers' own expectations and understanding of the actor. Additionally, Depp's angular face coupled with the ashen makeup of Burton's aesthetic and high-angled promotion shots for the film, lend the character an immature, if not childlike, demeanor that conforms subtly but consistently to cultural notions of cute. This conventionally *kawaii* appearance is first emphasized by Wonka's occupation but then subverted by his acutely odd behavior.[20]

Wonka enters the narrative as his five guests approach the thick iron gates of the chocolate factory. Slowly the iron doors slide open to reveal rich scarlet drapes. As the drapes pull back an elaborate mechanical carousel is revealed, adorned with dolls that mimic the slight distortion of the child form seen in *James and the Giant Peach*. The visual contrast between the heavy, imposing iron and the bright, loud carousel embodies a monstrous-cute paradox. The former connotes restraint and containment in its impenetrability while the latter denotes freedom and fulfillment. The dolls reach the pinnacle of monstrous-cute as they blink, move their rigid lower jaws and rotate in their fixed positions as they mime along to an inaugural song paying homage to Wonka. What should be childishly cute and fun becomes infused with monstrosity: the dolls are quite uncanny in their caricature of children, they blink and their mouths move but they remain out of time and ultimately restricted. More disturbingly these mechanical children were designed by an adult to praise him. As such, the dolls become a symbolic manifestation of a dominated child, forced to stand rigidly and to recite praises for a man who later rejoices in their destruction.[21] The five guests and their chaperones watch in bewilderment as pyrotechnics set the carousel alight and the high-pitched cheery song slows to a sinister distorted drone. As all movement stops the five guests stare in open-mouthed amazement at the melting dolls.[22] The version of childhood that Wonka creates through his carousel is viciously monstrous and yet entirely constructed by an adult, once again questioning the implicit opposition between the righteous adult and the repugnant child. The musical overture to this carousel scene, coupled with Wonka's obvious enjoyment of the destruction of childlike effigies, begins to construct the character as an adult embodiment of a monstrous child. Indeed, Wonka's solutions to each of the child-related problems that occur within the factory succinctly convey the sinister quality of the character: to rectify Mike Teavee's minuscule size, for example, he suggests using the taffy puller, a device that appears remarkably similar to an instrument of torture. Closely linked with Wonka's ambivalent attitude towards his child visitors is his unending desire to recreate the perceived magic of childhood in his confectionary. Adorning himself and his factory with startlingly bright colors and a variety of textures the confectioner effectively recreates childhood in an attempt to escape adulthood.

In an original interpretation Burton shows insights into Wonka's own bland and impoverished childhood. Wonka's early life is not restricted through lack of resources but rather through the strict rules imposed by his dentist father. With a muted palette, Willy is emotionally prevented from experiencing the joys of childhood, symbolized by his father's refusal to allow him to eat candy. In an act of rebellion that is both liberating and obstinately defiant, Willy secretly eats some candy and rediscovers the joys of childhood. He subsequently leaves home to be a confectioner in a final refusal of the sterile and dull version of adulthood his father represents. Using his father's negative example as motivation, Wonka constructs a transitional state somewhere between child and adult in which he can combine the joys of children with the ambition and success of adults. This liminal state is, however, inherently flawed as Wonka exists as neither a child nor an adult and his behavior is subsequently rendered strange and ultimately monstrous. Rather than foregrounding his own oddities, however, Wonka's discernibly childlike behavior both highlights the monstrosity of the children that visit his factory—who, with the notable exception of Charlie, are as egocentric as Wonka himself— and questions the role that adults play in the shaping of children's behavior. Whereas his Aunts did not adversely influence James, his father defines Wonka. Childhood is, in *Charlie*, a state of reproduction yet Wonka is neither a stable child nor a stable adult. In his search for an heir to his candy empire Wonka additionally, and perhaps more importantly, searches for emotional guidance to rectify his problematic categorization.

The guidance that Wonka is searching for appears in the form of Charlie, a child who behaves more adult than Wonka himself.[23] As the film begins and documents Charlie Bucket's (Freddie Highmore) life, the city and house in which he lives are portrayed in a reduced palette with everything appearing to be comprised of shades of grey and blue. The dullness of the scenes help to convey Charlie's impoverished existence but it also presents a similarly impoverished version of childhood that is visually contrasted to the bright, primary colors and possession-laden lives of the other children in the film. Childhood for Charlie is a state of lacking: color, contrast, money and material possessions. It is a time of known strife, identifiable need and negative emotional certainty.

Although the opening scenes suggest that Charlie's childhood is an impoverished one, he has kind and loving parents and his polite and humble behavior offer an alternative construct of childhood to the one proposed by Wonka or the other children.[24] Charlie retains the gleeful excitement of a child, decorating his small bedroom with the wrappers of chocolate he has eaten, yet also possesses maturity and manners. When the children are allowed to snack on the candy meadow in the factory and Augustus immediately heads for the chocolate river, Charlie demonstrates mature self-control as he picks single blades of grass to eat. When Mike Teavee expresses disbelief at Wonka's ability to transport chocolate electronically Charlie, when asked to go ahead, willingly retrieves the chocolate and takes only a small bite to taste it. Respectful at all times, Charlie embodies a positive view of childhood that shares more features with James's innocence in *James and the Giant Peach* than with Charlie's narrative peers.

Semantically, Wonka and Charlie occupy the same liminal space—a man with the mannerisms and attitude of a child and a child with the mannerisms and attitude of a man—and both appear to be outsiders in relation to their respective social categories. Charlie is contrasted to the monstrous children in the film and is set apart by his good behavior while Wonka is contrasted to the notion of righteous adults and is set apart by his childlike behavior. Although outcast for diametrically opposing reasons, Charlie and Wonka's status as outsiders reflects the problematic nature of social norms. As Howard Becker states, "different groups judge different things to be deviant" which necessarily challenges the legitimacy of the standards against which it is judged: what is "normal" for the group of children is "abnormal" for the group of adults.[25] As a result of their expulsion from the social groups that have created these oppositional versions of deviancy, Charlie and Wonka come together in such a way that their "deviations" compliment one another: they are juxtaposed, but as opposite sides of the same coin.

Fueled by a combination of greed and ambition, isolated by paranoia and an encompassing desire for self fulfillment and, as the carousel homage to his greatness can attest, exhibiting more than a little arrogance, Willy Wonka is a combination of the traits he abhorred in his child visitors. Subtly implicating his father as an influence upon his monstrosity, the unwanted traits of childhood become unified and rationalized in the flamboyant chocolatier and demonstrate the ways in which the metaphorical child is the progenitor of the adult that passes judgment. Charlie, on the other hand, represents a construct of childhood with hope for a positive outcome. His wisdom and compassion outweigh Wonka's innovation and isolation to the extent that Wonka's subtle monstrosity is clearly manifested in a single remark. After winning the opportunity to become Wonka's heir, Charlie asks if his family can come to the factory with him and Wonka instantly and gregariously replies, "Oh dear boy, of course they can't!"[26] The opening of the remark, coupled with Depp's smile and affirmative head movement, cue the viewer into expecting the last part of the phrase to be a welcome confirmation. Instead, Wonka's distorted monstrosity rises to the surface in his final declaration and the expectation that Charlie, a pre-teen boy, would willingly abandon his family in exchange for living in a chocolate factory with a middle-aged stranger.

As these two representations of childhood and adulthood converge in Wonka and Charlie they come to embody the dynamics of monstrous-cute. Through contrast to Wonka's monstrosity Charlie's goodness comes to the forefront of the term cute, and through Charlie's cuteness the elements of Wonka's monstrosity gain clarity. Moreover, the competing concepts of childhood meet within the liminal space between the definitions of monstrous and cute and exchange qualities such that Charlie's compassion and Wonka's ambition create a hybrid concept of child and adult in which both terms are continuously in contact. In this way "child" and "adult," "monstrous" and "cute" reveal facets of their opposite that were previously inaccessible in a truly uncanny exchange. This transient state of existence can be called neither adult nor child and yet it is both simultaneously, a liminal and oscillating state of developmental consciousness. What this reveals to the viewer, albeit insidiously, is the coherent and structured nature of the two opposing terms. Like monstrous and cute, the tangible significance of adult and child in *Charlie* lies in the specific textual and cultural constructions of the two categories. The terms are not automatically assigned concrete meanings but develop their meanings gradually and dynamically alongside one another.

If fiction for children has "a specific concept of children and childhood underpinning [it]" Burton's adaptations of Dahl's tales show us that the specific concept of childhood is by no means a universal constant.[27] In *James and the Giant Peach* childhood is constructed as a state of innocence encased in impending adult monstrosity. James' dealings with the monstrous-cute, and his ability to manipulate facets of both monstrosity and cuteness propel him towards a modulated version of adulthood in which he is neither and yet both at the same time. In *Charlie and the Chocolate Factory* childhood is represented as a state that is created by adults but also a state that influences the construction of the "adult" that eventually emerges from the child. The opposition of child and adult is not an opposition at all and is reconciled through the proximity of Charlie and Wonka in a monstrous-cute dynamic that highlights the constitutive role of one to the other.

The fluidity of the concept of childhood in both *James* and *Charlie* exposes an unknown quality to adult conceptualizations. There is, after all, no set pattern to growing up and an adult cannot always recall each and every formative moment of their childhood. Burton's monstrous-cute aesthetic thus becomes a key component in the visualization of Dahl's exploration of the fantastical qualities of childhood.[28] The resolutions posed in both films are not simple, definitive answers or judgments on the nature of either adults or children. Neither should they be taken as judgments upon the role of parents in the nurturing and development of children: parental responsibility has been variously constructed in both titles in such a way that there is no single preference presented to viewers and readers of these tales. James achieves a state that combines the positive elements of childhood with the empowering elements of adulthood while Charlie enters into a period of mutual development with his monstrous-cute opposite. The narratives neither pose conventional coming-of-age tales nor present any of the developmental options in an unambiguous way. Indeed, monstrosity in Dahl's work is often explicitly outside of the child yet implicitly within. Dahl's *Matilda* (1988), for example, is an infantilized reincarnation of the monstrous "witch" that haunts Stephen King's *Carrie* (1974). Matilda's psychic power is in juxtaposition with the physical monstrosity of Miss Trunchball who becomes the focus of monstrous manifestation within the narrative. Matilda is both hero—liberator of the child "prisoners" of Trunchball's school and of herself as she eventually lives with Miss Honey—and an anti-hero; a monster in her own right, but one who eventually outgrows her ability. The monstrous is made anti-monstrous through its self-educative defeat. Similarly, Burton's aesthetic commandeers the familiar and, through exaggeration and distortion, questions whether the familiarity once felt was ever a tangible reality.

What Burton's adaptations do succeed in doing, however, is raising an intricate web of questions relating not only to the representation of children—are they our salvation or truly monstrous?—but also to the ways in which adults construct their own understandings of children. The commentary provided by adult-created, child-centered fiction can only be read in a figurative light; these are not children *per se* but adult recreations of childhood experiences that serve to reveal as much about the *adults* who write and produce them as about the children they represent. Burton's ambiguous flirtation with parental responsibility can, in fact, be read as a direct challenge to the authority and sanctity of the child represented by adults in fiction for children. Burton's monstrous-cute aesthetic asks, as Dahl's source text did through a different medium, how far viewers can trust the representation of the liminal child and how much of the constructed child is actually projected adult anxieties. Like Dahl's child protagonists—James, Charlie, Matilda, the nameless hero of *The Witches*—Burton's interpretations oscillate between the negative and positive aspects of the child as both a figurehead of the future of humanity and the potential originator of the downfall of the parent generation. The pertinent question to ask here is whether the child has the capabilities to metaphorically represent either, or whether the adult mind that generated the symbol has wrapped its own half-recalled memories in the swaddling cloth of hindsight, ruminating on what it perceives to be the great potential of each adult-in-training. As both artists approach the same unknown space and transgress the boundaries of culturally familiar categories, the seamless transition from monstrous to cute to monstrous-cute exposes both the ambiguity in the construction of the child and the very spaces in which the characters move. It is due to the combination of their artistry and the inherently uncanny nature of the subject matter that Burton's adaptations of *James and the Giant Peach* and *Charlie and the Chocolate Factory* can explore, both overtly and subliminally, the innate and unavoidable contradictions contained within representations of childhood liminality.

Notes

1. Stephen T. Asma, *On Monsters: An Unnatural History of Our Worst Fears* (Oxford: Oxford University Press, 2009), 7. The term monster has been adopted by a number of literary and visual theory movements, including but not limited to feminism, disability studies and sexuality studies, but one of the recurring themes of the *monstrous* throughout most disciplines is the notion of otherness and of being outside the perceived norms of given group or society. As such, that which is different is often labeled *monster* and this essay draws upon this ambiguous undercurrent of difference when it applies the label to both children and adults in different contexts.
2. Jasia Reichardt, "Artificial Life and the Myth of Frankenstein," *Frankenstein, Creation and Monstrosity*, Stephen Bann, ed. (London: Reacktion, 1994), 136–157, 139.
3. The term ordinary is used here to highlight is symbiotic relation to the extraordinary quality of the monstrosity entailed in the monstrous-cute. Whereas historically,

monstrosity and its opposite may have been represented by the juxtaposition of the normal and abnormal, the assimilation of those terms by sexuality and disability studies have lead to an oppositional quality arising with one term being cast as positive and the other as negative. The abnormal stands as a refusal of the normal—itself a term that is heavily influenced by social structures—in a way that distances and differentiates the two. In contrast, the extraordinary nature of the monstrous-cute proves itself to be not an opposition but an evolution of the ordinary; it does not refuse one in favor of the other but combines both into a hybrid image. Moreover, the notion of ordinary as positive/extraordinary as negative is often challenged by the monstrous-cute of, for example, Emily Strange, Ruby Gloom and Pokemon, as the extraordinary is often preferential and eventually prevails.

4. Jeffrey Jerome Cohen, "Monster Culture (Seven Theses)," in *Monster Culture: Reading Culture*, Jeffrey Jerome Cohen ed. (Minneapolis: University of Minnesota Press, 1996), 3–25, 20.

5. Cohen, 4.

6. Children as portents of the future feature heavily in the contemporary Gothic tradition, from John Wyndam's science-fiction novel *The Chrysalids* (1955) to Stanley Kubrick's adaptation of Stephen King's *The Shining* (1980). Standing as a literal symbol of the future, they access the unknown and return to their creators, their parents, with knowledge that sets them apart from society. This is, of course, a development of the internalization of the monstrous that has occurred over the last century or so. While the classical Victorian Gothic of Mary Shelley's *Frankenstein* (1818) may find the monstrous in opposition to the ordinariness of society, the contemporary Gothic of the monstrous human—vampires, werewolves, psychopaths, children—finds the monstrous not simply in the *difference* between "us" and "them" but in the *similarities*. The contemporary Gothic showcases the monstrous but also reminds us that this monstrosity, this deviation, comes from nowhere other than ourselves, our social rules, our organic nature, or our anxieties about our future. Burton has often mobilized both forms of the monstrous in his work and, as in the case of *Edward Scissorhands* (1990), has questioned the validity of the notion of the visibly monstrous by demonstrating that true deviance is within the humans. It is not surprising, therefore, that a large portion of Burton's back catalogue involves the child or infantilized adult as protagonist.

7. Anthony C. Little, "Manipulation of Infant-like Traits Affects Perceived Cuteness of Infant, Adult and Cat Faces," *Ethology*, 118 (2012): 775–782. Accessed January 11 2014, DOI: 10.111/j.1439–0310.2012.02068.x

8. Lois Drawmer, "The Monster Under the Bed: Adult Anxieties of Childhood," *The Role of the Monster*, Niall Scott, ed. (Oxford: Inter-Disciplinary Press, 2010), 125–130, 126.

9. Maja Brzozowska-Brywczyńska, "Monstrous/Cute: Notes on the Ambivalent Nature of Cute," *Monsters and the Monstrous: Myths and Metaphors of Enduring Evil*, Niall Scott, ed. (Amsterdam: Rodopi, 2007), 213–228, 214.

10. Julia Kristeva, *Powers of Horror: An Essay on Abjection* (New York: Columbia University Press, 1982), 1. A similar attraction/repulsion dynamic can be found in Mikhail Bakhtin's notion of the carnivalesque, as discussed by Robert Stam in *Subversive Pleasures* (Baltimore: Johns Hopkins University Press, 1989), wider notions of the grotesque and many psychoanalytically inflected readings of contemporary horror film including Carol Clover's *Men, Women and Chainsaws* (Princeton: Princeton University Press, 1992).

11. Roald Dahl, *James and the Giant Peach* (London: Puffin, 1990), 7, 8.

12. *James and the Giant Peach*, directed by Henry Selick (Burbank, CA: Walt Disney Pictures, 1996), DVD.

13. The construction of adults as monstrous has a two-fold effect. Firstly, it enhances the projected difference between the child protagonist and the adult antagonists, drawing what becomes an almost fundamental distinction between the two without irrecoverably disassociating one from the other. Secondly, it allows the character roles of adult and child to symbolically represent a cultural anxiety that is, above all, internal. The anxiety is not *directly* concerned with the treatment or raising of children, but with the classical Gothic trope of correct continuation of society, direct inheritance and the implicit pressures that society places upon adults—as propagators and cultivists of our children— and children—as the promise of futurity. It is the fluid connection between the adult and the child, as the complete unit that will either strengthen or annihilate societal continuation, that is at stake in both Dahl's and Burton's characterizations of children and adults. It is a theme both return to frequently and it is one that can never be given a full answer simply because the process is continually ongoing and each new inception of the adult-child relation holds the same utopian/dystopian potential.

14. Despite the connotations of *peach* denoting sexual attractiveness, James' ritual of eating the flesh of the peach is not a symbolic sexually motivated act. It may be more related to the connotations of admiration and non-sexual enjoyment. The peach itself evidently plays a part in James' becoming, providing him with the tool to escape his Aunts and ultimately enact his own transition to adulthood. It is an agent in James' "coming of age," but it is not a wholly sexualized symbol.

15. Paul Wells, *The Animated Bestiary* (New Brunswick: Rutgers, 2009), 27.

16. Kristeva, 2.

17. Parental influence, or lack thereof, is a reoccurring theme for both Roald Dahl and Tim Burton. From Dahl's orphaned protagonist of *The Witches* (1983) to Burton's troubled Lydia in *Beetlejuice* (1988), children and their relationships with their parents and other adult figures have proved to be fertile ground for the particular brand of monstrous-cute employed by both artists. There are also subtle overtones of parental responsibility inscribed in both: that Lydia's preoccupied parents cannot see her emotional distress questions both the morality and the effectiveness of their nurturing skills, lending the film a subtle inflection of allegory as though the contention between the living Deetz's and the dead Maitland's were a metaphorical extension of Lydia's figurative growing pains. In Burton's adaptations too the moral responsibility of adults to correctly guide and influence children is implicitly reflected in the ambiguous construction of children, particularly in *Charlie*, as both innocent and monstrous; correctly influenced and running wild. The question that arises from this ambiguous presentation is one that never receives an answer: who, if anyone, is to blame for the monstrous child?

18. Roald Dahl's *Charlie and the Chocolate Factory* amlagamates the animal/human dichotomy in its descriptions of Willy Wonka. Clearly demarcating Wonka's perceptive acuity and his "difference" from the other adults, he is described as being "like a quick clever old squirrel from the park." Simultaneously human and animal, Wonka typifies a kind of subversive deviation from sociocultural norms that is cast as positive (he is a *clever* squirrel, after all) yet somehow deeply concerning. *Charlie and the Chocolate Factory* (London: Puffin, 1995), 81.

19. The nuances of Wonka as a monstrous incarnation in both book and film are perhaps succinctly encapsulated by Marilyn Manson's (Brian Warner) interest in the role and Depp's reputed use of the Manson persona as inspiration for his portrayal (originating, of course, from Depp and Warner's previous musical collaborations and their ongoing friendship).

20. The almost androgynous contours of Depp's cheekbones and eyebrows, together with the contrast between the pale skin and dark features of his face draws comparisons

to the *kabuki* or *noh* masks of Japanese musical theatre. Just as those masks enabled the actors to characterize their roles and communicate emotion, or a lack thereof, so too does Wonka's face cover up the fluid nature of his personality. Partially obscuring both gender and age, Wonka appears to perform his role as an adult while harboring a child-like outlook upon the events of the narrative.

21. The notion of control is avoided here for two reasons. Firstly, Wonka's symbolic attempt to control his mechanical children fails as they self-combust. Secondly, while traditional monsters invoke a crisis of control as they rampage through society wreaking havoc, the monstrous-cute invokes a subtle psychological crisis. The dynamic between the monstrous-cute is internalized and, by virtue of the fact that children and adults are *not* conceptually distinct, one seeking to control the other would involve imposing sanctions upon both. Indeed, Dr. Wonka's attempt to control his child fail; the parents' attempts to control their children at the factory fail; Wonka's own pseudo-attempt to control himself (by playing an "adult" role) fails. The only child that is controlled is Charlie, and he controls himself. Thus the child can be restrained and contained but it cannot be externally controlled and this uncontrollability forms part of their inherent monstrosity.

22. *Charlie and the Chocolate Factory*, directed by Tim Burton (2005; Burbank, CA: Warner Bros. Pictures, 2005), DVD.

23. The fact that Wonka seeks guidance from Charlie is a unique interpretation in the Burton adaptation. Neither the source text nor the original film version manifested the *lack* in Wonka that facilitated his need to find an heir who would not only continue his empire but also in some way complete his own transition from child to adult.

24. Undoubtedly, in both Dahl's and Burton's versions of *Charlie*, the representation of Charlie Bucket is infused with connotations of class. Charlie is not only morally different to his peers but also financially different and this is reflected in Burton's use of the monochrome palette to represent Charlie's house. What Charlie lacks in wealth he seemingly compensates for in maturity, good manners and empathy. There is, in the author's opinion, a specific and detailed criticism of capitalist materiality embedded in both versions of the tale whereby wealth and possessions are used as a signifier of a lack of humanity. While it is not within the scope of this essay to go into detail about the class ruminations present it should be noted that part of Charlie's cuteness and his monstrosity lies within his socioeconomic otherness to both his child peers and the adults (primarily Wonka) against whom he is characterized.

25. Howard S. Becker, *Outsiders: Studies in the Sociology of Deviance* (New York: The Free Press, 1973), 4.

26. There is a certain breed of oral monstrosity at work in Burton's interpretation of *Charlie*. Depp's distinctly toothy grin, Wonka's childhood braces, Charlie's father working in a toothpaste factory and Dr. Wonka's profession as a dentist all draw attention to the mouth. Add to this the explicit narrative of consumption and the juxtaposition between the consumerist *haves* and Charlie's *have not* status and the mouth becomes an important symbol in the relationship between child and adult. The mouth sustains, it provides but it also chastises and controls. This is an idea that also permeates Burton's *James*, as James' symbolic eating of the peach begins his attempt to escape the overbearing oral castigation of his Aunts, and his ultimate transition to adulthood. That Burton's adaptation ends with James orating his adventures to first New York city and then the child inhabitants perhaps suggests that the oral tradition is an important factor in propagating and recreating societal norms. Oral monstrosity, and oral resistance, may be the concomitant accompaniment to Burton's exploration of the relationship between his child and adult characters.

27. Drawmer, 126.

28. Roald Dahl's portrayal of childhood tends to oscillate between two poles of fanciful fiction: on the one hand childhood is viewed as a state of becoming the entails empowerment while on the other it is a somewhat subversive and potentially dangerous phase of life. The former is embodied most obviously by his child protagonists, who overcome various hardships and challenges to forge ahead with their inevitably successful lives. The latter, however, is implicit within the hardships those protagonists face and is often reflected in Dahl's ambiguous wordsmanship. In *James and the Giant Peach*, for example, Dahl plays with the multifarious meanings of "fantastic" in the exposition to James' adventure with the magical fruit. Stating that "there came a morning when something rather peculiar happened to him" Dahl stretches the signification of peculiar to its extreme with the italicized addition of "very." This emphasis augments the meaning of peculiar from the more innocent "uncommon" or "unusual" to the ambiguous "strange" or "queer." This movement between innocence and subversion is then ratified by Dahl's transition from "*very* peculiar" to "*fantastically* peculiar." Combining the strangeness of peculiar with the more emotive fantastic—which incorporate connotations from fanciful to grotesque—extends the potential meaning of the word. "Fantastically peculiar" can denote possible magical possibilities as easily as it can connote the carnivalesque grotesque. As such, the fantastical nature of childhood, for Dahl, lies in the complexities of magical possibilities juxtaposed with real-world dangers and potentials. The strange fellow that presents James with a bag of magical creatures is both a magician offering salvation and (implicitly and potentially, at least to the adults reading the story) a suspicious old man fraternizing with pre-teen children. Roald Dahl, *James and the Giant Peach* (London: Puffin, 1990), 10.

Bibliography

Asma, Stephen T. *On Monsters: An Unnatural History of Our Worst Fears*. Oxford: Oxford University Press, 2009.
Becker, Howard S. *Outsiders: Studies in the Sociology of Deviance*. New York: The Free Press, 1973.
Brzozowska-Brywczyńska, Maja. "Monstrous/Cute: Notes on the Ambivalent Nature of Cute." In *Monsters and the Monstrous: Myths and Metaphors of Enduring Evil*. Edited by Niall Scott, 213–228. Amsterdam: Rodopi, 2007.
Clover, Carol. *Men, Women and Chainsaws*. Princeton: Princeton University Press, 1992.
Cohen, Jeffrey Jerome. "Monster Culture (Seven Theses)." In *Monster Culture: Reading Culture*. Edited by Jeffrey Jerome Cohen, 3–25. Minneapolis: University of Minnesota Press, 1996.
Dahl, Roald. *Charlie and the Chocolate Factory*. London: Puffin, 1995 [1964].
_____. *The Witches*. London: Puffin, 2007 [1983].
_____. *Matilda*. London: Puffin, 2003 [1988].
_____. *James and the Giant Peach*. London: Puffin, 1990 [1961].
Drawmer, Lois. "The Monster Under the Bed: Adult Anxieties of Childhood." In *The Role of the Monster*. Edited by Niall Scott, 125–130. Oxford: Inter-Disciplinary Press, 2010.
Kafka, Franz. *The Metamorphosis and Other Stories*. New York: Dover, 1996.
Kristeva, Julia. *Powers of Horror: An Essay on Abjection*. New York: Columbia University Press, 1982.
Little, Anthony C. "Manipulation of Infant-like Traits Affects Perceived Cuteness of Infant, Adult and Cat Faces." *Ethology*, 118 (2012): 775–782 [accessed January 11 2014], DOI: 10.111/j.1439–0310.2012.02068.x

Reichardt, Jasia. "Artificial Life and the Myth of Frankenstein." *Frankenstein, Creation and Monstrosity*. Edited by Stephen Bann, 136–57. London: Reacktion, 1994.
Shelley, Mary. *Frankenstein*. London: Penguin, 2003.
Stam, Robert. *Subversive Pleasures*. Baltimore: Johns Hopkins University Press, 1989.
Wells, Paul. *The Animated Bestiary*. New Brunswick: Rutgers, 2009.
Wyndam, John. *The Chrysalids*. London: Penguin, 2008.

SECTION THREE

Technology, Artistry and Stardom

Converging Worlds
Neo-Victorianism in the Stop-Motion Films

Kara M. Manning

> While twentieth- and twenty-first-century film has played an ever-increasing role in returning modern audiences to the Victorian Age, fictions which pastiche that past are both prolific and popular. Ever and again modern and postmodern directors, screen-writers, authors turn back to the plots of the Victorians....
> —Judith Johnston and Catherine Waters[1]

> It's a funky old art form, stop-motion ... basically it's artists doing it and painting sets and making things. There's something very gratifying about that, something I love and never want to forget.... When it's done beautifully, you feel somebody's energy. It's something that computers will never be able to replace, because they're missing that one element.... There is something about stop-motion that gives it an energy that you don't get in any other form.
> —Tim Burton[2]

As a literature scholar whose primary interest is in 19th-century British fiction and proto-cinematic technologies, I generally cannot help but approach and interpret most visual media from the vantage point of a Victorianist, and this tendency has been encouraged in recent years by an ongoing phenomenon of Victorian-inspired television and cinema.[3] As my first epigraph suggests, we are constantly bombarded by creative reimaginings of 19th-century literature, history, and culture, and this essay argues that Tim Burton's films are very often engaged in such creative reimagining. While Burton acknowledges that his filmmaking has been largely influenced by the monster movies and special effects prominent during the Golden Age of Hollywood (usually considered as the period from the 1930s to the 1960s), it is also possible to detect Victorian genre conventions, aesthetic elements, and cultural concerns in many of his films, creating what Johnston and Waters describe as a pastiche of the Victorian past. Indeed, much of Burton's corpus might be considered *neo-Victorian* in that it frequently relies upon, revises, and redeploys nineteenth-century texts and/or cultural anxieties.

To be sure, some of his most recent directorial efforts have explicitly participated in adapting 19th-century literature to the big screen, even if mediated by previous adaptations. *Frankenweenie*, in both its 1984 short live-action form and its 2012 feature length stop-motion version, relies on Mary Shelley's iconic classic, *Frankenstein* (1818, 1831), and *Dark Shadows* (2012), along with its soap opera predecessor has an unmistakable lineage in Bram Stoker's perpetually living *Dracula* (1897). *Alice in Wonderland* (2010) hybridizes Lewis Carroll's 1865 and 1871 works,[4] while *Sweeney Todd: The Demon Barber of Fleet Street* (2007) has initial roots in *The String of Pearls, A Romance*, the penny blood attributed to Thomas Peckett Prest and published serially between 1846 and 1847. Adaptation aside, many other films appropriate Victorianism indirectly. For instance, *Tim Burton's Corpse Bride* (2005) has, in Burton's own words, "a somewhat Victorian feel, because … it sort of represents that kind of Victorian repression…. [T]hat kind of rigid structure of society where people are categorised and put into certain boxes."[5]

Burton is, perhaps, unconscious of just how (neo-)Victorian his corpus actually is, as virtually all of his films works with themes of categorization, repression, transgression, and alienation, issues that crop up repeatedly in Victorian fiction. Concerns over duality or dichotomous notions of the insider(self)/outsider(other), mainstream/underground culture, and the preservation/subversion of the status quo were frequently interrogated by Victorian writers, and these extremities, as well as the thresholds between them, are also constantly scrutinized by Burton. One need look only to films like *Corpse Bride* and *Alice* to recognize Burton's interest in crafting diverse versions of a lively, vibrant—and in these two examples, literal—underworld existing in marked contrast to the dull, drab reality of the "actual" world. In many cases, Burton's protagonists (e.g., Victor van Dort and Alice Kingsleigh) experience personal growth or catharsis in the underworld, allowing them to return to their real/surface existence as changed individuals who are primed for alternate ways of thinking, acting, and asserting identity. As in many a Victorian novel, however, Burton's characters often seem to end up more or less conforming to the status quo and/or performing a colonized version of the past (e.g., Victor, newly firm in his convictions, will marry Victoria; Alice, now independent and confident, will sail off to China). Plots typically wrap up quite neatly, and characters are often returned, albeit altered, to their original "boxes." Yet in the process Burton explores complex social and cultural issues, which remain uncertainly and uncomfortably with us despite his frequently happy endings. Such persistent and looming ambiguity is also characteristic of Victorian plots, especially those of the Gothic mode.[6]

A number of scholars and film critics have examined Burton's reliance on Gothic elements,[7] but his films have yet to undergo such scrutiny within a neo-Victorian context, an oversight that limits our understanding of how the nineteenth century is entangled in Burton's work. As Marie-Luise Kohlke and Christian Gutleben assert in the introduction to their recent collection, *Neo-Victorian Gothic* (2012), the current popularity and prevalence of both the neo-Victorian and the (neo-)Gothic has led to a convergence, indeed, a conflation of the two:

> *Neo-Victorianism is by nature quintessentially Gothic:* resurrecting the ghost(s) of the past, searching out its dark secrets and shameful mysteries, insisting obsessively on the lurid details of Victorian life, reliving the period's nightmares and traumas. At the same time, neo-Victorianism also tries to understand the nineteenth century as the contemporary self's uncanny *Doppelgänger,* exploring the uncertain limits between what is vanished (dead) and surviving (still living), celebrating the persistence of the bygone even while lauding the demise of some of the period's most oppressive aspects, like institutionalised slavery and legally sanctioned sexism and racism. Such are the very Gothic constitutive features of neo-Victorianism.[8]

My essay attempts to initiate a productive discussion of Burton's quintessentially neo-Victorian Gothicism by focusing on films that utilize the uniquely uncanny form of stop-motion animation. I argue that *Vincent* (1982), *Tim Burton's Nightmare before Christmas* (1993),[9] *Corpse Bride* (2005), and *Frankenweenie* (2012), by virtue of the stop-motion form, most keenly reflect Burton's engagement in what Victorian scholars Dianne F. Sadoff and John Kucich have called "postmodernism's privileging of the Victorian as its "other" or that time, place, and people by and against which we tend to understand and define ourselves.[10] I further contend that taken together these films represent a process of working through the tensions between past and present. That is, in resurrecting ghosts and reliving nightmares and traumas of the Victorian Gothic mode, Burton negotiates our continued—and sometimes troubled—proximity to nineteenth-century culture and literature.[11]

Stop-Motion and Victorian Visual Culture

Stop-motion animation—also known as stop-frame, stop-action and claymation—has a long, fascinating history, one that is bound up in the history of cinema, neither of which I can thoroughly delineate here.[12] Prior to examining Burton's films, however, it is necessary to briefly discuss the stop-motion form and to situate it within the Victorian period, during which it was first developed. Very basically, stop-motion is a cinematic technique whereby three-dimensional figures or objects are filmed one frame at a time as minute alterations are made to their positions, resulting in the illusion of movement when the frames are viewed sequentially at an appropriate rate (usually 24 frames per second).

Essentially, this is how all motion picture technology works: many individual "snapshots" of the subjects combine to produce what we perceive as movement. But with stop-motion animation, much of the action is never captured on film, as the form requires puppeteers to subtly manipulate inanimate objects between each frame. As Steve Tillis explains in "The Art of Puppetry in the Age of Media Production," "the manipulation of a stop-action figure does not take place in front of the audience (or of the film camera that is the stand-in for the audience), but is, quite literally, hidden away, taking place as it does between the individual frames of film. What the audience sees, as it views a stop-action film, is not the recorded image of movement, but the illusion of movement created through the recording."[13] This time-consuming process demands absolute precision on the part of the animator; one second of film footage requires 24 individual, subtle manipulations of the puppet subject, which can take hours to achieve effectively. The sheer intensity of the animation and filming procedure is one reason so few full-length features are made entirely in stop-motion.[14] The form has most often been used to create special visual effects in live-action films and advertisements. Burton, of course, has paid homage to the likes of Ray Harryhausen in relying on similar effects in live-action films such as *Pee-wee's Big Adventure* (1985), *Beetlejuice* (1988), and *Mars Attacks!* (1996).

Given its prominence in films of the 1930s through the 1960s, it might be easy to assume that the stop-motion form was a product of the 20th century. While these decades certainly saw rapid improvements in the form, the technique was actually first developed in the late Victorian period on the heels of the advent of cinema. A pioneer of filmmaking in France, Georges Méliès, accidentally discovered the possibilities of stop-motion in 1896 when his camera jammed and the subsequent footage showed "one set of vehicles and people appear[ing] to be substituted for another as if by magic."[15] This particular technique is now more properly known as stop-motion replacement, but Méliès and others quickly realized the potential for animating models or puppets using the same strategy. Many early stop-motion pictures, such as James Stuart Blackton's now-lost 1898 *Humpty Dumpty Circus*, brought children's toys and dolls to life.[16]

Filmmaking in general and stop-motion animation in particular evolved at the close of the Victorian era from a range of visual technologies and entertainments that were both widespread and popular over the course of the 19th century. Scientists often developed devices to study and explain visual phenomena. Scottish philosopher, scientist, and inventor Sir David Brewster, for instance, created the kaleidoscope in 1816 to demonstrate the principles of light polarization and multiple reflection. Similarly, John Aryton Paris, a British physician and medical researcher, is often credited as the inventor of the thaumatrope, a simple device that he used in 1824 to illustrate persistence of vision, the phenomenon by which still images can seem to unite or even to move.[17]

Originally conceived as scientific tools and visual aids to scientific discourse, these and a host of other devices—known as optical or philosophical toys—took a firm hold on the popular imagination and became standard fixtures in many households by mid-century. Public entertainments and spectacles were also wildly popular in the Victorian period, and these included puppet shows, theatre productions, and magic lantern shows. The photograph, the earliest of which was taken in 1826, was a significant form of visuality during the period, as well, creating both excitement and anxiety, as the Victorians were forced to confront themselves as mechanically and chemically produced "copies." From this rich visual culture grew modern motion picture technologies, such as the Lumière brothers' Cinématographe, which was unveiled in 1895. Several scholars have begun to explore the intersections between visual technologies and artistic endeavors, including how phantasmagoria, a very gothic form of magic lantern spectacle, influenced writers of the period. Andrew McCann, for instance, notes "literary texts ... can function like phantasmagorias, exemplifying and producing the slippage between the exterior and the interior, the world of mass culture and the world of the imagination, as they transmit visions into the mind of the reader."[18]

Charles Dickens made notable use of such narrative techniques; indeed, Karen Petroski has suggested that Dickens relied heavily on phantasmagoria, using "forms of description that explicitly put readers in a position resembling that of the spectators of the [phantasmagoric magic lantern shows]...—knowing that what they witness is illusion but nevertheless temporarily allowing themselves to believe in its reality and to be affected by it."[19] To illustrate the manipulation of both readers and characters by visions and illusions, Petroski cites examples of narrative "moments of perceptual confusion" from several of Dickens's works, most notably *A Christmas Carol*, which we shall see bears particular relevance to Burton's *Nightmare*.[20]

Neo-Victorianism in Burton's Stop-Motion Films

The Victorians were fascinated by spectacles and intrigued by the technological possibilities of both stopping and creating movement, of capturing and preserving moments in time. The stop-motion animation technique nicely reflects the Victorian desire to be entertained and surprised by visual "magic." Burton, too, seems enamored of such possibilities. Over the course of his (so far) thirty-year career, the filmmaker has returned repeatedly to the "funky old art form."

In one sense, his insistence on stop-motion resurrects and preserves a now largely dying art that was born during the Victorian period. For modern audiences, there is certainly something old-fashioned and disorienting about stop-motion, particularly since we have grown accustomed to the slick effects achieved by computer imagery and motion-capture. As the second epigraph above makes clear, Burton finds the beautifully potent and distinctly human energy of stop-motion to be at times preferable to CGI. The specter of the puppeteer, as well as the nineteenth century, survives in the finished stop-motion film: puppets, props, and sets radiate an uncanny vision—and version—of "real" life, as we perceive something of ourselves and of our shared past in the painstakingly crafted worlds or effects depicted via the form. In viewing the animation of lifeless objects, we experience an unusual reversal of the effect of gazing upon a Victorian-era photograph capturing in stasis a then-living individual. Stop-motion is a simultaneously pre- and post-mortem mode of visuality. From a purely technological perspective, stop-motion animation—and film in general—is always already neo-Victorian.

Burton's neo-Victorian sensibilities, however, encompass a great deal more than technical developments and cinematic strategies. It is, in other words, what Burton *does* with the form that reveals his (seemingly unconscious) investment in Victorian culture and literature. All of Burton's stop-motion films, for instance, make use of highly stylized puppets with very recognizable shapes and features. Most are caricatures or grotesques of the human figure, which often visually emulate Dickensian descriptions. Take, for example, the cadaverous lawyer Vholes, in Dickens's *Bleak House* (1853): "a sallow man with pinched lips that looked as if they were cold, a red eruption here and there upon his face, tall and thin, about fifty years of age, high-shouldered, and stooping. Dressed in black, black-gloved, and buttoned to the chin, there was nothing so remarkable in him as a lifeless manner..."[21] or, from the same novel, the depiction of plump Mrs. Pardiggle, a philanthropic "formidable style of lady, with spectacles, a prominent nose, and a loud voice, who had the effect of wanting a great deal of room. And she really did, for she knocked down little chairs with her skirts that were quite a way off."[22]

Such figures might be easily compared to Burton's designs for Jack Skellington, Victor van Dort, Mrs. Claus, and Mrs. van Dort, among others. Many of Burton's figures also resemble phantasmagoric subjects, as they either are skeletons or have skeletal features like sunken eyes, prominent cheekbones, and wan complexions. Sir David Brewster wrote of the "skeletons and other terrific figures" he saw projected by magic lantern during a nineteenth-century phantasmagoria and described the eerie effects achieved by making them "grow less and less" or "larger and larger"; Brewster was particularly stunned when the figures "suddenly advanced upon the spectators, becoming larger as they approached them, and finally vanished by appearing to sink into the ground."[23]

Burton's stop-motion figures are often manipulated in a similar fashion, sinking from or rising into view or seeming to grow larger. For example, we first meet Jack Skellington as he leaps, disguised as a scarecrow with a Jack-o-lantern head, into a bubbling well and rises slowly from the water in his tailored, black and white pinstripe suit and all his skeletal glory. The otherworldly, noxious-looking green light emanating from the bowels of the well casts eerie shadows over Jack and other nearby characters. Additionally, as Jack is attempting to explain Christmas to his cohorts during a town meeting, the last lines of his narrative song are delivered in a chilling voice, and he moves closer and closer to the crowd—and us—until his delightfully cackling skull with its vacant eye sockets looms large in our field of vision. Here again, the choice of color is remarkable, as Jack is bathed in a vibrant red, which prefigures his wearing of a Santa suit even as it demonizes him and his plans.

Clearly, *Nightmare* relies on the Gothic images and effects of the phantasmagoria, and this reliance was made even more pronounced when the film was re-released in 3D in October 2006. In this version, spectral bats, ghosts, and pumpkins leap out at the audience, and the already three-dimensional characters and sets have far more depth and perspective, effectively "surrounding" the viewer. A neo-Victorian Gothic quality is at play in all of Burton's stop-motion, and the aesthetic is also carried out in set designs, color palettes, and representations of othered worlds. Discussing each film in turn will help to tease out some of these neo-Victorian features, as well as the ways in which the films collectively negotiate the nineteenth-century past.

Perhaps lesser known than his later work, Burton's first stab at directing a film post-university was his 1982 stop-motion short *Vincent*. Only about six minutes long, the film tells the tale of seven-year-old Vincent Malloy, who exists almost entirely in his own imagination. The story is conveyed in verse, as narrated by Vincent Price, an idol of Burton's own youth, and is punctuated by the black and white stop-motion and accompanying music, both of which call to mind a gloomy Gothic tone. Alternately occupying roles as horror movie legend Price and master of the 19-century American Gothic Edgar Allen Poe, the young titular character imagines himself experimenting "so he and his horrible zombie dog / could go searching for victims in the London fog," a simultaneous allusion to both *Frankenstein* and Jack the Ripper, who terrorized London's East End in the 1880s. During the last few minutes of the film, Vincent's mother sends him to his room, where "his horrid insanity had reached its peak," and he falls "limp and lifeless down to the floor" as "he quoted 'The Raven' from Edgar Allen Poe." We might assume that his death is also a fantasy, but for this character, the present and past cannot coexist. His obsession with old horror films and especially the works of Poe undo him, indicating an insurmountable gap between the past and the present.

Nightmare might also be read in terms of such a tension, as the sepia-toned Halloween Town, reminiscent of an early photographic process called daguerreotype, presents us with a microcosmic version of the 19th century. From the mad scientist who creates and attempts to control female companions to the two-faced elected mayor who suspiciously resembles the British Houses of Parliament, from the monarchical Jack who deftly colonizes (perhaps *rips* off) Christmas Town to the suppressed Sally who craftily escapes her tower confinement, we enter a world that politically and socially resembles the Victorian period and that period's use of the Gothic literary mode. Significantly, Jack's version of Christmas—a Victorian Gothic version that smacks more of Dickens's *A Christmas Carol* than of the 1964 stop-motion classic *Rudolph, The Red-Nosed Reindeer*—is literally shot down by the real world, *our* contemporary world, and in the end is relegated to its place in history, occupying a safe distance as a holiday seen only once a year. Indeed, Jack's failed appropriation of Christmas horrifies the occupants of the real world and hangs over our heads in a manner somewhat akin to Marley's ghost, who haunts Ebeneezer Scrooge in Dickens's famous holiday story of negotiating the spirits of the past, present, and future.

Burton's Christmas Town, too, in its bright, shiny, round post–World War I industrial success and Coca-Cola commercialization, might be perceived as another version of the past, which is also maintained in its non-threatening moment in time. The particular traditions associated with each holiday must, for Burton's real world society, be held in check so as not to disrupt or subvert the relationship between past and present. The presence of the Victorian Gothic in Halloween Town's Christmas presents cannot be tolerated.

Very like *Nightmare, Corpse Bride* makes use of contrasting colors, which call to mind nineteenth-century photographic technologies. In fact, of the living world in *Corpse Bride*, co-director Mike Johnson says he and Burton wanted a color palette "close to a tin-type or daguerreotype," and the clothing styles and set designs clearly situate the upstairs world in the 19th century.[24] However, in an odd reversal, this rigid, drab world is made to correspond to contemporary actuality, as it *is* the world of the living, while the downstairs realm of the dead becomes the colorful, lively, instructive and, thus, potentially more acceptable Victorian past.

Still, despite the numerous border crossings made by Victor and Emily and the co-mingling of the living with the dead, the present with the past, the film concludes with the two worlds upholding a version of separate-though-perhaps-equal distance. Nevertheless, both the living and the dead bind us to the Victorian period via characters' names. Victor and Victoria clearly elicit the monarch, Queen Victoria, herself, while the van Dort's employee/servant, Mayhew, recollects the English journalist Henry Mayhew, well known for his sympathetic treatment of the urban lower classes in his collection of essays *London Labour and the London Poor* (1851). The eponymous corpse, Emily, surrounded by her tattered bridal dress and flowing veil remind us of the waiflike apparition at the window in Emily Brontë's *Wuthering Heights* (1847), and the phantasmagoric figure is also similar to sensational Gothic depictions of women in Wilkie Collins's novels *The Woman in White* (1860) and *The Moonstone* (1868).

Burton's black and white stop-motion remake of *Frankenweenie* offers us the possibility of the resurrected past occupying an important and necessary role in the present, as the twice-resuscitated "monster," Sparky, is finally recognized as a loyal and trustworthy member of the living family and neighborhood. Additionally, the film bridges the nineteenth-century past and the twenty-first-century present by engaging in adaptation and a process of cultural memory. Although the curious boy (another Victor) and patchwork dog (a canine version of *Nightmare's* Sally) are a rather domesticated version of Shelley's original treatment of human monstrosity and the ethical concerns created by scientific progress, we see signs of other cultural anxieties that have been handed down to us from the Victorians.[25] Victor's classmate, Toshiaki, embodies the stereotypical view of Asians as intelligent, technologically savvy, and suspicious or threatening. Toshiaki's role is a version of what Edward Said has famously termed Orientalism: "a Western style for dominating, restructuring, and having authority over the Orient."[26] Certainly, the empire-crazed Victorians were guilty of perceiving all things Oriental as either commercially-viable or culturally-unacceptable, and this limited, domineering way of thinking continues to haunt us. Toshiaki reminds us of the anxieties we share with the past, as does Elsa Van Helsing, whose name recalls the hunter of the invasive foreign threat, Dracula. Another character, Edgar "E" Gore occupies an interesting intermedial role, as he not only reveals Victor's reanimation technique to the rival classmates, but he also perpetuates the life of Igor, a figure who haunts the literary *Frankenstein*, though he appears only in film adaptations. On the one hand a touching story of a boy and his dog, *Frankenweenie* also asserts the ways in which the past is alive—reanimated—in our current moment.

Ending at the Beginning

Burton's stop-motion films might be considered simple family fare, and it is, perhaps, easy to find in his corpus a general adherence to the feel-good story, to the quirky, misunderstood outsider who elicits our sympathy, to the sweet, often romantic conclusion that leaves us feeling all is well. But to focus solely on these aspects is to obfuscate the complex neo–Victorian subject matter that often permeates the filmmaker's projects. When read in terms of longstanding social and cultural issues, Burton's *ouvre* looks less like a series of Hollywood hits and more like a scrapbook of Victorian anxieties. The fear of foreign invasion and acts of terrorism, variously represented, figure prominently in a number of his films—e.g., *Batman* (1989) and *Batman Returns* (1992), *Edward Scissorhands* (1990), *Nightmare*, *Mars Attacks!*, *Planet of the Apes* (2001), *Sweeney Todd*, *Frankenweenie* (2012), *Dark Shadows*—and create a point of connection between contemporary and Victorian concerns, as evidenced in such literary works as Stoker's *Dracula* (1897). Issues of patriarchal oppression, female autonomy, and gender roles sneak into films like *Batman Returns*, *Nightmare*, *Sleepy Hollow* (1999), *Corpse Bride*, and *Alice*, all reminiscent of the ways in which "the Woman Question" was treated in Victorian writing by both men and women. Additionally, anxieties over mental and physical illness and disabilities are rife in Burton (e.g., *Pee-wee*, the *Batman* films, *Big Fish* (2003), *Charlie and the Chocolate Factory* (2005), etc.), as well as in Victorian fiction, particularly the Gothic. As Antoine de Baecque notes, "Burton offers the spectacle of bodies that are damaged, bruised, primitive, sutured and bleeding, all having experienced death. This world rests on a tradition that Burton has perhaps done more than anyone else to revive: the gothic, a genre and a style that has long been an integral part of the fantasy world, and which has made its mark all the way through the literature about Frankenstein, and stories about the living dead."[27] In his reliance on the Gothic, Burton emphasizes the Victorians as a "living dead" people with whom we must constantly contend.

Like Jack Skellington, we must interrogate the phenomenon, asking ourselves "but what does it *mean*?!" One possible answer, as I have attempted to make clear here, is that the Victorians and their era continue to fascinate and speak to us, even if we are not entirely conscious of our obsession. As sociologist Avery F. Gordon has noted, "haunting is part of our social world, and understanding it is essential to grasping the nature of our society and for changing it."[28] The 19th century continues to haunt our ways of thinking, and we see Victorian ghosts in many of our post/modern endeavors, especially artistic ones. Burton pays homage not only to the great names of classic monster cinema, but he also resurrects the spirit of the Victorian literary and cultural imagination in ways that challenge us to understand and potentially change our society.

Notes

1. Judith Johnston and Catherine Waters, "Introduction: Victorian Turns, NeoVictorian Returns," *Victorian Turns, NeoVictorian Returns: Essays on Fiction and Culture*, Penny Gay, Judith Johnston, and Catherine Waters, eds. (Newcastle upon Tyne: Cambridge Scholars Publishing, 2008), 9.

2. Quoted in Mark Salisbury, ed., *Burton on Burton,* revised ed. (London: Faber & Faber, 2006), 118–19.

3. Strictly speaking, the Victorian period in England spanned the years of Queen Victoria's reign, from 1837 until her death in 1901. The decades leading up to her coronation are, therefore, not technically part of the historical "Victorian" era but are often included in discussions of Victorianism and neo–Victorianism, as the whole of the 19th century saw rapid change in many arenas (culture, industry, science, technology, literary genres, etc.). Some examples of the "Victorian-inspired" TV and film craze, then, might include adaptations of novels by Charles Dickens, as well as those by the earlier author Jane Austen (who died in 1817). Many films and mini/series are even more loosely based on the period, such as the BBC's *Jekyll* (2007; 6-part mini-series), *Whitechapel* (2009; 3-part mini-series), and *Ripper Street* (2012–), and NBC's *Dracula* (2013–).

4. In a previously published essay, I examine Burton's hybridized use of narrative and technology in *Alice*. See Manning (2011).

5. Quoted in Salisbury, *Burton on Burton*, 256.

6. Scholars often point to Horace Walpole's 1764 *Castle of Otranto* as the seminal Gothic text. During the Victorian period, the genre's popularity waxed and waned, but many writers incorporated gothic elements (isolated settings, ghosts or apparitions, physical or mental illness, and ominous atmospheres) into their work in order to explore individual and societal fears. See Botting (2001) for a useful introduction to the Gothic, its subgenres, and its continuous permutations.

7. See, for example, Allen (2010), Page (2007), Wisniewska (2003), and Woods (2007).

8. Marie-Luise Kohlke, and Christian Gutleben, "The (Mis)Shapes of Neo-Victorian

Gothic: Continuations, Adaptations, Transformations," *Neo-Victorian Gothic: Horror, Violence and Degeneration in the Re-Imagined Nineteenth Century*, Kohlke and Gutleben, eds. (Amsterdam: Rodopi, 2012), 4.

9. *Nightmare* was, of course, directed by Henry Selick; Burton co-produced the film with Denise Di Novi. A similar collaboration occurred with Selick's *James and the Giant Peach* (1996), which also uses stop-motion animation, though in combination with live action. I include *Nightmare* here because Burton was largely responsible for writing and conceptualizing the film and because it was done entirely in stop-motion.

10. Dianne F. Sadoff and John Kucich, "Introduction: Histories of the Present," in *Victorian Afterlife: Postmodern Culture Rewrites the Nineteenth Century*, ed. Kucich and Sadoff (Minneapolis: University of Minnesota Press, 2000), xi.

11. Because my particular focus here is on Burton's stop-motion, I do not address at length other films that also reflect a distinctly neo–Victorian Gothic flavor, such as *Sweeney Todd* and *Dark Shadows*. Certainly, these live action productions also revisit the 19th century.

12. For a comprehensive of the form's history, see Harryhausen and Dalton (2008). In his introduction, Tony Dalton notes that stop-motion is most commonly known in Europe as model (or puppet) animation.

13. Steve Tillis, "The Art of Puppetry in the Age of Media Production," *TDR: The Drama Review* 43, no. 3 (1999), 191.

14. Burton and Selick have done much to keep stop-motion alive, and recent years have seen an increase in stop-motion filmmaking.

15. Ray Harryhausen and Tony Dalton, *A Century of Stop Motion Animation: From Méliès to Aardman* (New York: Billboard Books, Watson-Guptill, Crown Publishing, Random House, 2008), 38.

16. Ibid., 39.

17. Burton fans will recall the prominent role played by the thaumatrope in *Sleepy Hollow* (1999). Ichabod Crane (Johnny Depp) also relies on visual devices he designed to better conduct his forensic investigations, such as the unwieldy magnifying spectacles. Interestingly, Burton's film is set in 1799, creating several historical inaccuracies that, nevertheless, emphasize the story's 19-century origin via American writer Washington Irving. Burton creatively reimagines the 1820 "Legend of Sleepy Hollow" in ways that are better suited to Victorian gothic narratives from the 1850s onward. Also of interest, is that Burton's anachronism, as well as the look of Ichabod's spectacles, might be considered steampunk. Though I would not go so far as to say that Burton's work generally participates in the genre or aesthetic, it is noteworthy that members of the steampunk community have adapted his adaptations to some degree.

18. Andrew McCann, "Textual Phantasmagoria: Marcus Clarke, Light Literature and the Colonial Uncanny," *Australian Literary Studies* 21, no. 2 (2003), 138.

19. Karen Petroski, "'The Ghost of an Idea': Dickens's Uses of Phantasmagoria, 1842–44," *Dickens Quarterly* 16, no. 2 (1999), 73.

20. Ibid., 88.

21. Charles Dickens, *Bleak House*, George Ford and Sylvère Monod, eds. (New York: Norton, 1977), 469.

22. Ibid., 93.

23. Quoted in Petroski, "The Ghost of an Idea," 72.

24. "Inside the Two Worlds," Bonus footage on *Corpse Bride*, directed by Tim Burton and Mike Johnson (2005; Burbank, CA: Warner Home Video, 2005), DVD.

25. Of course, various disciplines apply particular nuances of meaning to the term "monstrous." My use of the term follows Judith—now Jack—Halberstam in *Skin Shows: Gothic Horror and the Technology of Monsters*: "[T]he emergence of the monster within

Gothic fiction marks a peculiarly modern emphasis upon the horror of particular kinds of bodies.... In the modern period and with the advent of cinematic body horror, the shift from the literary Gothic to the visual Gothic was accompanied by a narrowing rather than a broadening of the scope of horror.... the visual register quickly reaches a limit of visibility" (3).

26. Edward W. Said, *Orientalism* (1978; New York: Vintage-Random House, 1994), 3.

27. Antoine De Baecque, *Tim Burton*, Imogen Forster, trans. (Paris: Cahiers du cinéma Sarl, 2011), 218.

28. Avery F. Gordon, *Ghostly Matters: Haunting and the Sociological Imagination* (1997; Minneapolis: University of Minnesota Press, 2008), 27.

Bibliography

Allen, Steven. "Bringing the Dead to Life—Animation and the Horrific." In *Fear Itself: Reasoning the Unreasonable*, edited by Stephen Hessel and Michèle Huppert, 87–95. Amsterdam: Rodopi, 2010.

Botting, Fred, ed. *Essays and Studies 2001: The Gothic*. Cambridge: D. S. Brewer, 2001.

De Baecque, Antoine. *Tim Burton*. Translated by Imogen Forster. Paris: Cahiers du cinéma Sarl, 2011.

Dickens, Charles. *Bleak House*. 1853. George Ford and Sylvère Monod, eds. New York: Norton, 1977.

Gordon, Avery F. *Ghostly Matters: Haunting and the Sociological Imagination*. 1997. Minneapolis: University of Minnesota Press, 2008.

Halberstam, Judith. *Skin Shows: Gothic Horror and the Technology of Monsters*. Durham: Duke University Press, 1995.

Harryhausen, Ray, and Tony Dalton. *A Century of Stop Motion Animation: From Méliès to Aardman*. New York: Billboard Books, Watson-Guptill, Crown Publishing, Random House, 2008.

"Inside the Two Worlds." Bonus footage on *Corpse Bride*. Directed by Tim Burton and Mike Johnson, 2005. Burbank: Warner Home Video, 2005. DVD.

Johnston, Judith, and Catherine Waters. "Introduction: Victorian Turns, NeoVictorian Returns." In *Victorian Turns, NeoVictorian Returns: Essays on Fiction and Culture*, edited by Penny Gay, Judith Johnston, and Catherine Waters, 1–11. Newcastle upon Tyne: Cambridge Scholars Publishing, 2008.

Kohlke, Marie-Luise, and Christian Gutleben. "The (Mis)Shapes of Neo-Victorian Gothic: Continuations, Adaptations, Transformations." In *Neo-Victorian Gothic: Horror, Violence and Degeneration in the Re-Imagined Nineteenth Century*, edited by Marie-Luise Kohlke and Christian Gutleben, 1–48. Amsterdam: Rodopi, 2012.

Manning, Kara M. "'That's the Effect of Living Backwards': Technological Change, Lewis Carroll's *Alice* Books, and Tim Burton's *Alice in Wonderland*." *Neo-Victorian Studies* 4 no. 2 (2011): 154–79. www.neovictorianstudies.com

McCann, Andrew. "Textual Phantasmagoria: Marcus Clarke, Light Literature and the Colonial Uncanny." *Australian Literary Studies* 21, no. 2 (2003): 137–50.

Page, Edwin. *Gothic Fantasy: The Films of Tim Burton*. London: Marion Boyars, 2007.

Petroski, Karen. "The Ghost of an Idea': Dickens's Uses of Phantasmagoria, 1842–44." *Dickens Quarterly* 16, no. 2 (1999): 71–93.

Sadoff, Dianne F., and John Kucich. "Introduction: Histories of the Present." In *Victorian Afterlife: Postmodern Culture Rewrites the Nineteenth Century*, edited by John Kucich and Dianne F. Sadoff, ix–xxx. Minneapolis: University of Minnesota Press, 2000.

Said, Edward W. *Orientalism.* 1978. New York: Vintage-Random House, 1994.
Salisbury, Mark, ed. *Burton on Burton,* revised ed. London: Faber & Faber, 2006.
Tillis, Steve. "The Art of Puppetry in the Age of Media Production." *TDR: The Drama Review* 43, no. 3 (1999): 182–95.
Wisniewska, Dorota J. "Strangers in the Strange Land: The Gothic Mode in Tim Burton's Films." *American Studies* 20 (2003): 143–56.
Woods, Paul A., ed. *Tim Burton: A Child's Garden of Nightmares, Revised Ed.* London: Plexus, 2007.

The Use of German Expressionism and American Exceptionalism

Peter C. Kunze

During his 1989 Farewell Address, President Ronald Reagan invoked the words of John Winthrop, one of the Puritan settlers of the Massachusetts Bay Colony, when he said

> I've spoken of the Shining City all my political life, but I don't know if I ever quite communicated what I saw when I said it. But in my mind it was a tall, proud city built on rocks stronger than oceans, windswept, God-blessed, and teeming with people of all kinds living in harmony and peace; a city with free ports that hummed with commerce and creativity. And if there had to be city walls, the walls had doors, and the doors were open to anyone with the will and the heart to get here. That's how I saw it, and see it still.[1]

Reagan's sentiment embodied the ethos of American exceptionalism, a self-aggrandizing sense of ingenuity and inimitability that can be traced through the American character as far back as the 19th century or to the very founding of the United States. Deborah L. Madsen, in her discussion of Benjamin Franklin and his *Autobiography*, notes, "What remained was the perception that America would continue to be judged by the other nations of the world to whom America would remain a model, a guide, a measure. And also a guardian of the inalienable rights of man, so recently enshrined in the Constitution."[2]

American exceptionalism, unsurprisingly, served to not only forge a nationalism domestically, but to legitimize political efforts and military actions abroad. This attitude manifests itself throughout American culture, beginning with American literature, but thereafter in art, music, and cinema. Following the humiliating defeat in Vietnam, conservative politicians countered American self-doubt by emphasizing the exceptionality of the United States and its ideological underpinnings; scholars such as Susan Jeffords and

William V. Spanos have studied the cultural manifestations of American exceptionalism in film and literature, respectively.[3]

Of course, not all artists corroborated this nationalist celebration of the status quo. In this essay, I focus on the early films of Tim Burton from 1982 to 1992 to discuss how the American way of life was not only criticized, but also shown to be contradictory.[4] To further this analysis, I hope to demonstrate how Tim Burton embraces the subversive German Expressionist style yet alters it to function within a capitalist studio system during a largely conservative cultural and political moment.

French film critic Aurélien Ferenczi refers to *Frankenweenie* as a pastiche of Whale's Frankenstein,[5] and the term "pastiche" seems to be one that critics are prone to employ in describing Burton's work. Yet if we understand it in the sense that Fredric Jameson does—as "blank parody"[6]—then such an assessment carelessly reduces the political import of Tim Burton's work, especially his early short films and features. More accurately, Burton appropriates the German Expressionist style and fuses it with the Hollywood aesthetic that demands clean and tidy stories with happy endings, such as *E.T. the Extra-Terrestrial* (Spielberg, 1982), *The Karate Kid* (Avildsen, 1984), *Back to the Future* (Zemeckis, 1985) and *Hoosiers* (Anspaugh, 1986).

Dismissing Tim Burton on the basis of his commercial success reveals an outdated allegiance to the Romantic notion of authorship, one which the pragmatics of the studio system easily debunk. A more nuanced (and practical) approach would appreciate Tim Burton's ability to adopt subversive styles and incorporate them into mainstream products without impairing their potential for success. Despite German Expressionism's often counter-hegemonic intentions, its stylistic complexity often alienated the group it aimed to awaken and inspire.[7] Burton's appropriation demonstrates one incarnation that attempts to marry avant garde aesthetics with the studio's necessity for popular consumption. While it may not spark a revolution, it does work to undermine the stale conventions that continue to anesthetize the mainstream audience by reifying the values and practices of the dominant ideology.

German Expressionism

The history of German Expressionist cinema is a contested one. Some misalign the rise of the Weimar Republic after World War I with its flourishing, but Thomas Elsaesser refutes such claims.[8] Stellan Rye and Paul Wegener's 1913 film *The Student of Prague*, for example, pre-dates the war.

One of the earliest analysts of the German Expressionist contribution to film practice was Siegfried Kracauer, whose 1949 book *From Caligari to Hitler* echoes the sentiment that the films are "macabre, sinister, morbid."[9] By making the camera "completely mobile," he claims German film directors innovated filmmaking as they "marshaled the whole visual sphere."[10] When one watches the landmark films, such as *The Cabinet of Dr. Caligari* (Wiene, 1920), *Nosferatu* (Murnau, 1922), and *Metropolis* (Lang, 1927), the striking visuals reveal a resounding defiance to the realistic representation one may find in similar films of the era. The asymmetry of the set designs in *Caligari*, a silent horror masterpiece about the manipulative Dr. Caligari (Werner Krauss) and his pawn, the sleepwalking Cesare (Conrad Veidt), or the use of shadows in *Nosferatu*, a seminal entry into the vampire film genre and precursor to *Dracula* (Browning, 1931), capture the disharmony celebrated by German Expressionism in its attempts to unsettle and alarm the viewer against the rule of the bourgeoisie. Through the manipulation of sets, lighting, and acting performances, German Expressionism refuted the staid conservatism of traditional realism in cinematic narrative. Nevertheless, defining the movement remains a difficult task, especially in terms of outlining its innovations and influence.

Linguistically speaking, one may see Expressionism as an inversion or response against Impressionism. While the Impressionist painters aimed to capture the perception of the object, Expressionist artists were more concerned with rescuing its true essence. Fueled with a revolutionary sensibility, these artists, according to John D. Barlow, "wanted to infuse everything with spirit (Geist) by an extravasation of their inner selves and because they wanted to bring out the true spirit of things and the world."[11] Expressionist stylization embellished, transformed, and subverted reality (and common notions about it) in order to raise a critical consciousness. "To a revolutionized people expressionism seemed to combine the denial of bourgeois tradition with faith in man's power freely to shape society and nature," Kracauer contends, viewing Expressionism as a German response to the "breakdown of their universe."[12] Whether the scheming doctor of *Caligari* or the immoral industrialist of *Metropolis*, the antagonists of these films revealed bourgeois machinations to control, subdue, and exploit the underclasses through physical force or ideological manipulation. Unsurprisingly, the triumphs of German Expressionist cinema were often the horror films that personified and dramatized fear or the science fiction films that created dystopian microcosms to speculate (cynically) about the future of the human race. Burton draws from both of these strains, crafting playful films that are both fantastic in their vision and satirical in their tone.

In its efforts to both alienate and unnerve its audience, German Expressionism creates an alternative world characterized by deviant behavior, distorted figures, and cold, sterile environments. J. P. Telotte observes that, deriving from the Expressionist tradition in the theater, the films employed "stylized sets, exaggerated acting, distortions of space, heavy use of shadows, irregular compositions that emphasize oblique lines, as well as specifically filmic techniques like low-key lighting, dutch angles, and composition in depth."[13] In *Nosferatu*, Count Orlok's exaggerated features include long fingers and ears along with sharpened teeth and an enlarged nose with a sharp hook. Donned in all black, his protracted movement abruptly contrasts the panic of his victims. Director F. W. Murnau often yields to menacing shadows to suggest Orlok's approach, both transforming his villain into complete darkness and signifying the subsequent unseen violence. The clashing movements of the characters and impeding of time's progression heighten the film's affect and forge a model for future horror films.

Aside from the German directors who immigrated to the United States during this time, the earliest influence of Expressionism in American cinema may be seen in the horror films of Universal Studios. One of the smaller outfits in early Hollywood, Universal benefited from the stark visual style that depended on smoke, shadows, mirrors, and unnatural backdrops. Indeed Frances Guerin argues the use of light and lighting "as compositional materials in the construction of mise-en-scène, agents in narrative progression, and bearers of discursive meaning" is German Expressionism's longest lasting effect on cinema.[14] The influence continued into film noir, and critic John D. Barlow traces the formal developments through the work of Orson Welles and Ingmar Bergman, suggesting the impact of German Expressionism not only in American and European filmmaking, but also in popular as well as art house cinema.[15] The style took advantage of the limitations of black-and-white photography by crafting images that beautifully captured on film the chiaroscuro of the finest painters. The introduction of color film as well as sound defused some of the visual power of German Expressionism, but various media clearly demonstrate its ongoing legacy, be it Art Spiegelman's graphic novel *Maus* or David Lynch's iconoclastic films. Without a doubt, German Expressionism remains, alongside the Italian Neo-realists of the 1940s and the French New Wave of the 1950s, one of the most distinctive and influential periods of artistic creation in film history. The work of Tim Burton testifies to relevance of German Expressionism today, perhaps just as much if not more than at the time of its original inception a century ago.[16] What is compelling about Burton's invocation of German Expressionism, though, is his ability to be simultaneously playfully subversive and commercially viable.[17]

Vincent *and* Frankenweenie

Vincent, a short film Tim Burton directed in 1982, reveals numerous cinematic influences on Burton's stylistic and narrative preferences. A comically morbid tale about a boy's obsession with the macabre, the title character's name alludes to the filmmaker's debt to horror star Vincent Prince, who serves as narrator and, years later, plays a featured role in *Edward Scissorhands*. Paying homage to *The House of Wax* (de Toth, 1953) and the Roger Corman's film adaptations of Edgar Allan Poe, *Vincent* channels the B-movies that laid the foundation for his personal aesthetic while invoking the German Expressionist style. The black-and-white photography along with stop-motion animation—that is, the meticulous moving and photographing of objects so as to make them appear animated on film—allow the budding director to play with shadows and light in his composition, while the character's stilted movement creates a figure who is grim, unusual, yet sympathetic. The opening shot features a brick wall and a silhouette of a curved tree, which vaguely resembles the cat that emerges from behind it. This exaggeration of nature echoes the gloomy stylization of German Expressionism, while allowing Burton to fuse in his own humor through the Dr. Seuss-like narration and the haunting repetition of the "The Streets of Cairo" on flute.

The protagonist, Vincent Malloy, seems reminiscent of *The Scream* by painter Edward Munch, an early influence on German Expressionism. With large white eyes and a narrow mouth agape, Vincent's physicality embodies the terror characteristic of the work of his heroes Vincent Price and Edgar Allan Poe and appears to be an early model for Victor Van Dort of *Corpse Bride* (2005). He descends into a nightmarish world, where reality spins, strange creatures wander about, and doors take on a shape more appropriate for funhouse mirrors. Burton manages the light and dark, fueled in part by the dramatic organ music, to capture the tortured existence Vincent has created for himself. Vincent fails to escape and collapses dead, as Price whispers "Nevermore" and the screen fades to black. More spectacular than satirical, *Vincent* nevertheless promises the highly visual worlds Burton will create in his future work: ones populated by freaks and loners, the shallow and the misunderstood.

Though I contend Burton's early films make clear allusions to German Expressionist cinema, it remains clear that its influence on Burton, at least in part, is filtered through the Universal horror films that made the earliest American uses of the style and arguably sanitized its subversive potential for a mass audience. Obviously *Frankenstein*, especially the 1931 adaptation by James Whale, continues to be the most resonant source in Burton's aesthetic, palpable in the 1984 live short film *Frankenweenie* and its 2012 extension into an animated feature as well as the looser adaptation one finds in *Edward Scissorhands*. In the former texts, Burton embraces the Frankenstein narrative not so much as man's wrestling with God (and his attempts to replicate His powers), but as an effort to chronicle and understand a young boy's struggles to cope with the realities of death.

Though not as satirical as Burton's early features, the short film *Frankenweenie* nevertheless captures the narrow-mindedness and capacity for violence of small-town America. The neighbors eventually relent on their aggressive efforts to "banish" Henry and his resurrected dog, but not after one resident shockingly sets fire to the miniature windmill, which serves as sanctuary to the pursued innocents. Echoing the windmill where Frankenstein's monster (allegedly) dies in *Frankenstein*, Burton locates this windmill on a miniature golf course, a symbol of suburban recreation in a supposedly tranquil small town. *Frankenweenie* transfers the setting from an unnamed Germanic village in the nineteenth-century to contemporary suburbia, thereby underscoring the film's subtly critical agenda (later much clearer in films like *Edward Scissorhands*).

Beetlejuice

Though *Beetlejuice* is not based on a screenplay by Burton, the director's second feature film nevertheless continues his obsession with the strange, subversive, and disorderly. Beetlejuice (Michael Keaton) finds himself in limbo between the living, who find him crass, and the dead, who find him untrustworthy. He lives in Adam Maitland's (Alec Baldwin) model of Winter River, Connecticut (the town where the film is set), and Beetlejuice busies himself luring flies, promoting his bio-exorcist services, and flirting crudely with women, including the prostitutes Juno (Sylvia Sidney) plants there to distract him.

With *Beetlejuice*, Burton moves out of the suburbs we see in his previous films and into rural New England, yet his attacks on narrow-mindedness and pretention remain the same. A busybody real estate agent (Annie McEnroe) tries to convince Adam and his wife, Barbara (Geena Davis), to sell their large house because it is too big for a childless couple, enforcing the pervasive American mythos of the nuclear family unit. The greatest target of the film's satirical rage is Delia Deetz (Catherine O'Hara), who reluctantly moves to Connecticut to appease her husband, Charles (Jeffery Jones).

A status seeker and artist of dubious talent, Delia attempts to please the uppity New Yorker types she surrounds herself with: her interior decorator, Otho (Glenn Shadix); her agent, Bernard (Dick Cavett); and Charles's primary backer, Maxie Dean (Robert Goulet). The Maitlands attempts to rid their house of the living people who "haunt" it, and this assault on Charles and Delia, of course, is an assault on Reagan-era yuppies: shallow capitalists who pursue wealth and prestige at the expense of their souls and any sense of sincerity or authenticity. Indeed, the Deetzes—save their daughter, Lydia (Winona Ryder), whose Burtonesque combination of melancholy and grimness wins the Maitlands' affections—make a concerted effort to exploit their spectral roommates to advance their careers and respectability among the urban elite. Such ill-guided pursuits provide Burton with the chance to showcase his love of shadows, the grotesque, and Expressionist set design, as the Maitlands and Beetlejuice bend reality to the alternating delight and terror of their "victims."

In one terrifyingly delightful moment, Beetlejuice transforms his head into a merry-go-round as his arms unfurl to become the huge mallets used for hitting the bells at carnivals, thus dispatching a cheerfully unaware Maxie Dean and wife through the ceiling. This slapstick moment yields to a wedding sequence with Beetlejuice in a tacky maroon tuxedo and his reluctant bride Lydia in a red dress—surely the stuff nightmares. Delia's hideous abstract sculptures come to life, and soon restrain Delia and Charles, making them victims of their own shallow posturing. The hearth transforms into an asymmetrical door frame straight out of German Expressionism, and a small skeletal figure emerges to preside over the ceremony. The exaggerated, even grotesque, décor mirrors the distastefulness of Delia and Charles's pretentious self-presentation, their superficial cross-class performance that desperately yearns for middle class acceptance. Despite Beetlejuice's attempts to prevent interruption, Barbara eventually rides a surreal sand snake through the ceiling, and it consumes Beetlejuice.

This outlandish sequence shows the childlike wonder that preoccupies Burton's directorial style, combining horrific figures with a comical sensibility. Beetlejuice is defeated, but so too are Charles and Delia, who learn to embrace rural life and disavow their blatant commercial ambitions and, symbolically, Reagan-era greed. (This, of course, does not prevent the film from becoming one of Burton's biggest box office successes, at the time.)

Batman *and* Batman Returns

Like his first feature film, *Pee-wee's Big Adventure*, the 1989 movie *Batman* saw Tim Burton returning to characters which were not wholly his own, but rather previously existing popular culture icons. Nevertheless, in *Batman* one finds Tim Burton's distinctive aesthetic at work, drawing in part from the German Expressionism present in his earliest films. While *Edward Scissorhands* offers in-depth character studies set against the backdrop of a conformist suburban culture, *Batman* is lighthearted and rather uncomplicated in terms of its satirical bite. Aside from a brief backstory—Bruce Wayne's parents were murdered in a robbery, and Batman arises to avenge them and all wrongdoing in Gotham—*Batman* offers little character development beyond asserting the goodness of Bruce Wayne (Michael Keaton) and the evilness of Jack Napier (Jack Nicholson).

Bruce Wayne is a wealthy industrialist, an unlikely protagonist for Tim Burton, whose films generally disdain the greed and ambition that seems requisite for the participants of corporate America. Burton compromises for this shortcoming by portraying Bruce Wayne as a Jay Gatsby–type: a reluctant party host who seemingly longs for more, particularly in the form of heterosexual romance. Vicki Vale (Kim Basinger) offers such a possibility, in a character who balances an admirable professional ambition with a consistent need to be saved from the treachery of malevolent males. In short, the ideal for Bruce Wayne: a consummate professional who nevertheless needs the masculine protection he can provide. This fairly conventional love story is the stuff of Hollywood blockbusters, and in this rather attractive pairing the Expressionist influence is nonexistent.

The most immediate evidence of Expressionism comes in the rendering of Gotham itself, a stand-in for New York City that seems to collapse an idealized mid-twentieth century vision of city life into contemporary times. Even the Mayor (Lee Wallace)—a straight-talking, balding, older man with grey hair—bears resemblance to New York's mayor at the time, Ed Koch. The scope of the sets, however, demonstrates a re-creation of an urban landscape on the scale of Fritz Lang's *Metropolis*. The city is populated with soaring statues, like the mirror images of kneeling lever operators in *Batman Returns*, that give the city a cold feeling, emphasizing the mechanical and systematic operations of the city Lang underscores in his film masterpiece. Shadows abound and steam from the street grates is omnipresent, creating an environment that obscures what lies beneath and conjures an air of mystery and malice.

The recent incarnation of Batman under the direction of Christopher Nolan offers a stark contrast to the figure Burton depicts in the initial films in the franchise, revealing the stylistic and thematic differences between the directors. As conservative commentators Andrew Klavan and Ross Douthat have noted,[18] Nolan's Batman (Christian Bale) may be read as a stand-in for

President George W. Bush, who battles villains like the Joker (Heath Ledger), Bane (Tom Hardy), and Miranda (Marion Cotillard) in a veritable War on Terror. Batman's efforts to protect the public are read as vigilantism, a brief plot point in Burton's *Batman Returns* that the resolution quickly redeems. Indeed Burton's films are not (nor do they intend to be) the conservative political allegories some argue Nolan has offered. While *Batman* combined the darkness of Batman comics with the black comedy of Burton, the sheer unease Jack Nicholson's performance may have inspired in the late 1980s now reads as almost camp compared to the trenchant cynicism of *The Dark Knight* (Nolan, 2008) and *The Dark Knight Rises* (Nolan, 2012).

The villains of Batman are perhaps the clearest narrative indication of Expressionist influence. The Joker's disfigured grin recalls the eerie smile of Gwynplaine (Conrad Veidt), the protagonist of Paul Leni's 1928 Expressionist masterpiece, *The Man Who Laughs*. (Veidt also portrayed Cesare, the somnambulist in *The Cabinet of Dr. Caligari*). When the Joker terrorizes an art museum, he noticeably prevents one of his goons from defacing Francis Bacon's painting, *Figure with Meat*. A gruesome re-interpretation of Diego Velázquez's portrait of Innocent X, the painting echoes Expressionistic conventions, though Bacon himself was not an Expressionist. Finally Oswald Cobblepot (Danny DeVito), also known as The Penguin, sneers his blackened teeth, flirts shamelessly with women, and consumes raw fish. J. P. Telotte notes that Expressionist characters "mov[e] in a stilted and eerily unnatural fashion"[19]; Cobblepot's menacing waddle and grotesque appearance seemingly conflates the striking figures of Count Orlok and Dr. Caligari. Perhaps most notably, the name of the menacing industrialist of *Batman Returns*—Max Schreck (Christopher Walken)—reveals the film's debt to German Expressionist cinema. Not only was Max Schreck the star of F. W. Murnau's *Nosferatu*, but the word "schreck" resembles the German word for means "horror," *Schrecken*. And the "shock" of Schreck physically manifests itself in his shock of white hair, rendering him both unusual and sinister.

Batman Returns may, in fact, be a revision of the relative silliness of *Batman*. While the first film offers a visual (and comic) delight, the second film is more damning in its discussion of corporate greed and more nuanced in its examination of monstrosity. Cobblepot suggests that he and Schreck are monsters, but his monstrosity is physical while Schreck's is behavioral. Cobblepot's struggles against a society that privileges the so-called able-bodied and Selina Kyle (Michelle Pfeiffer) as Catwoman's attempts to counter the macho sexism of Schreck, Cobblepot and even Wayne underscore the ideological oppressions that marginalize populations of American society in their efforts to maintain a society that actively marginalizes women and individuals with disabilities.

Perhaps counterproductively, the film seems to reduce Catwoman to a sexual object—donning a skintight vinyl suit with stitching a la Frankenstein's monster—even as she attempts to use her sex appeal to both resist her demoralization at work and empower herself against male aggression, sexually and physically. In this manner, *Batman Returns* allows Burton to subvert exceptionalist notions of equality regarding gender or physical ability. Alienated from society, much like Frankenstein's monster, these characters violently react; though their resistance takes an unacceptable form, it is not unprovoked, allowing Burton to deconstruct the clear good versus evil binary he established in *Batman*. In the process, Burton illustrates the hypocritical tendency of American society to depend on the othering of minority groups while simultaneously laying claim to ideals of life, liberty, and the pursuit of happiness.

Edward Scissorhands

Admittedly, *Edward Scissorhands* appears in 1990 between Tim Burton's blockbuster Batman films, but it was the first project that seems to recapture the visionary work in his short films. *Pee-wee's Big Adventure* was obviously based on the character Paul Reubens created and performed, *Beetlejuice* was the creation of screenwriters Michael McDowell and Warren Skaaren, but *Edward Scissorhands* was his first feature film story he received screen credit for. Watching *Edward Scissorhands* nearly twenty years later, it may be his purest film and his masterpiece; undoubtedly, it is the film that beautifully encapsulates the Burton aesthetic, combining various strains we have seen throughout his early work: a protagonist who is a misunderstood outsider living in a narrow-minded community, a childlike fascination with the strange and the grotesque, a tongue-in-cheek humor that wavers between ironic and campy, an embrace of Gothic conventions and German Expressionist style. Like *Frankenweenie*, *Edward Scissorhands* revises and updates *Frankenstein*, but the modern period Burton transports the film to appears to be both 1960s and 1980s simultaneously. For Russell A. Potter, such an effort testifies to the film's postmodern aesthetic: "In the commodity-fetishism of Burton's suburbs, chronology is deliberately scrambled, such that commodities, like the clip-art cutouts of postmodern collages, drift about in their own free play of signification."[20] Potter's reading potentially dislodges the film from its historical context and renders it apolitical. Yet I would argue that the collapse of time in Burton may attest to the fact that the tranquilizing conformity of the postwar years returned under Reagan—at least a nostalgia to reconstruct such a non-existent past did.

Of course the film also reconstructs Burton's past, and the influence of German Expressionist horror films and the Universal films they influenced is substantial. The blunt contrast between the pastel-colored "little boxes" that populate the neighbor and the dark Gothic castle on the hill emphasize the otherness of Edward and his life. He was invented, and his creation echoes Dr. Frankenstein's creation of the Monster. While Frankenstein rejects his creation, Edward's creator (Vincent Prince) loves him, though he dies before he can give Edward human-like hands, leaving Edward with the titular scissorhands. With his pale skin, shock of black hair, and garb of black leather and chains, Edward resembles not only his real-life creator Tim Burton, but also the somnambulist Cesare from *The Cabinet of Dr. Caligari*.

Burton revises this narrative, of course: while Dr. Caligari manipulates Cesare into becoming a homicidal maniac who terrorizes the village, Edward is a benign soul who first invokes fear, then fascination, and finally anger. This response cycle to Edward reveals how the idyllic suburban life nevertheless harbors hatred and stupidity, and Edward's innocuous efforts to help are quickly exploited by self-interested residents, each of whom is determined to outdo the other. Joyce (Kathy Baker), who finds validation in a string of extramarital flirtations, attempts to seduce Edward, much to his confusion and her embarrassment. Indeed, the "monstrous" Edward becomes a screen unto which the petty suburbanites project their desires, suspicions, and curiosities; in the process, the befuddled Edward feels homeless. This sharp condemnation the banality of small town life speaks to Burton's upbringing in Burbank, California—a self-described "pit of hell"[21]—and the relative prosperity of America in the late 1980s. Turning to the oppositional potential offered by German Expressionism, Burton stunningly captures it through his interplay of darkness and light, perhaps best scene as Kim (Winona Ryder) twirls in the "snow" generated by Edward's ice sculpting. These disparities are again ably illustrated in the final scene in the castle, where Edward, left in the shadows, creates the snow that falls on the elderly Kim's home. His efforts reveal his ongoing affection for her, and his bittersweet efforts to recapture the serenity of the night she danced for him. Love, romantic or platonic, becomes the only means of redemption for his dark outsiders, since assimilation into society is not possible, nor even desirable in Burton's realities.

The true individualist, Edward, like Huck Finn before him, must retreat from society in order to achieve any form of salvageable happiness. Burton poignantly celebrates this selfless decision, while lambasting the society that both celebrates the individual, yet ultimately makes his exile an existential necessity. Therein Burton illustrates a key paradox to the conservative vision of individualism: a cultural which demands conformity by normative standards nevertheless claims to celebrate outliers, rebels, and iconoclasts who take a bold stance. In reality, this bold stance cannot threaten the status quo, who maintain power through a manipulation of the masses, rather than a physical and political separation from them.

Conclusion

The legacy of German Expressionism endures throughout Burton's more recent work, from the shadowy world of *Ed Wood* (1994) to the embellished set designs of his literary adaptations, including *Sleepy Hollow* (1999), *Charlie and the Chocolate Factory* (2005), and *Alice in Wonderland* (2010). Certainly the synergy of the macabre and the comic continues to be his primary mode of storytelling. Yet, as Burton develops and the United States seemingly moved beyond the staunch conservatism and false opulence of the 1980s, the political urgency of his work seems to have diminished. Only *Corpse Bride* (2005) was a wholly original feature film, while the bulk of his productions have been adaptations of novels, a trading card series, a television series, and a musical. Burton seems to have transitioned more into a Jamesonian vision of pastiche, perhaps a reflection of his unapologetic embrace of a commercial aesthetic or a larger cultural shift away from the naïve exceptionalist narrative of Reagan-era conservatism. Whether this move, certainly an understandable one in contemporary conglomerate Hollywood, pays homage to the influence of German Expressionism or debases its initial subversive intentions is a matter of person opinion. It goes without saying, however, that Burton's work, in a postmodern period characterized by remakes and recycling, continues to imprint his distinctive, eclectic style on these often-told tales of the past. Perhaps that remains the most productive and practical option for the auteur at the dawn of the twenty-first century, where the Shining City on the Hill appears as a distant illusion.

Notes

1. Quoted in Michael Reagan and Jim Denney, *The City on a Hill: Fulfilling Ronald Reagan's Vision for America* (Nashville: Thomas Nelson Publishers, 1997), 5.
2. Deborah L. Madsen, *American Exceptionalism* (Jackson: University Press of Mississippi, 1998), 37–38.
3. Susan Jeffords, *The Remasculinization of America: Gender and the Vietnam War* (Bloomington: Indiana University Press, 1989), and William V. Spanos, *American Exceptionalism in the Age of Globalization* (Albany: SUNY Press, 2009).
4. Although not discussed in this essay due to space constraints, Burton's first feature

film, *Pee-wee's Big Adventure*, does feature some German Expressionist techniques, particularly in the nightmare sequence. I do not, however, believe it is substantive enough to warrant extended consideration compared to Burton's more representative gothic work.

    5. Aurélien Ferenczi, *Tim Burton*, Trista Selous, trans. (Paris: Cahiers du cinéma Sarl, 2010), 12.
    6. Fredric Jameson, *Postmodernism, or, The Logic of Late Capitalism* (Durham, N.C.: Duke University Press, 1991), 17.
    7. J. P. Telotte, "German Expressionism: A Cinematic/Cultural Problem," in *Traditions in World Cinema*, edited by Linda Badley, R. Barton Palmer, and Steven Jay Schneider (New Brunswick, N.J.: Rutgers University Press, 2006
    8. Thomas Elsaesser, *Weimar Cinema and After: Germany's Historical Imaginary* (New York: Routledge, 2000), 18.
    9. Siegfried Kracauer, *From Caligari to Hitler: A Psychological History of the German Film* (Princeton: Princeton University Press, 2004), 3.
    10. Ibid., 3.
    11. John D. Barlow, *German Expressionist Film* (Boston: Twayne, 1982), 19.
    12. Kracauer, 68.
    13. Telotte, 16.
    14. Frances Guerin, *A Culture of Light: Cinema and Technology in 1920s Germany* (Minneapolis: University of Minnesota Press, 2005), 13.
    15. Barlow, 179–186 and 198–204.
    16. The lingering influence of German Expressionism can also be found in films like *Blade Runner* (Scott, 1982) and *The Crow* (Proyas, 1994), as well as the work of David Cronenberg and Christopher Nolan.
    17. It is worth noting that while German Expressionism lingers in Burton's more recent work, especially *Sweeney Todd* (2007), the satirical bite seems to have softened. Perhaps that is a reflection of his career's trajectory or the sociopolitical climate; regardless, it is beyond the scope of this essay, which examines the early work in its historical milieu.
    18. Consult Andrew Klavan, "What Bush and Batman Have in Common," *Wall Street Journal*, July 25, 2008 and Ross Douthat, "The Politics of *The Dark Knight Rises*," *The New York Times*, July 23, 2012.
    19. Telotte, 17.
    20. Russell A. Potter, "Edward Schizohands: The Postmodern Gothic Body," *Postmodern Culture* 2, no. 3 (1992), par. 22.
    21. Tim Burton, qtd. in Kristian Fraga, "Introduction," in *Tim Burton: Interviews* (Jackson: University of Mississippi Press, 2005), x.

Bibliography

Barlow, John D. *German Expressionist Film*. Boston: Twayne, 1982.
Douthat, Ross. "The Politics of *The Dark Knight Rises*." *The New York Times*. July 23. 2012.
Elsaesser, Thomas. *Weimar Cinema and After: Germany's Historical Imaginary*. New York: Routledge, 2000.
Ferenczi, Aurélien. *Tim Burton*. Trista Selous, trans. Paris: Cahiers du cinéma Sarl, 2010.
Fraga, Kristian. "Introduction," in *Tim Burton: Interviews*. Kristian Fraga, ed. Jackson: University of Mississippi Press, 2005: vii–xxii.
Guerin, Frances. *A Culture of Light: Cinema and Technology in 1920s Germany*. Minneapolis: University of Minnesota Press, 2005.

Jameson, Fredric. *Postmodernism, or The Logic of Late Capitalism*. Durham. N.C.: Duke University Press, 1991.

Klavan, Andrew. "What Bush and Batman Have in Common," *Wall Street Journal*. July 25. 2008.

Kracauer, Siegfried. *From Caligari to Hitler: A Psychological History of the German Film*. Princeton: Princeton University Press. 2004.

Madsen, Deborah L. *American Exceptionalism*. Jackson: University Press of Mississippi. 1998.

Potter, Russell A. "Edward Schizohands: The Postmodern Gothic Body." *Postmodern Culture* 2. no. 3 1992: 30.

Reagan, Michael, and Jim Denney. *The City on a Hill: Fulfilling Ronald Reagan's Vision for America*. Nashville: Thomas Nelson Publishers, 1997.

Spanos, William V. *American Exceptionalism in the Age of Globalization* Albany. SUNY Press, 2009.

Telotte, J. P. "German Expressionism: A Cinematic/Cultural Problem," in *Traditions in World Cinema*. Linda Badley, R. Barton Palmer, and Steven Jay Schneider, eds. New Brunswick, NJ: Rutgers University Press, 2006: 15–28.

"I'm Not Finished"
Gender Transgression and Star Persona in Edward Scissorhands

Deborah Mellamphy

In the 200th episode of *South Park*, which first aired in the U.S. on April 14th 2010, the show's creators Trey Parker and Matt Stone acknowledge and parody the close working relationship of Tim Burton and Johnny Depp. In an episode that sets out to poke fun at a large number of celebrities, Tom Cruise's character asks Burton why he casts Depp in "all" of his films and asks "if you're that in love with Johnny Depp, you should just have sex with him already."[1]

Over the past 22 years, the collaborations of Tim Burton and Johnny Depp have produced some key cinematic images and have addressed some fundamental theoretical issues. Their collaborations *Edward Scissorhands* (1990), *Ed Wood* (1994), *Sleepy Hollow* (1999), *Tim Burton's Corpse Bride* (2005), *Charlie and the Chocolate Factory* (2005), *Sweeney Todd: The Demon Barber of Fleet Street* (2007), *Alice in Wonderland* (2010) and *Dark Shadows* (2012) were largely critical and box office successes, contributing to the immense stardom that Burton and Depp have both achieved. While most studies of the two individuals have briefly alluded to their collaborations,[2] no critical study exists that focuses exclusively on the closely connected issues of gender and star theory that are central to their collaboration. Depp is fascinating within a Hollywood context due to the physical and gender ambiguity of his characters and star image.

In this essay I will comment on how Burton collaborates with Depp to reference, subvert and parody the star's persona in an over-stated hyperbolic performance through images of transgressive gender in the interest of producing a comedic act, which also reveals the actor's self-aware subversion of established gender imagery. In this task, I will examine their first collaboration *Edward Scissorhands* due to its destabilization of gender norms. The casting of Depp introduces an important arena of intertextuality into the film, as his star persona exposes some interesting dynamics for a contemporary audience cognizant of star types. I will do this through a reading of the text that makes visible the complexities inherent in the operation of dominant gender ideology and I will analyze the extent to which the narrative, Depp's performance and *mise-en-scène* explore gender ambiguity. In doing so, I will also examine how the male body is socially and visually constructed and approach questions of cinematic pleasure in current theoretical discourse and how these might pertain to *Edward Scissorhands*. Such a reading opposes the approach of critics such as Mark Salisbury, Kristian Fraga and Roger Ebert[3] who have considered the Burton/Depp collaborations as highly commercial films that reinforce dominant cultural ideas and images.

Masculinity in the 1990s

As many have argued, the beginning of the 1990s marked a change in the way masculinity was portrayed onscreen in American culture, as male actors and their characters became more fragile in comparison to the muscular performances of the 1980s, a development that seems linked to changing social attitudes towards masculinity and gender difference.[4] These changes have been discussed in scholarly works including *Screening the Male* (1993), *Male Trouble* (1993) and *Acting Male: Masculinities in the Films of James Stewart, Jack Nicholson, and Clint Eastwood* (1994) and such works have shown that the male image on the cinema screen is as significant historically and as complex, and multiple, as the female. Such work uses existing feminist and psychoanalytical cinematic thought to reinvent cinematic discourse and challenge inherent ideological systems by focusing on examining the representations of problematic and often paradoxical masculinity, the eroticized male image and "hard" and "soft" images of masculinity; hard in their strong, muscular bodies but soft in their emotional vulnerability and "effeminateness." Cohan and Hark write in the introduction to *Screening the Male* that:

> film theory has for the most part confidently equated the masculinity of the male subject with activity, voyeurism, sadism, fetishism, the story, and the femininity of the female subject with passivity, exhibitionism, masochism, narcissism, and spectacle. In this scheme of the homologous differences of power, stability, and wholeness of masculine subjectivity at the expense of femininity seem all too axiomatic and, thus, universal and uncontestable.[5]

Cohan and Hark argue that contrary to being universal, masculinity in cinema often incorporates many of the characteristics traditionally associated with femininity and vice versa. In addition, Judith Butler argues that both masculinity and femininity are socially constructed identities. Butler's theory builds on the work of Joan Riviere,[6] who considered femininity as a culturally necessitated masquerade. Since the publication of Butler's theory, there has been more consideration of how masculinity can also be linked to performance. Masculinity has been exposed as multi-layered and can be considered as a constructed masquerade, a mask that can be put on, and taken off, so that both masculinity and femininity are no longer established biological facts but are now social and cultural performances open to transgression. This revision of the masculine persona has deconstructed "masculinity" and revealed man's acknowledgement of his repressed femininity. As Dennis Bingham has argued in *Acting Male: Masculinities in the Films of James Stewart, Jack Nicholson and Clint Eastwood*, masculine domination represents not biological nature but artifice and it is becoming more difficult for men to convince themselves and others of their indestructibility, demonstrating the fragility of patriarchal gender constructions.[7]

In addition, several critics, including Steve Neale have illustrated that the male body can become the object of fetishistic scopophilia and can be passive, allowing others to gaze at his image.[8] Neale, drawing on D.N. Rodowick,[9] emphasizes the denial of the eroticism of the male body through onscreen instances of combat such as the gun battle or the fight. Through such strategies, the filmmaker makes onscreen male characters subjects of the voyeuristic gaze, for both the audience spectator and other male characters, which represses homosexual desire. In these instances, male activity becomes pure spectacle and the narrative temporarily freezes to recognize the pleasure of the exhibition of the male body. Neale argues that, "We are offered the spectacle of male bodies, but bodies unmarked as objects of erotic display."[10] Yet, in addition, Neale discusses several of Douglas Sirk's melodramas from the 1950s, including *All That Heaven Allows* (1955) and *Written on the Wind* (1956), in which Rock Hudson is clearly marked as the object of the erotic look in (diegetically) scenes that display his body and, implicitly, feminize him, thus acknowledging the fetishization of the male body.

Depp is fascinating within this theoretical context due to the physical and gender ambiguity of his characters and star persona. Depp began his career in the 1980s, an era full of contradictions in terms of images of masculinity. This was a decade that has been most noted by Yvonne Tasker and Susan Jeffords for its use of hyper-masculine images and themes. Stars such as Arnold Schwarzenegger, Sylvester Stallone, Bruce Willis and Jean-Claude Van Damme became popular in the decade. Tasker and Jeffords link these images of muscular masculinity with the rise of neo-conservativism under the Reagan and Bush administrations, at which time these tough male bodies became nationalist symbols.[11] Alternatively the 1980s was also a decade of rebellion linked with youth culture in the form of the Brat Pack. In films such as *The Breakfast Club* (1985), *St. Elmo's Fire* (1985) and *Pretty in Pink* (1986). Members of the Brat Pack such as Rob Lowe, Andrew McCarthy, Emilio Estevez, Matt Dillon and Robert Downey, Jr., were constructed as rebellious male pin-ups who offered an alternative and more vulnerable youthful form of masculinity.[12]

This more vulnerable image of masculinity became most significant during the 1990s as the Queer Movement opened up a space for multiple masculinities and resulted in less macho and muscular images of masculinity becoming acceptable in Hollywood. Stars including River Phoenix, Leonardo DiCaprio and Keanu Reeves, as well as Depp, became the sex symbols of the decade and represented a new type of sexual fluidity. Jess Cagle notes that "androgyny chic has ushered in a new brand of movie star: Johnny Depp, Leonardo DiCaprio, and Keanu Reeves would all once have been sissies."[13] Drawing on Neale's theories, Depp's body can be read as similarly eroticized and the focus of fetishistic scopophilia in several of his films, including *Edward Scissorhands*. This essay wishes to explore the undoing of established gender norms and to read, with consideration of a reopened dialectics, the contemporary performativity of gender that is exposed in onscreen representations of gender transgression in *Edward Scissorhands*.

Within the Hollywood star system, Depp belongs to the tradition of the male star who embodies a version of masculinity that is accommodating in its vulnerability and gentleness rather than being overly imposing and aggressive.[14] He began his career in the 1980s with roles that depicted him as a sex symbol and a male pin-up, such as in *A Nightmare on Elm Street* (1984) and in the television series *21 Jump Street*, the latter of which he starred in from 1987 to 1990. It was an image he was unhappy with and one that he attempted to discard through more transgressive and gender subversive performances. His most ambiguous role before *Edward Scissorhands* was in John Waters' *Cry-Baby* (1990), a musical that depicted Depp as the quintessential "song and dance man" a highly feminized image of masculinity.[15] Indeed, his performance in this film profoundly marked him out as spectacle, signifying a feminine element to his performances and persona, a trend that his later performances, particularly within Burton's films, rely on. I argue that Depp has built his persona on the tropes stereotypically considered "feminine" including exhibitionism, narcissism and masquerade, thus making his performances highly camp, theatricalized, and ambiguous in regards to representations of onscreen masculinity. Each of Burton's films helped to establish this persona and subsequently became custom-made star vehicles to sustain this star image.

Defining Awkwardness: Ambivalence in Edward Scissorhands

Based on an image reportedly originally conceptualized by Burton as a teenager,[16] *Edward Scissorhands* is the first collaboration between Burton and Depp that features a character that defies the notion of a stable gender or social identity, as well as confusing modes of spectatorship, desire and identification. Burton and Depp have revealed that they initially decided to work together as both claim to have identified with the awkward character of Edward Scissorhands. Burton explains that the image:

> was linked to a character who wants to touch but can't, who was both creative and destructive—those sort of contradictions can create a kind of ambivalence.... I just felt I couldn't communicate. It was the feeling that your image and how people perceive you are at odds with what is inside you.[17]

This is a theme that has pervaded their work together and stems from Burton's reported awkwardness growing up and Depp's rejection of his image as teen heartthrob. As Edward Scissorhands, Depp firmly establishes his star persona as one associated with ambiguity and contradictions.

As Edward Scissorhands, Depp plays a supremely vulnerable character who subversively undercuts aspects of traditional masculinity and Depp's image reveals androgyny as a subversive image. In his behavior the most radical way that Edward is stereotypically feminized is in his embodiment of physical and emotional feminine weakness and vulnerability. Depp's character is portrayed as an emotionally and psychologically vulnerable character in this society, signified by his obvious discomfort and passiveness as a result of his outsider status. His body language is extremely uncomfortable; this is signified by his ineptness with his hands and body as he keeps nicking his own face, has difficulty eating and putting on clothes. He also frequently walks into objects and furniture, seeming nervous and apprehensive. His vulnerability is further signified by his submission to other characters[18]; he becomes an easily manipulated utensil in the Boggs home and performs menial household tasks such as cutting hedges, opening cans and chopping vegetables. He is also easily led to perform acts that he knows are wrong, as when he breaks into Jim's house. He later reveals that he did it simply because Kim asked him to, illustrating his submission to her. His ultimate show of vulnerability occurs at the end of the film when he banishes himself from society, instead of attempting to assimilate, a choice that could be read as a masochistic, self-punishing act. In these displays, *Edward Scissorhands* demonstrates formal and narrative patterns structurally linked with self-abasement. Edward/Depp is thus placed in the passive, feminine position in his submission to the wishes of both male and female characters, thus subverting the gender-defined, socially assigned positions of masculine/feminine and power/powerlessness.

A further significant element of Depp's performance that signifies his submissiveness is his appearance as an infantile character, one that often relies on others to care for him. For example, Peg dresses him and tucks him into bed at the beginning of the film, while several women feed him at the neighborhood barbeque. Gaylyn Studlar argues that masochism and the willingness of either male or female characters to confer power to others involves a governing infantile scenario.[19] Studlar postulates that in the pre–Oedipal period of development, the mother is the object of the child's fantasized introjection, on which the child depends, creating a "dual unity and complete symbiosis between child and mother."[20] In the infantile stage of dependence, pleasure involves submission to the mother's body and gaze.[21] By relying on others, chiefly Peg who resembles a maternal imago figure, Edward is placed in a culturally feminine position, disavowing phallic power and defying the values of patriarchal society. He seems to exist in a pre–Oedipal stage of development, embodying "feminine" masochism and offering subversive possibilities of pleasure in Hollywood cinema, posing a threat to prevalent norms of how masculine stars are portrayed onscreen.

Edward's voice is another important element of his ambivalence, as it is soft, falsetto and is stereotypically feminine and passive, even child-like, as opposed to the deep commanding voice associated with masculine actors such as Humphrey Bogart and Spencer Tracey. Edward remains largely silent throughout the film and his dialogue when it is used is minimal and functional, comprised of short sentences and often single words. For centuries, silence has been a feminine ideal, laid down by patriarchal Christian tradition in the last decades of the Seventeenth century.[22] This tradition considered the virtues of silence, with its connotations of obedience and submission as essentially feminine. As a result, the silent woman became an accepted ideal, while it was understood that men were to be anything but silent in order to control others and to be subjective.[23]

Edward Scissorhands is also portrayed as being physically weak, as the tightness of his suit highlights the thinness of Depp's body and his lack of musculature, a visual signifier that Richard Dyer links with the effeminate male and hence feminine body. In his study of the male pin-up, Dyer observes that "muscularity is the *sign* of power-natural, achieved, phallic."[24] His lack of muscles marks Depp's body as an ambiguous site that does not conform to that of the domineering male. His face is also ambiguous as it is completely void of hair and his complexion is extremely pale, indicating his visible vulnerability and frail character, suggesting feminization. Indeed, the association between whiteness and femininity is long rooted in visual culture. In the Renaissance paintings of Sandro Botticelli such as *The Birth of Venus* (c. 1485) and *Young Woman in Mythological Guise* (c. 1480/1485), the ideal image of Renaissance female beauty is depicted as possessing pearly white skin. Early Renaissance Christianity believed a woman's outward appearance and inner soul were inextricably linked and that white skin demonstrates a virtuous character.

This association of pale skin and effeminateness and vulnerability is very strongly recognized in Victorian and Gothic literature, most notably in Emily Bronte's *Wuthering Heights* (1847). The character of Linton Heathcliff is contrasted with the dark-skinned Heathcliff, the latter the personification of subjective and authoritative masculinity in the novel. Conversely, Linton is described as a "pale, delicate, effeminate boy"[25] and a "whey-faced whining wretch,"[26] thus equating him with the other female characters who are also described as pale and unhealthy. Linton's sickly appearance is what makes him effeminate and his character perfectly exposes the Victorian ideal of dark, healthy masculinity versus pale, delicate femininity, as the epitome of male beauty was tanned skin, as seen in Bronzino's *Portrait of a Young Man* (c. 1517/1518). This dichotomy is also apparent in cinematic depictions of the sexes, with the "whiteness" represented by pale female skin and blonde hair being the apotheosis of male desirability. One need only examine the images of Lillian Gish and Marilyn Monroe to realize how Hollywood codes of glamour lighting were developed in relation to white women to emphasize their whiteness. Back lighting and soft-lighting were reserved for female characters to make them appear innocent, almost angelic and translucent, thus fetishizing their bodies. By turning Depp's naturally dark skin pale, Burton has consciously made him look sickly and has related him to representations of onscreen femininity and the effeminate male, thus contributing to literal and metaphorical passivity, also coded as feminine. In addition, in the final scene shared by Depp and Ryder's characters it is clearly Depp that is lit with soft lighting, while Ryder is largely in shadow. Depp's face is lit with bright light, resembling the lighting used to portray the vulnerability of the bodies and faces of female images.[27]

It cannot be denied that Depp's character can be read as an androgyne.

Stella Bruzzi states that sex, gender and sexuality are in the foreground regarding the representation of the androgyne. Bruzzi argues that,

> the most refined form of sexual attractiveness (as well as the most refined form of sexual pleasure) consists in going against the grain of one's sex. What is most beautiful in virile men is something feminine; what is most beautiful in feminine women is something masculine.[28]

Bruzzi here suggests that the androgyne renders gender boundaries fluid, arguing that the figure defies the notion of a stable gender or social identity, thus subverting established culturally approved modes of normative gender identity. She also contends that cinematic representations of androgyny can signify a highly erotic and desirable figure that appeals to both sexes and is eroticized due to his/her ambiguity, allowing the figure to transgress a stereotypical understanding of the male/active, female/passive dichotomy regarding cinematic spectatorship: "On the androgynous body is enacted ambiguity, the diminution of difference, and what is manifested is a softening of the contours-between corporality and metaphor, male and female, straight and gay."[29] As a result, Bruzzi suggests that figures of ambiguous gender enable multiple patterns of desire and modes of spectatorship both diegetically and extra-diegetically.[30] The androgyne becomes a mysterious and elusive figure, able to transgress boundaries and occupy the murky middle ground or unknown space between the categories of male and female, thus signifying an alluring defiance against gender norms.

Edward Scissorhands is undoubtedly the primary spectacle in the film: he draws all eyes, male and female and onscreen and off, towards his body largely because his black costume and pale appearance makes him a vivid contrast to the monochrome and pastel colors of the neighborhood and the bright colors worn by the suburban women, allowing him to defy the conventions of his society. In several scenes in the film, Edward/Depp looks in the mirror, providing a double image of himself. In one instance he looks at his reflection in Kim's room and the mirror is itself framed by magazine cuttings of eyes and faces, resembling the gaze of an audience. Edward is in a sense making himself the focus of an audience of eyes, while also looking at his own reflection in the mirror. Later in the film when Kim enters her bedroom and looks in the mirror, her reflection of her own image is disrupted by the reflection of Edward in her bed, signifying his location as central spectacle of the scene and narrative.[31] He is further made spectacle within the diegesis by becoming a local celebrity and by the fact that reporters and television cameras follow him after he has been released from prison. In many scenes, his costume exceeds its function and becomes an entity to be looked at. Edward usually simply nods or shakes his head, using his body, which the audience and other characters must watch closely to deduce his feelings. With silent characters more attention must undoubtedly be paid to their bodies in order to interpret their images and reactions. He is consciously specularized through the composition of the film, as he is regularly framed by windows, doors and arches both in suburbia and in the creator's castle to further draw the filmgoer's eye to his presence onscreen. Such framing also represents the character's entrapment within the perceived monotony of suburban life and his gender otherness within such a society.

Discussing the vulnerable male onscreen, Michael DeAngelis argues that James Dean's alienation is emphasized by his confinement to the edges of the CinemaScope frame and in his placement in the extreme foreground of deep focus compositions, which places him in a different visual plane to other characters, signifying his difference.[32] In contrast to this, Depp's character is constantly positioned in the center of the screen while both sides of him are symmetrically identical, literally positioning him onscreen as the compositional center of attention, suggesting that his body can be the focus of fetishistic scopophilia. This occurs throughout the film, as when Edward is walking down the corridors of the Boggs' home, is sitting at the dinner table, is being seduced by Joyce and is being held at the police station. This composition allows the audience to focus on his image completely. The numerous close-ups of Edward/Depp's face also allow him to become spectacle, as they highlight the softness, delicateness and beauty of his face. Depp is shot in a much tighter frame than any other character and this intensifies his constructed image that is somewhat removed from the normal rules of continuity shooting. These extreme close-ups usually allow for audience identification with the character, as "the audience is drawn into an empathetic attachment with the character's situation."[33] They stereotypically connote intimacy with the character and allow access to his subconscious, thus heightening the character's vulnerability and allowing the audience to empathize and to sympathize with a character who resembles a stereotypical repulsive horror monster. Thus, Edward's appearance as a "freak" intersects with his gender transgression, thus forcing the audience to question social and cultural norms.

Edward/Depp's body is fetishized as a result of being the primary spectacle. Masochism's passivity is associated with becoming the object of the active (or sadistic) look. In this manner, Edward Scissorhands becomes the object of fetishistic scopophilia, reversing Mulvey's outdated theory and signifying the male's "to-be-looked-at-ness,"[34] illustrating that the male star can be fetishized by both male and female and heterosexual and homosexual audiences. There is no doubt that Edward/Depp is coded as a sexual "fetishized" object. His black suit is central to this argument as it functions not only to disguise his physical sex but also to turn him into a fetishized spectacle.

Leather and PVC are commonly fetishized items by both heterosexual and homosexual society, thereby adding a sexual and erotic element to Edward's androgynous appearance. The desire for Edward within the diegesis is clear, as the women yearn for him sexually, especially and most prolifically Joyce, who attempts to seduce him. Joyce's desire for Edward is apparent in the scene when Edward cuts and styles her hair. Being touched by the androgynous figure is the "single most thrilling experience" of Joyce's life, signifying that these characters recognize the eroticism of the androgyne. This female yearning also demonstrates the power of the female gaze, illustrating that it does possess the power of action. This desire and his fetishization culminates in the scene when he is the subject of a television talk show. He is the spectacle of the studio, television and cinematic audiences, which are made up of male and female spectators in all three arenas and he is the focus of curious desire. It is a female studio audience member that asks if he has a girlfriend and the male host then reiterates the question, probing him for an answer. Therefore all audiences, including the television host recognize that he is a sexually erotic and alluring character.

The fetishization of Depp's body assumes forms of theatricality that subvert the mechanisms of cinematic voyeurism and identification. Edward mimics and participates in both the masculine and feminine activities that he observes without gendered or sexist judgment. In an early scene, he mirrors the movements of Bill Boggs, the father figure, as he cuts a hedge and in a later scene Edward participates in a barbeque that has been organized by Bill. Yet at other times in the film, Edward mimics and becomes involved in stereotypically female activities and activities incited by female characters such as dog grooming and hairdressing. He performs these tasks as easily as he performs male activities and without gender consciousness. These ambiguities subvert patriarchal power relations and heterosexual norms, illustrating that desire is mobile and transgresses identities, positions and roles, significant here due to the mainstream appeal of the film. They also demonstrate that male or female characters or stars can occupy either side of these relationships and that they are not determined by biological sex or gender. This suggests the socially constructed nature of the patriarchal idea of the masculine/feminine, sadistic/masochistic model and demonstrates that all of these are performances. This transgression and relationship of power can reflect the complexity of man's (and woman's) existence in patriarchal society. These transgressions of the masculine/feminine dichotomy, as well as the cinematic techniques that were established to uphold stereotypical representations of both sexes, illustrate the fluidity of gender boundaries, roles and representations, demonstrating their existence as social constructs and thus supporting Judith Butler's theory of all gender as performance.

Depp as Hollywood Star

The study of the stardom of Depp and how Burton portrays him reveals the significant tensions that dominate contemporary notions of the star in Hollywood. This essay has suggested that we should rethink our preconceptions about contemporary stardom. I do not presume that Depp presents the only possible formulation of movie masculinity in Hollywood today, but his immense fame and box-office draw do make him a significant example of contemporary Hollywood stardom. In addition, his particular display of both masculine and feminine traits and his "effeminate" appearance make him a significant example of transgressive gender display in Hollywood. Although masculinity has not been neglected as a social discourse, particularly since the 1990s, I have illustrated through an examination of Depp's masculinity, Hollywood's ongoing problems in its construction of gender. This is not only applicable to his characters but also to Depp's star persona, which gives concrete expression to the paradox and ambivalence of a gender representation that is unfixed, unstable and that relies on transgression. Depp is defined by his ambiguities, by multiple and conflicting possibilities of identity that persistently exist in a state of tension that can never be resolved. He is a star who can be considered effeminized but who is also posited in the dominant position as "leading man," demonstrated most clearly in the *Pirates of the Caribbean* films. Depp's difference from his contemporaries including Tom Cruise, Brad Pitt, and Robert Downey, Jr., in films including the *Mission: Impossible* franchise (1996, 2000, 2006, 2011), *Fight Club* (1999), and the *Iron Man* films (2008, 2010, 2013) respectively, demonstrates how his persona is not linked with the stereotypical male action star.

My analysis has suggested that it is possible for a male character, and star, to be placed within the vulnerable, masochistic position, as well as occupying the governing active position; a position that brings with it the potential for subversive commentary. Although largely known for his small "quirky" independent roles, when Depp does star in mainstream box office films, such as Burton's, this "quirkiness" is increasingly incorporated. I argue that his performances as Captain Jack Sparrow in the *Pirates of the Caribbean* films borrow heavily from his performances that embody gender fluidity in Burton's films and the ambiguous star persona that was created alongside such performances. He strategically constructs a variety of positions of spectatorial access to his star persona: his existence as a "sex symbol" acknowledges the existence of both heterosexual and homoerotic gazes.[35] Tellingly, the success and popularity of his persona shows the importance and appeal of this type of transgressive cultural and media construction within contemporary society, while also unveiling the tensions surrounding current images of masculinity in culture.

The collaborations between Burton and Depp seem keen on making Depp less attractive and more "weird." Depp has played many conventionally "sexy" characters throughout this career, including Don Juan in *Don Juan DeMarco* (1995), Roux in *Chocolat* (2000), and Cesar in *The Man Who Cried* (2001), that encouraged his sex symbol image but the primary function of Depp's performances in Burton's films in terms of Depp's star persona is to allow him to counteract this image and to subvert strict star categories, enabling him to show his range beyond such roles. An examination of Depp's star image, I argue, challenges Dyer's concept that the star is constructed according to a system of "structured polysemy."[36] Such a system dictates that a star can only be read according to a very limited range of factors and as a limited amount of characters.[37] It becomes clear that the opposite is the case in relation to *some* stars, primarily Depp.

Burton/Depp and the Fluidity of Gender

Burton and Depp's questioning of gender norms makes audience members more aware of the construction of outdated gender norms and images and proposes alternative possibilities of social order. It can be argued that they wish to make their viewers more socially aware of the operations of these gender systems rather than discard these systems altogether. I propose that the main aim of Burton and Depp's collaborations, at least within the parody of gender categorization, is to provide instances of pleasure for audience members who recognize the constructedness of such categories. This does not simply propose that their films are mere entertainment; these incongruities are certainly politically charged, making fun of society's own acceptance and propagation of these norms. In a way, these films propose alternative and incongruous images so that we can laugh at ourselves while also becoming aware of the political issues involved in gender norms, making viewers aware of the *possibility* of change. Burton and Depp's collaborations portray possibilities of resistance to normative constructions of socially assigned gender roles, demonstrating that, in terms of gender, mainstream film can experiment with gender forms and images and can question the reception of and identification with filmic characters.

As Murray Pomerance has argued, Depp "leaves us with ... the suspicion that masculinity does not exist."[38] By understanding the contradictions involved in the Burton/Depp films, we will be better able to recognize the paradoxes and complexities of all cultural representation and the reductionist nature of much of the theory used to interpret such images. Though this essay has focused on *Edward Scissorhands*, the theory is applicable to Burton and Depp's other characters including Ed Wood, Ichabod Crane, Willy Wonka, and Sweeney Todd, all of whom embody a certain gender fluidity. This essay has tried to suggest the difficulty of reading and fully interpreting, not only the images contained in the Burton/Depp films, but gendered images, male or female, in all cinema and media representation. In contemporary intertextual and self-reflexive multimedia society, the integration of many areas and levels of meaning make a reading of such films an intricate and dynamic process.

Notes

1. *South Park: The Complete Fourteenth Season*, directed by Matt Stone and Trey Parker (2010; Hollywood, Calif: Paramount Home Entertainment, 2011), DVD.

2. For information on Burton see for example, Ken Hanke, *Tim Burton: An Unauthorized Biography of the Filmmaker* (Los Angeles: Renaissance, 1999). Salisbury, ed., *Burton on Burton* (London: Faber, 2006). Helmut Merschmann, *Tim Burton: The Life and Films of a Visionary Director* (London: Titan Books, 2000). For information on Depp see for example, Brian J Robb, *Johnny Depp: A Modern Rebel* (London: Plexus, 2004); Denis Meikle, *Johnny Depp: A Kind of Illusion* (Surrey: Reynolds, 2004); Nigel Goodall, *The Secret World of Johnny Depp* (London: Blake, 2006); Christopher Heard, *Depp* (Toronto: ECW P., 2001).

3. Mark Salisbury refers to Burton's work as an "identifiable brand" known as "Burtonesque" that came with the benefit of Hollywood clout (xviii). Kristin Fraga comments on Burton's "weaknesses" that many academic critics feel have rendered him more of a visual opportunist than a complete filmmaker (vii). Fraga also labels Burton's work as "Hollywood" (viii) and says that by the end of the summer of 1989, Burton was a fullblown "player" in the Hollywood industry (ix). See Kristin Fraga, *Tim Burton: Interviews* (Jackson: University Press of Mississippi, 2005). In addition, see Roger Ebert, "Batman," *Chicago Sun-Times* June 23 1989.

4. This is reminiscent of the male characters portrayed in the 1950s by stars including Marlon Brando, James Dean and Montgomery Clift.

5. Steven Cohen and Ina Rae Hark, *Screening the Male: Exploring Masculinities in Hollywood Cinema* (London: Routledge, 1993), 3.

6. See Joan Riviere, "Womanliness as a Masquerade," in *Formations of Fantasy*, ed. Victor Burgin, James Donald and Cora Kaplan (London: Methuen, 1986), 35–44.

7. Dennis Bingham, *Acting Male: Masculinities in the Films of James Stewart, Jack Nicholson, and Clint Eastwood* (New Jersey: Rutgers University Press, 1994), 4.

8. As Freud maintained in "Three Essays on the Theory of Sexuality" (1905), looking contains both passive and active elements. This is an eroticized gaze that is used to repress the memory of the moment when the male child first realizes that the mother does not have a penis; this in turn evokes in the male child a castration complex. For the adult male, the eroticized gaze directed towards the woman fetishizes her, turning her into a phallic substitute. See Sigmund Freud and James Strachey, *Three Essays on the Theory of Sexuality* (New York: Basic Books, 1975).

9. D.N. Rodowick, "The Difficulty of Difference." *Wide Angle* 5.1 (1982), 4–15.

10. Steve Neale, "Masculinity as Spectacle: Reflections on Men and Mainstream Cinema," in *Screening* the Male: *Exploring Masculinities in Hollywood Cinema*, ed. Steven Cohan and Ina Rae Hark (London: Routledge, 1993), 18.

11. See Susan Jeffords, Hard Bodies: Hollywood Masculinity in the Reagan Era (New Brunswick: Rytgers, 1994) and Yvonne Tasker, *Spectacular Bodies: Gender, Genre, and the Action Cinema* (London: Routledge, 1993).

12. There is a lack of research on representations of whiteness in Burton and Depp's work, both separately and together and the racial implications of their representations of otherness.

13. Cagle, Jess, "America Sees Shades of Gay," *Entertainment Weekly*, 8 September 1995, 24.

14. Erinn C. Gilson argues that "vulnerability is more fundamentally a form of openness than a form of passivity" (129), which acknowledges a distinction between the terms vulnerability and passivity and which implies that vulnerability is a more active form of passivity. See *The Ethics of Vulnerability: A Feminist Analysis of Social Life and Practice* (London: Routledge, 2013).

15. See Steven Cohan, "'Feminizing' the Song-and-Dance Man: Fred Astaire and the Spectacle of Masculinity in the Hollywood Musical," *Screening the Male: Exploring Masculinities in Hollywood Cinema*, Steven Cohan and Ina Rae Hark, eds. (London: Routledge, 1993). and Gaylyn Studlar, "Valentino, 'Optic Intoxication,' and Dance Madness" *Screening the Male: Exploring Masculinities in Hollywood Cinema*, eds. Steven Cohan and Ina Rae Hark (London: Routledge, 1993). Both of these articles argue the musical genre "feminizes" the song-and-dance man through spectacle. This is a performance he would return to in *Sweeney Todd: The Demon Barber of Fleet Street*.

16. For a discussion on the generation of this image see Mark Salisbury, ed., *Burton on Burton* (London: Faber, 2006), 87.

17. See Mark Salisbury, *Burton on Burton* (London: Faber, 2006), 87.

18. I distinguish between passivity and submissiveness according to agency. Submissiveness implies being submissive to an agent/another individual, while passivity does not necessarily involve a conscious state of submissiveness to another individual or group.

19. Gaylyn Studlar, *In the Realm of Pleasure: Von Sternberg, Dietrich, and the Masochistic Aesthetic.* (New York: Columbia University Press.1988), 25.

20. Gustav Bychowski, "Some Aspects of Masochistic Involvement," *Journal of the American* Psychoanalytic Association. 7 no. 2 (1959), 260.

21. This primacy of the mother within the masochistic dynamic can be used to call attention to contradictions, patriarchal assumptions and the overall inadequacy of Freudian and Lacanian based psychoanalytic film theory. Studlar argues that this is due to the fact that "masochism's psychoanalytic structure shows that psychoanalytically oriented film theory must integrate the actuality of maternal influence and authority into its consideration of spectatorship" 30.

22. Marina Warner, *From the Beast to the Blonde: On Fairy Tales and Their Tellers* (London: Vintage, 1994), 29.

23. Sartre and Husserl took self-awareness to be an essential feature of subjectivity;

"To be a subject is to be in the mode of being aware of oneself" (Hua). According to Heather Albanesi, a theory of gender subjectivity asks how the man experiences masculinity (2). In "Gender as a Personal and Cultural Construction," (1995) Nancy Chowdorow theorises the process by which an individual creates their own sense of gender through conscious and unconscious attachment to some gender images, while dismissing others. Within the classic patriarchal dichotomy of male/female proposed by Freud, Mulvey and other theorists, the male gaze objectifies female characters through fetishistic scopophilia, thereby denying women their subjectivity and granting male characters (and audience members) authority and subjectivity.

24. Richard Dyer, *Stars* (London: British Film Institute, 1979) 132, emphasis in original.
25. Emily Brontë, *Wuthering Heights* (New York: Penguin, 1994), 245.
26. Op. cit. 256.
27. Although my focus here is on Depp's performance in *Edward Scissorhands*, his appearances in *Charlie and the Chocolate Factory* (2005), *Sweeney Todd: The Demon Barber of Fleet Street* (2007), *Alice in Wonderland* (2010), and *Dark Shadows* (2012) can also be noted for his characters' extremely pale skin. In each of his performances, his slender and waiflike body suggests physical weakness and fragility, thus feminising each character, and, in each case, his pale face further signifies ill health, a lack of masculine vigour and the implication of "feminine" weakness.
28. Stella Bruzzi, *Undressing Cinema: Clothing and Identity in the Movies* (London: Routledge, 1997), 108.
29. Op. cit. 176.
30. Ed Sikov defines the term diegesis as "the world of the story" in *Film Studies: An Introduction* (New York: Columbia University Press, 2010), 91.
31. It is only in the ice-sculpting scene of the film that another character, in this instance Kim is allowed to be spectacle. In this scene, Kim dances in slow-motion through the snow and ice generated by Edward's sculpture. The narrative is momentarily paused as the camera pans around Kim's body first from a low-angle and then in a close-up of her face and hands.
32. Michael DeAngelis, *Gay Fandom and Crossover Stardom: James Dean, Mel Gibson, and Keanu Reeves* (Durham: Duke University Press, 2001), 49.
33. Bill Nichols, *Representing Reality: Issues and Concepts in Documentary* (Bloomington: Indiana University Press, 1991), 156.
34. Laura Mulvey, "Visual Pleasure and Narrative Cinema" in *Film Theory and Criticism: Introductory Readings*, eds. Leo Braudy and Marshall Cohen (New York: Oxford University Press, 2004), 841.
35. See Michael DeAngelis, *Gay Fandom and Crossover Stardom: James Dean, Mel Gibson, and Keanu Reeves* (Durham: Duke University Press, 2001).
36. Richard Dyer, *Stars* (London: British Film Institute, 1979), 3.
37. It is important here to acknowledge the recent change in stardom with the marked difference between Star Studies and Celebrity Studies, celebrity becoming a term to refer to figures in "reality" television. Peter A. Lawlor has argued that "Celebrity, in the most obvious sense, is the lowest form of fame." See Peter A. Lawlor, "Celebrity Studies Today." *Society* 47 no. 5 (2010) 419–423.
38. Murray Pomerance, *Johnny Depp Starts Here* (New Brunswick, NJ: Rutgers University Press, 2005), 174.

Bibliography

Bingham, Dennis. *Acting Male: Masculinities in the Films of James Stewart, Jack Nicholson, and Clint Eastwood*. New Jersey: Rutgers University Press, 1994.

Botticelli, Sandro. *The Birth of Venus*. c. 1483. Uffizi Gallery, Florence.
_____. *Young Woman in Mythological Guise*. c. 1480/5. Stadelsches Kunstinstitut, Frankfurt.
Brontë, Emily. *Wuthering Heights*. 1847. New York: Penguin, 1994.
Bronzino, Agnolo. *Portrait of a Young Man*. c. 1517/8 The Metropolitan Museum of Art, New York.
Bruzzi, Stella. *Undressing Cinema: Clothing and Identity in the Movies*. London: Routledge, 1997.
Butler, Judith. *Gender Trouble: Feminism and the Subversion of Identity*. Thinking Gender. New York: Routledge, 1990.
Bychowski, Gustav. "Some Aspects of Masochistic Involvement." *Journal of the American Psychoanalytic Association* 7.2 (1959): 248–73.
Cagle, Jess. "America Sees Shades of Gay." *Entertainment Weekly*, 8 September 1995, 20–31.
Cohan, Steven, and Ina Rae Hark, eds. *Screening the Male: Exploring Masculinities in Hollywood Cinema*. London: Routledge, 1993.
DeAngelis, Michael. *Gay Fandom and Crossover Stardom: James Dean, Mel Gibson, and Keanu Reeves*. Durham: Duke University Press, 2001.
Dyer, Richard. *Stars*. London: British Film Institute, 1979.
Freud, Sigmund, and James Strachey. *Three Essays on the Theory of Sexuality*. New York: Basic Books, 1975.
Jeffords, Susan. *Hard Bodies: Hollywood Masculinity in the Reagan Era*. New Brunswick: Rutgers, 1994.
Mulvey, Laura. "Visual Pleasure and Narrative Cinema." In *Film Theory and Criticism: Introductory Readings*, edited by Leo Braudy and Marshall Cohen, 837–48. New York: Oxford University Press, 2004.
Neale, Steve. "Masculinity as Spectacle: Reflections on Men and Mainstream Cinema." In *Screening the Male: Exploring Masculinities in Hollywood Cinema*, edited by Steven Cohan and Ina Rae Hark, 9–20. London: Routledge, 1993.
Nichols, Bill. *Representing Reality: Issues and Concepts in Documentary*. Bloomington: Indiana University Press, 1991.
Penley, Constance and Sharon Willis, eds. *Male Trouble*. Minneapolis: University of Minnesota Press, 1993.
Pomerance, Murray. *Johnny Depp Starts Here*. New Brunswick: Rutgers University Press, 2005.
Riviere, Joan. "Womanliness as a Masquerade." In *Formations of Fantasy*, edited by Victor Burgin, James Donald and Cora Kaplan, 35–44. London: Methuen, 1986.
Rodowick, D.N. "The Difficulty of Difference." *Wide Angle* 5.1 (1982): 4–15.
Studlar, Gaylyn. *In the Realm of Pleasure: Von Sternberg, Dietrich, and the Masochistic Aesthetic*. New York: Columbia University Press, 1988.
Tasker, Yvonne. *Spectacular Bodies: Gender, Genre, and the Action Cinema*. London: Routledge, 1993.
Warner, Marina. *From the Beast to the Blonde: On Fairy Tales and Their Tellers*. London: Vintage, 1994.

Films Referenced

The Absent-Minded Professor. Directed by Robert Stevenson. 1961. Burbank, CA: Walt Disney Home Video, 2003. DVD.

Alice in Wonderland. Directed by Tim Burton, 2010. Burbank, CA: Buena Vista Home Entertainment/Walt Disney Studios Home Entertainment, 2010. DVD.

Batman. Directed by Tim Burton, 1989. Burbank, CA: Warner Home Video, 2005.

Batman Returns. Directed by Tim Burton, 1992. Burbank: Warner Home Video, 2005. DVD.

Batman Returns. Directed by Tim Burton. 1992. Burbank, CA: Warner Home Video, 2 disc Special Edition, 2009. DVD.

Beetlejuice. DVD. Directed by Tim Burton. 1988. Burbank, CA: Warner Home Video, 2008. DVD.

Big Eyes. Directed by Tim Burton. 2014. Beverly Hills, CA: Anchor Bay Entertainment, 2015

Big Fish. Directed by Tim Burton. 2003. Culver City, CA: Columbia TriStar Home Entertainment, 2004. DVD.

Blade Runner. Directed by Ridley Scott. 1982. Burbank, CA: Warner Home Video, 2007. DVD.

Bride of the Monster. (1955), Directed by Edward D. Wood, Jr. 1955. Burbank, CA: Rhino Entertainment, 1996. Deluxe Ed Wood Angora Box Set. VHS.

The Cabinet of Dr. Caligari. Directed by Robert Wiene. 1920. Chatsworth, CA: Image Entertainment, 1997. DVD.

Charlie and the Chocolate Factory. Directed by Tim Burton. 2005. Burbank, CA: Warner Bros. Pictures, 2005. DVD.

Chocolat. Directed by Lasse Hallström. 2000. Santa Monica, CA: Lions Gate Home Entertainment, 2011. DVD.

Citizen Kane. Directed by Orson Welles. 1940. Los Angeles, CA: Turner Home Entertainment, 2001. DVD.

A Clockwork Orange. Directed by Stanley Kubrick. 1971.Burbank, CA: Warner Bros., 2011. DVD.

Corpse Bride. Directed by Tim Burton. 2005. Burbank, CA: Warner Home Video, 2006. DVD.

The Crow. Directed by Alex Proyas. 1994. Santa Monica, CA: Miramax Lionsgate, 2012. DVD.

Cry-Baby. Directed by John Waters. 1990. Universal City, CA: Universal Studios Home Entertainment, 2005. DVD.

The Dark Knight. Directed by Christopher Nolan. 2008. Burbank, CA: Warner Home Video, 2008. DVD.

The Dark Knight Rises. Directed by Christopher Nolan. 2012. Burbank, CA: Warner Bros. Pictures, 2012. DVD.

Dark Shadows. Created by Dan Curtis. 1966. Orland Park, IL: MPI Home Video, 2012. DVD.

Dark Shadows. Directed by Tim Burton. 2012. Burbank, CA: Warner Home Video, 2012. DVD.

Dark Shadows: The Revival. Created by Dan Curtis. 1991. Beverly Hills, CA: MGM Video and DVD, 2009. DVD.

Dirty Harry. Directed by Don Siegel. 1971. Burbank, CA: Warner Bros., 2010. DVD.

Don Juan DeMarco. (1995), directed by Jeremy Leven. 1995. Los Angeles, CA: New Line Home Video, 2012. DVD.

Dracula. Directed by Todd Browning. 1931. Los Angeles: Universal Pictures, 2002. DVD.

E.T. the Extra-Terrestrial. Directed by Steven Spielberg. 1982. Universal City, CA: Universal Studios, 2012. DVD.

Ed Wood. DVD. Directed by Tim Burton.

1994. Burbank, CA: Touchstone Home Entertainment, 2004. Special Edition DVD.

Edward Scissorhands. Directed by Tim Burton, 1990. Los Angeles, CA: Twentieth Century–Fox. 2007. DVD.

Flying Saucers over Hollywood: The Plan 9 Companion. Directed by Mark Patrick Carducci. 1992. Birmingham, AL: Atomic Pictures, 2000. VHS, out of print.

Frankenstein. Directed by James Whale. 1931. Universal City, CA: Universal Studios, 1999. DVD.

Frankenweenie (feature length). Directed by Tim Burton, 2012. Burbank, CA: Walt Disney Home Entertainment, 2013. DVD.

Frankenweenie (original short). Directed by Tim Burton, 1984. Bonus Material. *Tim Burton's The Nightmare before Christmas*. Burbank: Buena Vista Home Entertainment/Walt Disney Studios Home Entertainment, 2008. DVD.

The French Connection. Directed by William Friedkin. 1971. Los Angeles, CA: Twentieth Century–Fox, 2005. DVD.

Glen or Glenda? (alternate title: *I Changed My Sex*). Directed by Edward D. Wood, Jr. 1953. Burbank, CA: Rhino Entertainment, 1996. VHS, Deluxe Ed Wood Angora Box Set.

The Godfather Part II. Directed by Francis Ford Coppola. 1974. Hollywood, CA: Paramount, 2008. DVD.

Hoosiers. Directed by David Anspaugh. 1986. Beverly Hills, CA: MGM, 2000. DVD.

House of Wax. Directed by André de Toth. 1953. Burbank, CA: Warner Home Video, 2003. DVD.

James and the Giant Peach. Directed by Henry Selick. 1996. Burbank, CA: Walt Disney Pictures, 1996. DVD.

The Karate Kid. Directed by John G. Avildsen. 1984. Culver City, CA: Sony Pictures Home Entertainment, 2005. DVD.

Klute. Directed by Alan J. Pakula. 1971. Burbank, CA: Warner Bros., 2005. DVD.

The Man Who Cried. Directed by Sally Potter. 2000. London: Universal Pictures UK, 2003. DVD.

The Man Who Laughs. Directed by Paul Leni. 1928. New York, NY: Kino Video, 2003. DVD.

Mars Attacks! Directed by Tim Burton, 1996. Burbank: Warner Home Video, 1997. DVD.

Metropolis. Directed by Fritz Lang. 1927. New York, NY: Kino International, 2010. DVD.

Nightmare Before Christmas, The. Directed by Henry Selick. 1993. Burbank, CA: Walt Disney Studios Home Entertainment. 2010. DVD.

Nightmare on Elm Street, A. Directed by Wes Craven. 1984. New York City, NY: New Line Home Entertainment, 2006. DVD.

Nosferatu. Directed by F.W. Murnau, 1922. Chatsworth, CA: Image Entertainment, 2001. DVD.

The Omen. Directed by Richard Donner. 1976. Los Angeles, CA: Twentieth Century Fox, 2006. DVD.

Pee-wee's Big Adventure. Directed by Tim Burton, 1985. Burbank: Warner Home Video, 2000. DVD.

Plan 9 from Outer Space. Directed by Edward D. Wood, Jr. 1958. Burbank, CA: Rhino Entertainment, 1996. VHS, Deluxe Ed Wood Angora Box Set.

Planet of the Apes. Directed by Tim Burton. 2001. Beverly Hills: Twentieth Century–Fox Home Entertainment, 2001. DVD.

Serpico. Directed by Sidney Lumet. 1973. Hollywood, CA: Warner Home Video, 2002. DVD.

The Shining. Directed by Stanley Kubrick, 1980. Burbank, CA: Warner Home Video, 2001. DVD.

Shrek. Directed by Andrew Adamson and Vicky Jenson. 2001. Universal City, CA: Dreamworks Home Entertainment, 2011. DVD.

The Silence of the Lambs. Directed by Jonathan Demme. 1991. Los Angeles, CA: MGM Video and DVD. 2007. DVD.

Sleepy Hollow. Directed by Tim Burton. 1999. Hollywood, CA: Paramount Home Video, 2000. DVD.

South Park: The Complete Fourteenth

Season (2010). Directed by Matt Stone and Trey Parker. 2010. Hollywood, CA: Paramount Home Entertainment, 2011. DVD.

The Student of Prague. Directed by Stellan Rye. 1913. West Conshohocken, PA: Alpha Video, 2004. DVD.

Sunday Bloody Sunday. Directed by John Schlesinger. 1971. Beverly Hills, CA: MGM Video and DVD, 2003. DVD.

Sweeney Todd: The Demon Barber of Fleet Street. Directed by Terry Hughes. 1982. Burbank, CA: Warner Home Video, 2004. DVD.

Sweeney Todd: The Demon Barber of Fleet Street. Directed by Tim Burton. 2007. Universal City, CA: Dreamworks SKG, 2008. DVD.

Tim Burton's Corpse Bride. Directed by Tim Burton and Mike Johnson, 2005. Burbank: Warner Home Video, 2012. DVD.

Tim Burton's The Nightmare before Christmas. Directed by Henry Selick, 1993. Burbank: Buena Vista Home Entertainment/Walt Disney Studios Home Entertainment, 2008. DVD.

Tootsie. Directed by Sydney Pollack. 1982. Hollywood, CA: Columbia Pictures Corporation, 2001. DVD.

21 Jump Street: The Complete Series. (1987–1981). Fox TV. Golden Valley, MN 2010. Mill Creek Entertainment.

Vincent. Directed by Tim Burton, 1982. Bonus Material. *Tim Burton's The Nightmare before Christmas*. Burbank: Buena Vista Home Entertainment/Walt Disney Studios Home Entertainment, 2008. DVD.

Willy Wonka and the Chocolate Factory. Directed by Mel Stuart. 1971. Hollywood, CA: Warner Home Video, 2011.

About the Contributors

Kimiko **Akita** is an associate professor in the Department of International and Cultural Studies at Aichi Prefectural University in Aichi, Japan. She has also taught in the School of Communication at University of Central Florida. Her research on gender and cross-cultural issues has appeared in books and journals including *Challenging Images of Women in the Media, Queer Media Images, Women and Language,* and *Japan Studies Review.*

Susan M. **Bernardo** teaches at Wagner College, where she is a professor of English. She co-authored *Ursula K. Le Guin: A Critical Companion,* and edited *Environments in Science Fiction: Essays on Alternative Spaces.* Earlier articles on Tim Burton's films appeared in *Film/Literature Quarterly.* She has also published on C.J. Cherryh's *Cyteen* and presented papers on Edith Nesbit's stories and Oscar Wilde's fairy tales. She is working on a book on *Star Trek: Voyager.*

Johnson **Cheu** is the editor of *Diversity in Disney Films* (McFarland, 2013). He has published work in disability studies, media studies, and popular culture studies in places like *The Journal of Popular Culture* and *Different Bodies: Disability in Film and Television.* His poetry and essays have also appeared in several journals and anthologies. He is an assistant professor in the Department of Writing, Rhetoric, and American Cultures at Michigan State University.

Sarah **Downes** holds a PhD from Loughborough University, where her dissertation was "Bodily Sensation in Contemporary Extreme Horror Film." Her primary research interests are contemporary horror film, alternative visual cultures and the Gothic. She is particularly interested in the ways in which extreme imagery connects with the reader/viewer through sensorial stimulations.

Brian D. **Holcomb** is an academic specialist in the College of Arts and Letters at Michigan State University. He teaches classes that combine twentieth century literature, art, and drama, as well as courses in gender and sexuality; mentors faculty on active learning pedagogy; and helps to develop hybrid and online courses. He received a PhD in English from Michigan State University, and has published articles on documentary theatre and on PG Wodehouse.

Rick **Kenney** is a professor and chair in the Department of Communications at Georgia Regents University. His specialties are media ethics and Japan studies. He has been published in the *Journal of Mass Media Ethics; Queers in American Pop Culture; Diversity in Disney Films* and *Japan Studies Review.* He is vice president of the Japan–U.S. Communication Association, a division of the National Communication Association.

Pamela **Krayenbuhl** is a Mellon Interdisciplinary Fellow and PhD candidate in screen cultures at Northwestern University. Her dissertation examines the intersection of dance cultures with commercial film and television cultures in midcentury America. She has presented her research on intermediality and media history before the Society for Cinema and Media Studies, the Society of Dance History Scholars, and elsewhere.

Peter C. **Kunze** earned a PhD in English from Florida State University and is working on a PhD in media studies from the University of Texas at Austin. His research examines the children's culture industry, specifically the animation renaissance since the 1980s, as well as sincerity and authenticity in contemporary television, film, and new media narratives.

Kara M. **Manning** is completing a PhD at the University of Southern Mississippi. Her dissertation draws together her research interests in Victorian literature and film studies. Previous publications include "'That's the Effect of Living Backwards': Technological Change, Lewis Carroll's *Alice* Books, and Tim Burton's *Alice in Wonderland*," which appeared in a 2011 special issue of *Neo-Victorian Studies*.

Rachel S. **McCoppin** is a professor of literature at the University of Minnesota Crookston. She is the author of *The Lessons of Nature in Mythology* (McFarland, 2015) and is writing a book on the cycles of nature in the hero's journey. She has published articles on mythology and comparative literature in many edited collections and her work has appeared *Symbiosis, Studies in American Humor, Studies in the Novel,* and *World Literary Review*.

Deborah **Mellamphy** completed a PhD in the School of English, University College Cork, Ireland, in 2010. Her thesis is titled "Hollyweird: Gender Transgression in the Collaborations of Tim Burton and Johnny Depp." She has taught undergraduate and postgraduate courses at UCC and has published journal articles and chapters on film, television, and video game studies. She works as a technical writer.

Lance **Norman** teaches literature, humanities, drama, and performance at Michigan State University and Lansing Community College. He has published essays on diverse figures of the modern and contemporary stage including Martin McDonagh, Harold Pinter, and Eugene O'Neill. His most recent work embraces the lenses of performativity and phenomenology to theorize the inherent theatricality in popular film and contemporary celebrity culture.

Lori **Parks** is a visiting assistant professor of art history at Miami University, Ohio. She received a PhD at the University of Reading (UK) and her area of research is focused on the body from an interdisciplinary perspective. Recent projects include co-editing a special issue on food for the *European Journal of*

American Culture and a chapter in *For His Eyes Only? The Women of James Bond* (forthcoming).

Lisa K. **Perdigao** is a professor of English at the Florida Institute of Technology. Her research and teaching interests are in the areas of American literature, YA literature, television, and film. She is the author of *From Modernist Entombment to Postmodernist Exhumation* and co-editor, with Mark Pizzato, of *Death in American Texts and Performances*. She has published articles on *Buffy the Vampire Slayer*, *Dollhouse*, *Community*, *Firefly*, and *Fringe*, among others.

Elizabeth Leigh **Scherman** holds a PhD in communication from the University of Washington and teaches at Bates College in Tacoma, Washington. Her research focuses on representations of identity in children's cinema, particularly disability. Her publications include essays in *Disability Studies Quarterly*, *The Galaxy Is Rated G* (edited by R.C. Neighbors and Sandy Rankin, McFarland, 2011) and *The Worlds of Farscape* (edited by Sherry Ginn, McFarland, 2013).

Gael **Sweeney** teaches creative nonfiction and cultural studies in the Writing Program at Syracuse University and has written on topics ranging from Elvis as a White Trash icon, *Queer as Folk* and Sherlock Holmes/Dr. Watson fandoms, to the queer significance of *The Lion King's* Timon and Pumbaa, Hugh Grant, and male supermodels.

Index

abjection 59, 166, 170, 178, 181
abnormality 30, 39, 42–43, 52, 174, 178
"According to Plan" 74
adaptation 4, 21, 39, 46, 66, 85, 87–88, 90, 92, 94, 96, 98, 100–101, 103–104, 106, 108, 110, 112, 114, 116–120, 122–126, 128–130, 132, 135–136, 138, 140, 142, 144, 146, 148, 150–166, 168, 170, 172, 174–180, 182, 185, 192–196, 202–203, 209
adulthood 171, 173, 175–176, 179–180
aesthetic 64, 68, 118, 123–124, 129, 132, 151, 155, 157, 165–167, 170, 172, 176–177, 184, 190, 195, 199, 202, 205, 207, 209, 225, 227
afterlife 61–62, 195–196
alcoholism 17
Alger, Horatio 89
Alice in Wonderland 48, 86, 100, 151, 163, 185, 196, 209, 212, 226, 229, 234
alienation 66, 185, 220
Althusser, Louis 103, 106, 114–115
ambivalence 56, 83, 104, 108, 110, 113, 173, 178, 181, 216–217, 222
androgyne 70, 81, 179, 215–216, 218–219, 221
angora 3, 8–10, 12–17, 229–230
animation 59, 83, 140, 163, 166, 169, 171–172, 186–189, 195–196, 202, 234
Anoedipal 83–84
Anspaugh, David 199, 230
Antoine 193, 196
archetypal 21–22, 24–32, 34
Ari 109–114
assimilation 47, 178, 208
atypical body 4, 36, 39, 41, 46–48
Aunt Sponge 165, 168, 171
Aunt Spiker 165, 168, 171
auteur 150–152, 161, 209
autopsy 60–61, 63, 67–68

Bacon, Francis 206
Baker, Kathy 27, 208
Bakhtin, Mikhail 56, 67–68, 162, 178
Baldwin, Alec 203
Bale, Christian 205
Baltus 72–73, 76
Bambi 22

Banford, Beadle 139, 142
Barlow, John D. 200–201, 210
Barnabas 117, 119–121, 123–126, 128–132
Bashford, Allison 63, 68
Basinger, Kim 205
Bassil-Morozow, Helena 21, 34–35, 49–50, 52, 163–164
Batman 3–4, 68, 70–72, 75–77, 79–80, 82–84, 100, 132, 152, 193, 204–207, 210–211, 224, 229
Batman Returns 4, 16, 57, 70–72, 74–76, 79, 82–84, 86, 100, 121, 132, 144, 193–194, 196, 204–207, 229
Baudrillard, Jean 99, 104, 109–110, 114–115
Beauregarde, Violet 32, 35, 45–46, 51, 155, 157, 161
Beck, Bernard 51–52
Becker, Howard S. 174, 180–181
Beetlejuice 132, 147, 179, 187, 203–204, 207, 229
"Belly of the Whale" 23, 31–32, 34
Benjamen, Bergery 50, 52
Benjamin, Walter 98
bestiality 114, 179, 182
Bhabha, Homi 104, 114–115
Big Fish 4, 86–89, 91–92, 94–95, 98–101, 152, 193, 229
Bingham, Dennis 214, 224, 226
Blackness 50, 52, 103
Blade Runner 210, 229
blindness 28, 169
Bloom, Will 86–99
Blue Hawaii 17
Bodylore 68–69
Bogart, Humphrey 217
Bonham Carter, Helena 38, 52, 71, 92, 94, 100, 125, 132
Boogeymen 18
Botticelli 218, 227
bourgeois 200
Brando, Marlon 118, 224
Breckinridge, Bunny 9–10, 15, 16, 18
Broadway 67, 136, 138
Brontë, Emily 192, 226–227
Bucket Family 38–39, 48, 160
Burton, Tim 1, 3–6, 8, 10–11, 13–14, 16–45,

237

47–56, 59–61, 63–64, 66, 68, 70–72, 82–83, 86–115, 117–119, 123–173, 175–180, 184–197, 199–210, 212–213, 215–216, 218, 222–225, 229–231, 233–234
Bush, George 42, 215
Bush, George W. 18, 206
Butler, Judith 18, 67, 214, 222, 227
"By the Sea" 134–159
Byzantium 125

The Cabinet of Dr. Caligari 200, 206, 208, 210–211, 229
Cagle, Jess 215, 225, 227
Calloway, Amos 91, 100
camp 18, 20, 51–52, 119, 122–124, 129, 131, 133, 206, 215
Campbell, Joseph 4, 21–23, 27, 29–35, 138
capitalism 4, 57, 67–68, 70–71, 73–75, 77, 79–83, 103, 105–106, 110, 114, 116, 123, 163, 210–211
carnivalesque 162, 178, 181
Carroll, Lewis 185, 196, 234
Cartesian 57
Catwoman 71–72, 76–77, 79–80, 83–84, 132, 206–207
Cesare 200, 206, 208
CGI 189
Changlings 52
Charleston, SC 1, 3
Charlie and the Chocolate Factory 4, 21, 30, 36–37, 41, 44–53, 68, 100, 150–152, 154–155, 158, 160–164, 166, 171–172, 174–177, 179–181, 193, 209, 212, 226, 229, 231
childhood 4, 31–33, 41–43, 50–53, 55, 58, 60, 65, 86, 89–90, 156–157, 165–168, 171, 173–178, 180–181
Christianity 218
Chrysalids 178, 182
CIA 148
CinemaScope 220
Citizen Kane 15–16, 156, 229
Clarke, Marcus 195–196
Clarke, Roger 49–52
claymation 186
Clift, Montgomery 224
A Clockwork Orange 154, 229
Cobblepot, Oswald 71, 78, 80, 206
The Coen Brothers 162, 164
Cola 191
Coleridge, Samuel Taylor 130, 133
Collins (Dark Shadows) 117, 119–123, 125–129, 131–132, 192
colonialism 39, 107, 112, 114, 151, 158
The Corpse Bride 3–4, 71, 73–75, 78, 81, 83, 185–186, 192–193, 195–196, 202, 209, 212, 229, 231

Crane, Constable 54–55, 57, 60–61, 63–64, 73, 75
Crane, Ichabod 54–55, 58, 61, 63, 66, 71, 73, 76, 81, 83, 195, 224
Craven, Wes 230
cripple 40, 44, 48
Cronenberg, David 210
Crudup, Billy 86, 89
Cruise, Tom 212, 222
Cry-Baby 215, 229
cure 37, 41, 45–46, 48, 52
Curtis, Dan 117, 130, 132, 229
Cyborgs 59, 67–68

daguerreotype 191–192
Dahl, Roald 3–4, 31, 36, 39, 41–42, 45, 47, 49–53, 150–153, 157–158, 162, 164–166, 168, 175–181
Dante 100
Dark Shadows 4, 18, 24, 117–119, 123–125, 127–133, 185, 193, 195, 206, 210, 212, 226, 229
Davidson (Planet of the Apes) 90, 102, 107–114, 201, 210, 230
Davis, Lennard J. 30, 35
deafness 30, 35
Dean, James 224
deconstruction 88, 94, 98–99, 101
Deetz, Delia (*Beetlejuice*) 179, 203
deformed 52, 166
Deluxe, Giles 229–230
Demme, Jonathan 169, 230
Depp, Johnny 3–5, 8, 11, 13, 16–20, 25, 38, 42, 44, 51–52, 54, 71, 86–87, 117–118, 123–125, 127–133, 136, 138–139, 147, 149, 151, 156–157, 162–164, 171–172, 175, 179–180, 195, 212–227, 234
Derrida, Jacques 88, 90, 94, 98–101
Descartes, Rene 57, 67
deviance 14, 36, 38, 42, 44, 46–49, 83, 174, 178, 180–181, 201
DeVito, Danny 71, 100, 206
diagesis 139
dialectic 38, 154, 166–167, 215
Dialogics 162, 164
DiCaprio, Leonardo 215
Dickens, Charles 188–189, 191, 194–196
diegetic 131, 214, 219
Dietrich, Marlene 225, 227
différance 90
Dionysian 61
disability 1, 4, 28, 30, 34–36, 41, 44, 46, 49–50, 52–53, 177–178, 233, 235
Disney 2, 4, 8, 19, 52, 66, 155, 162–164, 178, 229–231, 233
diversity 28, 32, 233
"Do the Clam" 17

Dr. Jekyll & Mr. Hyde 194
Dr. Seuss 202
Dolores 10–15, 17
Don Juan DeMarco 223, 229
Donner, Richard 230
Doty, William G. 21, 34–35
Downey, Robert, Jr. 215, 222
Dracula 55, 66, 131, 169, 185, 193–194, 200, 229
drag 9–10, 13–14, 18
Dreamworks 147, 230–231
Dunlop, Blair 42
Dyer, Richard 217–218, 223, 226–227
dynamism 171
dystopianism 179, 200

Eastwood, Clint 213–214, 224, 226
Ebert, Roger 19, 112, 114, 163–164, 213, 224
Ebook 83
Ed Wood 3, 8–20, 209, 212, 224, 229–230
Edelstein, David 148
Edward Scissorhands 3, 5, 21, 25, 42, 44, 47, 49–53, 68, 86–87, 98, 100, 178, 193, 202–203, 205, 207, 212–213, 215–217, 219–220, 224, 226, 230
effeminate 213, 217–218, 222
Elfman, Danny 37, 52
Elmo 215
Elsaesser, Thomas 199, 210
embodiment 28, 49, 58, 66, 68, 173, 216
empire 19, 77, 140, 173, 180, 193
enlightenment 30, 34, 55, 61, 64–65, 67, 69
entrapment 114, 220
"Epiphany" 140, 145
eroticism 214, 221
Essel, Eileen 38
ethology 178, 181
Everyman 38
evil 37, 58, 72, 76, 78, 136, 142, 144–146, 148, 153, 167, 178, 181, 207
exceptionism 5
expressionist 199–202, 204–208, 210

fairy tales 3, 41, 46, 52, 55, 66, 76, 83–84, 87, 89–90, 115, 152, 162, 164, 166, 175–176, 209, 225, 227, 233
fandom 226–227, 235
Fanon, Franz 104, 114–115
fantastic 41, 64, 68, 86, 96–97, 100, 171, 176, 181, 200
feminine 58, 71, 75, 138, 213–219, 221–222, 226
feminism 18, 177, 227
feminist 67–68, 73, 213, 225
fetish 8–9, 11–14, 59, 207, 213–215, 218, 220–221, 225–226
Fleming, Victor 100

Foucault, Michel 66
Francis 22–25
Frankenstein 27, 44, 53, 65–66, 86, 146, 177–178, 182, 185, 191, 193–194, 199, 202–203, 207–208, 230
Frankenweenie 3, 6, 47, 52, 163, 185–186, 192–193, 199, 202–203, 207, 230
freak 13, 50, 155, 202, 220
Freud, Sigmond 70, 84, 225–227
Fry, Jordan 40, 132, 157

Gallagher, Gina 98
Galswells, Pastor 74
Garland Thomson, Rosemarie 52–53, 148
gay 8–10, 12, 18–20, 194, 196, 219, 225–227
German Expressionism 4, 198–205, 207–211
Gilgamesh 34
Girl Happy 17.
Gish, Lillian 218
Glen or Glenda? 8–9, 12–14, 18–19, 230
globalization 115, 163, 209, 211
Gloop, Augustus 35, 39, 45–46, 51, 174
gobstopper 154
Gordon, Avery F. 134, 146, 148, 194, 196
Gotham 72, 74, 76–80, 205
gothic 35, 55, 70–71, 75, 82–84, 99–101, 117, 119, 122, 130, 133, 145, 178–179, 186, 188, 190–197, 207–208, 210–211, 218, 233
Goulet, Robert 204
Grave Robbers from Outer Space 15
The Great Gatsby 124, 205
"Green Finch and Linnet Bird" 142
Gremlins 162
grotesque 26, 51, 56, 62, 68–69, 83–84, 162, 164, 178, 181, 204, 206–207
Guattari, Felix 57, 67–68
Guerin, Frances 201, 210
Guerrero, Ed 50, 52

Halberstam, Judith 195–196
Halloween 42, 191–192
haunting 4, 122, 194, 196, 202
Heathcote, Bella 125, 130–131
Herman, Pee-wee 3, 21–26, 28–32, 34, 42, 187, 193, 204, 207, 210, 230
heteronormative 10–11, 14
Highmore, Freddie 30, 36, 52, 174
Hitchcock, Alfred 162
Hitler, Adolf 200, 210–211
Hoffman, Dustin 42
Hollywood 9–12, 14–17, 49, 53, 82, 98, 118, 131–132, 147, 149–150, 152, 171, 184, 193, 199, 201, 205, 209, 212, 215, 217–218, 222, 224–225, 227, 230–231
homogenous 38–39

Index

horseman, (headless) 54–59, 63–66, 72–73, 75–76, 81, 83
Hughes, Terry 147–148, 231
hybridity 80, 103–104, 106, 108, 112

IMAX 155
Impressionism 200
inclusion 25, 29–30, 33, 65
insanity 15, 18
intertextuality 162, 213

Jack the Ripper 146, 191, 194
Jackson, Michael 42, 156
James and the Giant Peach 165, 168–170, 179–180
Jameson, Fredric 114, 116, 199, 209–211
Johanna 141–144, 168
"Johanna" 142–143
Johnson, Tor 10, 15–16
Jorgensen, Christine 11, 13
Josephine (*Big Fish*) 90–91, 94, 96
Josette 120–123, 126, 128–132
Jung, Carl 34–35, 49, 52, 163–164

Kafka, Franz 169, 181
kawaii 165–167, 169, 172
Keanes (Big Eyes) 3
Keaton, Michael 71, 147, 203, 205
Kim (*Edward Scissorhands*) 27–30, 98, 205, 208, 216, 219, 226
Klute 154, 230
Kracauer, Siegfried 200, 210–211
Kristeva, Julia 166–167, 170, 178–179, 181
Kubrick, Stanley 178, 229–230
Kucich, John 186, 195–196
Kyle, Selina 72, 76–77, 79, 206

labor 50, 77, 159
Lacanian 121, 225
"Ladies in Their Sensitivities" 142
Landau, Martin 10, 18
Lang, Fritz 205, 230
Lange, Jessica 90
Ledger, Heath 117, 133, 206
Levinson, Barry 87, 98, 101
Lincoln, Abraham 102, 112
Linton, Simi 218
Lionsgate 229
Lovett, Mrs. 132, 135, 137, 140, 143, 147–148
Lugosi, Bella 10, 13, 15–16, 169
Lumet, Sidney 230
Lumière 188
Lynch, David 162, 164, 201

macabre 200, 202, 209
Madagascar 104
madman 62, 77, 135, 137, 141–142, 144–145

madness 134, 136–138, 141–145, 148, 225
Madonna 78
Maggie (*Dark Shadows*) 119–124, 126–131
magic 51, 53, 58, 81, 93, 98, 165, 169, 173, 187–190
Mars Attacks! 19, 87, 187, 193, 230
Marxism 72, 123
Masbath (*Sleepy Hollow*) 63, 65, 68, 76
masculinity 12, 71, 77, 81, 83–84, 157, 213–216, 218, 222–227
masochism 213, 217, 220, 225
masquerade 214–215, 224, 227
Mayne, Judith 106, 114–116
McGregor, Ewan 86
Mead, George Herbert 98,
melancholy 32, 204
Méliès 187, 195–196
melodrama 117–119, 133
Mephistopheles 123
Metropolitan 227
MGM 229–231
mimicry 103–105, 109, 113
Miramax 229
misfit 1, 3, 10–11, 13, 15–17, 38, 44, 47–48, 76
Mr. Toad 66
modernism 99, 101, 105, 107, 114, 164
modernity 104–105, 115
Mohr, Joshua 2, 6
Monroe, Marilyn 218
monsters 4, 34, 41, 45, 50, 59, 67–68, 115, 134, 146, 165–167, 169, 177–178, 180–181, 195–196, 206
monstrosity 44, 166–169, 171–173, 175–178, 180, 182, 192, 206
monstrous-cute 4, 44, 165–167, 169, 171–172, 175–181
Moviephone 19
Moyers, Bill 21
Muir, John 20
Mulvey, Laura 220, 226–227
Murnau 200–201, 206, 230
mythography 34–35
mythology 21, 33–35, 57, 100, 234
Mythosphere 35

NAACP 158
Nabokov, Vladimir 99
Napoleon 78
narcissism 72, 213, 215
nationalism 83, 115, 198–199, 215
Neale, Steve 214–215, 225, 227
neoliberalism 159, 164
neovictorian 189, 194, 196
Nichols, Bill 226–227
Nicholson Jack 205–206, 213–214, 224, 226
The Nightmare Before Christmas 42, 47, 49, 162–163, 169, 186, 230–231

nihilism 155
"No Place Like London" 137
Nolan, Christopher 205–206, 210, 229
Norden, Martin F. 28, 34–35
norm 11, 49, 144, 166, 171; *see also* norms
normal 10, 13, 16, 18, 20, 30, 38–49, 51, 77, 129, 131, 174, 178, 220
norms 22, 60, 71, 79, 136, 151, 161, 166, 174, 177, 179–180, 212, 215, 217, 219–221, 223
Nosferatu 118, 200–201, 206, 230
nostalgia 106–107, 110, 113–114, 150, 163, 207

The Odyssey 34–35
Oedipal 217
Oompa Loompas 31–32, 35, 39–40, 44, 158–160, 163
Orientalism 192, 196–197
other 1–4, 7, 9–10, 12–14, 16, 18, 20–22, 24–26, 28–34, 38, 40–46, 48, 50, 52, 56, 58–60, 62, 64, 66, 68, 72–74, 76–84, 88, 100, 103–104, 108–110, 112–113, 115, 119, 121, 124, 126, 129–131, 133–134, 137–145, 147, 151, 154–157, 160, 166–167, 169–171, 174–176, 178–181, 184–186, 188–190, 192, 195, 198, 208, 214, 216, 218, 220–221, 224, 226; *see also* otherness
otherness 22, 24–25, 27, 31, 56, 129, 177, 180, 208, 220, 225
outsider 3, 7, 10, 12, 14, 16–18, 20, 22, 24, 26, 28, 30, 32, 34, 38, 40–42, 44, 46, 48, 50, 52, 56, 58–60, 62, 64, 66, 68, 72, 74, 76, 78, 80, 82, 84, 87, 128, 145, 153, 185, 193, 207, 216; *see also* outsiders
outsiders 3, 50, 54, 71, 93, 135, 174, 180–181, 208

Page, Edwin 88, 99, 101, 196
Parker, Sarah Jessica 10, 13, 20
Parker, Trey 212, 224, 231
Pastor, Louis 74
patriarchy 71–75, 79, 81–82, 193, 214, 217, 221, 225–226
Peckett 185
Pee-wee's Big Adventure 21–22, 25–26, 34, 204, 207, 210, 230
Peg (Edward Scissorhands) 25–26, 29–30, 44, 217
performativity 122, 215, 234
Pericles 106–108, 112–113
persona 5, 87, 117–118, 126–127, 129, 169, 179, 212–216, 222–223
personhood 125, 130
personification 169, 218
phallic 217–218, 225
Phantasmagoria 188, 190, 195–196
phenomenology 234

Pickering 63
Pirates of the Caribbean 8, 155, 222
Pirelli, Adofo 136–137, 142–143
Pixar 4
Planet of the Apes 4, 9, 17, 20, 102–115, 193, 230
Poe, Edgar Allan 3, 191, 193, 202
Pokemon 178
Pollack, Sidney 231
Pomerance, Murry 224, 226–227
PopWatch 20
postcolonialism 103–104, 109, 111–113, 158–159
post-Jungian 50
postmodernism 35, 87–88, 96, 98–101, 103–107, 112–116, 184, 186, 195–196, 207, 209–211, 235
poststructuralism 88, 98, 101
postwar 207
Potter, Russel A. 35, 207, 210–211
Presley, Elvis 17, 235
"Pretty Women" 142–143
Price, Vincent 18, 86, 191, 202
Prometheus 53
psyche 21, 28, 32
psychedelic 155
psychiatry 19
psychic 10, 21, 65, 176
psychoanalysis 59, 122, 133, 178, 213, 225, 227
psychopaths 178
psychotherapy 34–35
Puritan 58, 198
Pygmalion 130
pygmies 158

queer 9–11, 13, 17–18, 20, 181, 215, 233, 235
quest 4, 21–23, 25, 27, 29, 31, 33, 35, 63, 66, 81, 92, 131
Quixote 16
quixotic 123

Rabelais and His World 67–68
race 1, 4, 21, 40, 49, 53, 102–103, 111, 115–116, 140, 151, 158–159, 163, 186, 200, 225, 234
radical 59, 87, 119, 130, 170, 216
rationality 57–58, 63, 111, 136, 159, 170
"The Raven" 191
readaptation 161–163
Reagan (presidential era) 198, 204, 207, 209, 211, 215, 225, 227
realism 13, 96, 99, 101, 105, 114, 118, 200
reception 74, 98, 101, 224
redemption 44–46, 51, 55, 136,
Reeves, Keanu 215, 226–227

remake 102–104, 120, 123–124, 131–132, 150, 152, 162, 164, 192
remasculinization 209
repulsion 167, 178, 220
Reubens, Paul 22
rhetoric 5, 33, 122, 162, 164, 233
Ridley, Scott 229
Robb, Anna Sophia 32, 45, 157
"Rock-a-Hula, Baby" 17
Roof, Dylann 5
Rudolph, the Red-nosed Reindeer 191
Ryder, Winona 27, 52, 98, 204, 208

Salinger, Diane 24
Salisbury, Mark 20, 49–50, 52, 66–68, 162–164, 194, 197, 213, 224–225
Sally (Nightmare) 191–192
Salt, Veruca 35, 40, 45–46, 154, 172
Sammond, Nicolas 163–164
Sandra (*Edward Scissorhands*) 67–68, 91–92, 96
Sartre, Jean Paul 98, 225
Satan 24
scars 26, 33, 65
schizophrenia 57, 67–68
schizophrénie 67–68
Schreck, Max 206
Schwarzenegger, Arnold 214
scopophilia 214–215, 220, 226
The Scream (painting) 202
Scrooge, Ebeneezer 191
Sedgwick, Eva Kosofsky 20
Selick, Henry 162, 166, 178, 195, 230–231
Selznick, David 12
semiotics 122
sepia 55, 137
Serpico 153, 230
Sesame Street 169
sexism 186, 206
sexuality 8–10, 19, 76, 83, 120, 164, 177–178, 219, 225, 227, 233
Shapiro, Joseph 46, 52–53
Shelley, Mary Wollstonecraft 44, 53, 146, 178, 182, 185, 192
Sherlock 235
Shildrick, Margaret 58, 67–68
Shrek 46, 51–52, 230
Sidney, Sylvia 203
The Silence of the Lambs 169, 230
Silverman, Kaja 131, 133
Simone (*Pee-wee's Big Adventure*) 24–25
simulacra 103–106, 108–110, 112–115, 118
Sirk, Douglaas 214
Skellington, Jack 190, 194
Sleepy Hollow 4, 54–57, 59–76, 78, 80–84, 193, 195, 209, 212, 230
Slugworth 153–155

Snow White 51, 98
Sondheim, Stephen 134, 136, 140, 145–149
Sontag, Susan 20, 123, 125, 131, 133
Sony 99, 230
Sorrento, Matthew 62, 68–69
Spanos, William V. 199, 209, 211
Sparky 192
spectacle 15, 27, 61, 136, 188, 193, 213–215, 219–221, 225–227
spectatorship 106, 115–116, 216, 219, 225
Spectre 92–93, 95–97, 99–100
Spiegelman, Art 201
Spielberg, Steven 199, 229
Stafford, Barbara Maria 61, 67, 69
Stallone, Sylvester 214
Stam, Robert 162, 164, 178, 182
stardom 4, 183, 186, 188, 190, 192, 194, 196, 200, 202, 204, 206, 208, 210, 212, 214, 216, 218, 220, 222, 224, 226–227
steampunk 134, 147, 195
STEM 2
stereotype 28, 31, 79, 112, 153, 156–159, 169, 192, 215–217, 219–222
Stewart, James 163, 213–214, 224, 226
stigmata 46, 67–68
Stoker, Bram 131, 185, 193
stop-motion technology 1, 3–4, 184–193, 195–196
Stoppard, Tom 66–68
Stuart, Mel 4, 150–164, 187, 231
subjectivity 17, 109–110, 120, 122, 151, 213, 225–226
suburbia 25–27, 31, 203, 207, 220
subversion 18, 82, 119, 167, 170, 172, 178–179, 181–182, 185, 191, 199–203, 207, 209, 212, 215–217, 219, 221–223, 227
supernatural 54–55, 58–60, 64, 71, 75, 81, 119
Sweeney Todd 3–4, 8–9, 11, 13, 15, 17, 19, 100, 132, 134–137, 139–149, 185, 193, 195, 210, 212, 224–226, 231, 235

Taylor, George 102–103
Taylor, Noah 38, 52, 160
Teachout, Terry 137, 147, 149
Teavee, Mike 35–36, 40, 45, 157, 161, 172–174
Telotte, J.P. 201, 206, 210–211
Thade 102, 108–110, 112–114
Tobias (*Sweeney Tood*) 144–145
Tomorrowland 163–164
Tootsie 42, 231
transgender 9
transsexual 9, 11, 13–14, 18
transvestism 8–14, 18–19
trope 12, 46, 51, 131–132, 179
Truffaut, François 161, 164

Trunchball 176
Turner, Bryan 56, 66–67, 69
Turpin, Judge 135, 139, 141–144, 148

uncanny 16, 88, 100, 120, 128–129, 170, 172, 175, 177, 186, 189, 195–196
underworld 24, 27–28, 33–35, 74, 76, 82–83, 185
Universal Studios 10–11, 50, 52, 147, 201–202, 208, 229–231
utopia 28, 34, 76, 179

Vale, Vicki (Batman) 205
Vampira 10, 16
vampire 117–120, 124–126, 128–132, 169, 178, 200, 235
Van Brunt, Brom 58
Van Damme, Jean-Claude 214
Van Dian, Casper 58
Van Dort 71, 82, 185, 190, 192, 202
Van Garrett 71–73, 76
Van Helsing, Elsa 193
Van Tassel 56–58, 64–65, 71–73, 75–76, 78, 81
Veronica (*Dark Shadows*) 20, 126, 130
Vicky (*Dark Shadows*) 125–130, 132, 230
Victorianism 68, 71, 74, 78, 134, 140, 142, 145–147, 178, 184–196, 218, 234
Vidal, Gore 19, 193
Vietnam 153–155, 198, 209
vigilantism 206
villain 23, 25, 27, 29, 39, 201
Vincent 186, 190, 202, 231

Wahlberg, Mark 102, 107
Walken, Christopher 71–72, 206
Wallace, Daniel, 86–90, 93, 95, 99–101, 205

Washington, Irving, 54, 66–68, 70, 81, 83–84, 195
Watergate 153–155
Waters, John 184, 194, 196, 215, 229
Watson, Emily 71
Waugh 88, 99, 101
Wayne, Bruce 68, 71–72, 76, 205–206
Weimar Republic 199
Weinstock, Jeffrey 19–20
Welles, Orson 8, 10, 13, 15–16, 170, 179, 182, 201, 229
werewolves 124, 178
Western 34, 55–56, 58, 63, 66, 81, 88, 103, 157, 192
Whale, James 65, 199, 202, 230
Wheeler, Hugh 134, 145–149
whiteness 103, 115, 218, 225
Wiest, Dianne 25, 44, 52
Wilder, Gene 151, 156
Willy Wonka 3, 30, 36–40, 42, 47, 52, 150, 152–156, 158, 162–164, 171–173, 175, 179, 224, 231
Winslow, Norther 97
Winters, Victoria 125–129, 131
Winthrop, John 198
witchcraft 64
The Wizard of Oz 100
Wonkavision 157
"Worst Director" 8, 16–19, 177, 181
Wuthering Heights 192, 218, 226–227
Wyndam, John 178, 182

Young, Katherine 62, 68–69

Zemeckis, Robert 199
zombie 191

www.ingramcontent.com/pod-product-compliance
Ingram Content Group UK Ltd.
Pitfield, Milton Keynes, MK11 3LW, UK
UKHW011435100725
460636UK00016B/340